Manna From Heaven

Inspirations of Faith, Love, Wisdom
And
Motivation

Gwenith Miles Lewis

Gift Edition

Two Harbors Press

THE MEANING OF MANNA

Anything badly needed that
Comes unexpectedly
Into your life
To give divine and spiritual

Substance.

Webster's Dictionary

Two Harbors Press
212 3rd Avenue North, Suite 290
Minneapolis, MN 55401
612.455.2293
www.TwoHarborsPress.com

ISBN - 978-1-936198-86-3
ISBN - 1-936198-86-x
LCCN - 2010934736

Typeset by James Arneson

Printed in the United States of America

DEDICATION

I dedicate this volume to all who read its pages. May you awaken each morning with a song in your heart.

May you have peace of mind, good health, and a great enthusiasm for life.

May you think well of yourself and know you can accomplish every dream and every goal.

May your thoughts be filled with love and gratitude while you count your many blessings.

Contents

2. MOTIVATION AND CHANGE

3. GOD AND SERVICE

4. FAMILIES ARE FOREVER

5. POEMS WITH WISDOM

6. ON THE LIGHTER SIDE

7. AMERICA THE BEAUTIFUL

ACKNOWLEDGEMENTS

Through the years, I have collected many excellent materials: poems, talks, and inspirational articles. I have used these materials for class instruction and for motivational writings. A sincere effort has been made to trace the ownership of selections used in this collection of materials, and to give proper credit to the copyright owners. If any error or omission has occurred, it is inadvertent, and I would like to make corrections for future editions, provided that written notifications are made.

My grateful acknowledgement and thanks to Joy Saunders Lundberg for her two poems *My Grandma, and My Grandpa.* My grateful acknowledgment to the Lundberg Company, of Provo, Utah, for permission to reprint her poetry.   .

"The Holy Bible," King James version, for reference material.

My gratitude and thanks to my publishing team. Working with them was a special, enjoyable experience. They were all so dedicated and helpful.

Grateful acknowledgement is given to the Laguna Beach and Laguna Hills branches of the Orange County Public Library. My appreciation is given to the librarians and assistants for their research and dedication.

My gratitude and special thanks to Ms. Marie Toth, of Executive Assistance, Laguna Hills, CA, for her assistance, experience and expertise.

I wish to express my deep, personal thanks to: James J. Gillis, Sara Havranek, Marjorie and Lawrence Lee, Charlene Nelson, and Darrell E. Moses for their talents, their abilities, friendship, and kind thoughts on my book jacket.

I am lovingly grateful to my son, Darrel Lewis, for his editing and computer skills in helping to make this book a reality and for his expertise.

I am indebted to my husband, William S. Lewis, for his sound counsel, reviews, guidance, and editing: for permission to use his prize-wining photograph of the Balloon Festival in Albuquerque, New Mexico, for my book jacket: for his devoted help in putting this work together.

My sincere gratitude to Lawrence Lee for giving me permission to use his writing, A Once Proud Land. My best wishes to the Lee family for a lifetime of love, friendship and service. You are the best of souls.

I am indebted to Gus Gedatus, my able editor, through his family values and sound counsel caught the vision of what I was striving to accomplish and found the way to promote my book. My sincere thanks Gus. To Danielle Adelman, Author Coordinator, one marvels when one witnesses her dedication and steadfastness in all her labors and are privileged to benefit from her pleasing personality. Thank you Dani, you are one special, lovely lady.

TRIBUTE TO MY FAMILY

*M*any years ago, Rabindranath Tagore, wrote these stirring words:

"The song I came to sing remains unsung, I have spent my life stringing and unstringing my instrument."

My fate may have been the same as Tagore's, had I not been blessed from the heavens above. My Creator gave me the privilege to be born in a home with two creative parents Benjamin Miles and Theo Robinson Miles. Material things were never plenty, but love and their time was given in great amounts. We were introduced to literature, art, music, dance lessons (my parents could not afford) and the wonderful joy of reading. Wherein, I found the treasures I have compiled and enjoyed for a lifetime.

Not enough can be said about Bill and our sixty plus years together. The joy turned into a family, stalwart and true-in their personal lives: David and Melody, Darrel, Sheri and Bob. Then we were joined with grandchildren: Trevor (Jack), Ryan, Megan, Nathan, Rayna, Derek, Kristina and James, they are the "whipped cream on the glorious cake." Each generation brings more love and fun – now we have four great-grandchildren to enjoy (with more to come, I hope). Life is beautiful. It is true-*"Families are Forever."*

Gwenith Miles Lewis

INTRODUCTION

Manna From Heaven is a writing featuring a selection of my thoughts and a collection of writings, poetry, and literature from the wisdom of writers of the past who have gained the admiration and appreciation for their genius over decades of time. The gems of this collection of educational and inspirational information has been molded into this book for the purpose of teaching formulas for life-changing opportunities, while gaining spiritual strength, and for providing suggestions for motivational improvements.

Manna From Heaven is a volume written for all religions. Thoughts are provided for all who believe in a divine or superhuman power to be obeyed and worshipped as a Creator, whether Christian, Jewish, Buddhist, Islamic or other. The reader will notice it is a collection where you will find some whimsical humor and enjoyable poetry. This volume was designed just for browsing when time is short. It was created to give one something uplifting to think about.

God is our greatest hope for peace in this world. In our thoughts we must have a spirit of brotherhood. We must love one another. Criticism of another's faith in God, as well as, their skin color is an un-godly practice. Under our God-inspired Constitution we are given the privilege to worship God according to the dictates of our conscience. The souls of many great men and women have been lost in the carnage of war, in the interest of preserving such freedom. God, in turn, loves all his children regardless of race or religion.

This book is a beginning step for parents to achieve the training for teaching moral character to their children. The outside influences such as television and the loss of instruction once given in the schools, churches and homes, leave children with moral illiteracy. Some children live in homes where no moral training is present. Their loss of basic manners and moral character are turning our educational facilities into chaotic conditions. Additionally, poor character training progresses into the following generation many times exacerbating the weakness. Adults must see this need in their children and set the example of character. Good books, stories, poems, and music can be used to start children on the road to moral training and literacy. It is my sincere hope that the material in this group of examples will give parents ideas to build on if we are to strengthen our homes and family units. We must guard our thoughts and actions. We need older and successful examples as our role models for parenting. We need the knowledge of modern skills such as self-esteem training and motivational materials to produce strong willed families.

In the last pages of this book, I have given priority to *America the Beautiful*. The United States of America is the jewel in God's glorious world. Not only is she the 'Land of the Free' and the 'Home of the Brave,' she stands as a beacon of hope and protection to men and women who yearn for freedom and equality.

The United States of America was one of two new continents discovered six hundred years ago; the smallest of the two continents, that later became the United States of America, was undeveloped land inhabited only by the Native Americans. The United States is a land which developed into an economical giant. Due to the efforts and the sacrifices of men and women who immigrated to find freedom, a place to worship, raise their family and earn a living in a new country, free from taxes, a church run government and less domination from growing governments, overcrowded areas where there was no land or opportunity to provide for their families or to escape famine. These goodly people found a rich, pristine area in which the Government was providing "homestead rights" to the immigrants and dedicated men who fought in the Revolutionary War. The "bloody war" was necessary to keep our county free of domination and produce a country that could be molded into a democracy.

Introduction

The "Framers of the Constitution" patterned it through their optimism, generosity, self reliance, free enterprise, and under the grace of God, were outstanding men of achievement. Men who put their new government before their own safety, their families safety and comfort. I hope you will appreciate hearing about their wisdom, wonderful vision and accomplishments which are noted in this volume.

CHAPTER ONE

Virtues

FAITH IS OUR ASSURANCE
OF A BRIGHT FUTURE

Faith is more than a belief, it is an abundant power. In the New Testament, the Apostle Paul taught that *"faith is the substance of things hoped for and the evidence of things not seen,"* Hebrews 11:1. To have faith we must also trust. When human trust tends to waiver, our faith can remain as strong as ever. Therefore, faith is a most powerful force in our life. Faith is a principle in which action and power are shown. When we exercise faith, we show our hope for something that we have yet to obtain.

Faith is a gift of God, given to us as a reward for living the best we can. Every conceivable good thing we do affects our faith. The ruling force in our life is a result of our behavior and desire to keep God's commandments. Conversely, where good is not found religious faith is not found.

Faith is always apparent when righteousness is present, and the greater the measure we receive the greater the growth of our faith. It will redirect the course and direction of life towards obedience of God's laws. We are rewarded with spiritual growth and faith beyond measure when we are mindful of Gods laws. In our personal lives, as we exercise our faith, we find that we are constantly learning and building our faith. One cannot fail to grow when we experience great knowledge when faith is rewarded in times of confused and turbulent surroundings and we turn to the one source of help, our God.

We can experience a growing faith that is continually being enriched by prayer. We should not be afraid to show and tell of our faith. Perhaps, others need to hear such words and to know that they are not alone in their beliefs. Indeed, you may at times be taunted for your belief in God, nevertheless, secretly you may be commended more that you would believe.

Like a seed that becomes a mighty oak tree, faith keeps growing and getting stronger year by year. Let us believe in the miracles and expect them in times of need when we call on God.

Sad is a person who goes through life without the comfort of faith. I am reminded of the story of Mark Twain. He was known as a vocal critic of man's ties with God. Mr. Twain arrived home one evening, having been gone from his home on a world tour. He was relating his many experiences in Europe and having met Kings and Queens, and the delight of having been entertained by royalty.

His young daughter listening to his many tales commented, "Pretty soon you will know everybody but God, won't you Papa?"

It is said that the great John Wesley was leading a discussion one day with a group of religious notables on the subject of faith. When he asked the gentlemen to define the word faith, no one had a good answer. At last, a woman hearing the discussion stood and spoke these words, "Faith is taking God at his word." Mr. Wesley spun around in his chair and faced the woman. "That will do," said Wesley, "It is enough for all of us."

Mr. Wesley must have been touched by the simple words

of this woman. She knew that she was a child of God. She did not need to be reminded that she was in God's presence. One can feel the inner knowledge that she knew her source of love, comfort, health, strength, and protection. This kind of awareness, so beautifully stated, is "enough for all of us."

One thing that comes clear to the enlightened mind is that there are laws that keep life and all living endeavors in proper balance. The scientists refer to them as natural laws. When we live by these natural laws, such as faith, with God, we can accomplish great things, heal the sick, give comfort to a troubled mind, restore order in our homes, and restore hope when family problems overwhelm us. Discovering these laws brings progress, enabling us to obtain higher levels of service and commitment to each other and to our God. Faith is needed in our families and personal lives.

You will agree with me that we live in an unsettled world. As we all anticipate, the problems will multiply and become more intense, as our population increases and men continue in ungodly principles toward selfish endeavors, and, worse yet, forget God their maker. We need to learn how to deal with the harsh facts of physical and emotional changes in the world around us. We must learn to contend with the changing weather conditions, governmental control, taxation, gangs and lawlessness, without our coming apart or cracking under the strain of it all. We must, through faith, have the resiliency to live beyond these struggles, and show love and service to our neighbors around us.

It is apparent that we must broaden and magnify our faith. We do this by understanding that true faith must lead to action. For example, the Holy Bible used by Christians, helps renew our understanding of faith in general. In the Epistle of James, Chapter 2:24, *"Ye see then how that by works a man is justified, and not by faith only."* Likewise in James 2:26, *"For as the body without the spirit is dead, faith without works is dead also."*

3

It is essential that we seek knowledge and learning by exercising our faith.

Faith is the first principle of religious belief and it is the foundation of righteousness and the principle of action in all intelligent endeavors. With "faith" we enter the pathway to the heart and that action gives us the courage to learn and progress in all of our goals. Without faith we could never accomplish learning and I am speaking here of "faith in one's self." All capacities to learn involve faith in your self-esteem, judgments, actions, and desires. Faith is needed by anyone wishing to succeed.

> *Experience is called the most eloquent preacher, but it never has a large congregation, because the greatest sermon we will ever preach will be the sermon of our lives.*

Anon.

LIFE'S PURSUIT

In our earthly mortality,
God has given each one of us,
as his children, our free agency.

We have two guests to entertain,
the body and the spirit.
That which we feed the body
shall not live,
But that which we feed the spirit
shall live forever.

Author unknown.

Virtues

FAITH

Faith that withstood the shocks of toil and time;
Hope that defied despair;
Patience that conquered care;
And loyalty, whose courage was sublime;
The great deep heart that was a home for all,-
Just, eloquent, and strong
In protest against wrong;
Wide charity, that knew no sin, no fall;
The Spartan spirit that made life so grand,
Mating poor daily needs
With high, heroic deeds,
That wrested happiness from Fate's hard hands.

Louisa May Alcott

THE LOOM OF TIME

Man's life is laid in the loom of time
To a pattern he does not see,
While the weavers work and shuttles fly
Till the dawn of eternity.

Some shuttles are filled with silver threads
And some with threads of gold,
While often but the darker hues
Are all that they may hold.

But the weaver watches with skillful eye
Each shuttle fly to and fro,
And sees the pattern so deftly wrought
As the loom moves sure and slow.

God surely planned the pattern:
Each thread, the dark and fair,

5

Is chosen by His master skill
And placed in the web with care.

He only knows its beauty,
And guides the shuttles which hold
The threads so unattractive,
As well as the thread of gold.

Not till each loom is silent,
And the shuttles cease to fly,
Shall God reveal the pattern
And explain the reason why

The dark thread were as needful
In the weaver's skillful hand
As the threads of gold and silver
For the pattern which He planned.

Greek Myth

THE OLD MUSICIAN

The following story, true in every detail, is told of the late Charles Francois Gounod, the French musical composer, who possessed a very kind heart in addition to his musical genius. On Christmas evening, in 1837, an old man carrying a stout stick walked slowly through the most fashionable quarter of Paris. His right arm pressed to his side an oblong object wrapped in a checkered cotton handkerchief. He was very thin, poorly clad and shivering. He was buffeted about by the scurrying crowds, apparently at a loss which way to turn. He untied his checkered handkerchief and disclosed a violin and a bow. Raising the instrument, he started to play a sentimental strain, but the result was only harsh and inharmonious sounds. With a sob he sank to his knees. "Oh, God," he prayed. "Why can I no longer play?"

Three young men came down the street singing a tune which was popular among the students of the "Conservatory of Music." One of them accidentally knocked off the old man's hat, and a second, stumbled against his leg. The bareheaded old violinist rose proudly to his feet.

"Pardon, mister," said the third young man. "I hope we did not hurt you." The speaker picked up the man's hat. "No," was the bitter answer. The young man saw the violin. "You are a musician?" "I once was," he replied. Two large tears trickled down the old man's face. "What is the matter? Are you ill?" The old man faltered for a moment; then he held out his hand to them. "Give me a trifle for the love of that God who dwells in the high heavens. I can no longer earn anything by my art. My fingers are stiff, I am in want and my daughter is dying of consumption."

Down in his pockets went each of the trio. They were poor students. Their combined capital was found to be six sous and a package of gum.

"This won't do," declared the student who had apologized for the accident. "We want more than this to relieve our fellow artist. A pull together will do it. You, Adolphe, take the violin and accompany Gustave, while I go around with the hat."

A ringing laugh was the answer. They pulled their hats over their faces and turned up their coat collars to avoid recognition. Adolphe took the violin from the old man's trembling hands. The first notes of the "Carnival of Venice" floated out upon the night air. Such masterful music did not customarily come from the instruments of street players. Windows of the Royal houses flew up and heads were trust out of the openings. Strollers coming down the street stopped. And those who had gone on retraced their steps. Soon a good sized crowd had gathered. Gustave sang the favorite "Cavatina" from "La Dame Blanche" in a manner that held the audience spell-bound. It "rained money" when the song was finished.

"One more tune," whispered the treasurer of the enterprise. "Bring out those bass notes of yours, Adolphe. I'll help you out with the baritone part, Gustave, my brave tenor." "We'll finish up with the trio from *"Guillaume Tell."* And mind, now, we're singing for the honor of the Conservatory, as well as, for the sake of a brother artist."

The three young men played and sang, probably as they never played and sang in their life after. The most critical of audiences was enthralled.

Life came back to the old man. He grasped his stick, and, adopting it as a baton, used it with the air of one having authority. He stood transfixed when they had finished; his face lighted up; his eyes glistened.

The proceeds of the entertainment netted 500 francs. Many of the wealthy listeners had thrown gold pieces into the old battered hat. They gave the old man his hat and its contents, and wrapped up the instrument in the old checkered handkerchief.

"Your names, your names, " the old man gasped. Give me your names that I may bless them on my death bed."

"My name is Faith,: said the first.

"My name is Hope," said the second.

"And mine, Charity," said the treasurer of the enterprise.

"You do not know mine," continued the old man, regaining his voice. "Ah, I might have been an impostor, but I am not. My name is Charles. For ten years I directed the opera at Stransburg. It was I who led in *"Guillaume Tell."* Since I left my native land, misfortune has followed me. With this money my daughter and I can go to the country and there she will recover her health, and I will find a place to teach. You-all of you will- be truly great."

"Amen," was the hearty response of the students, as they shook the good man's hand. Despite their attempts as disguising, the young men had been recognized by one who afterwards told the tale.

They were known to fame in later years as Gustave Roger, the great tenor; Adolphe Herman, the great violinist, and Charles Gustave, the great composer. So the old man's prophecy was fulfilled.

Author unknown

God has a design for our lives. We may not understand what God has in mind, but it is up to us to us to improve that pattern we are to follow.

WE MUST HAVE FAITH

*W*e must have faith! What is God striving to do with us? He is preparing us to live with him when we leave this earthly estate. Word for word and precept by precept God wants us to recognize that we are one of His children, regardless of race, creed or position, He loves us all equally. If we fail to carry this message to the world we may find that man-kind may destroy each other. We shall all return to him but those with a faith in God will be more prepared. Having faith in the Lord, means we are relying on Him and are striving to do His will. All we need to do is sincerely and devotedly call upon Him for help. Let us ask God in faith with nothing wavering, to help cure our troubled world.

In keeping with my intention not to be partial in my writing, I wish to remind you that my words are intended for God's children of all faiths. I use reference material from the Holy Bible because it was the vehicle used in my training by goodly and loving parents, and I follow the faith of my mother and father. I want to remind you when I use my Christian doctrine, please would you listen to my message and substitute the religious doctrine you practice and are comfortable using, just as one is more comfortable in the vernacular they were born with. I would like to pass on this advice, it too comes from the Bible in James 1:5-6. It carries a truthful statement for all human inhabitants of the earth.

"If any of you lack wisdom, let him ask of God, that giveth to all men liberally, and upbraideth not; and it shall be given him."

"But let him ask in faith, nothing wavering. For he that wavereth is like a wave of the sea driven with the wind and tossed."

In regard to exercising faith we may need repentance from past sins and mistakes. With a sincere heart and steady mind ask God for forgiveness. Then be merciful with yourself. Forgive yourself – this is a divine commandment. It helps to know *"The Lord seeth not as man seeth – the Lord looketh on the heart."*

1Samuel 16:7
King James Version, Holy Bible

FAITH

Nothing in life is more wonderful than faith-
the one great moving force which we can
neither weigh in the balance nor
test in the crucible.
Sir William Osler

WE UNDERSTAND SO LITTLE

*O*nce there were two young brothers who had spent all their lives in the city, and had never even seen a field or pasture. So one day they decided to take a trip into the countryside. As they were walking along, they spied a farmer plowing, and were puzzled about what he was doing.

"What kind of behavior is this?" they asked themselves. "This fellow marches back and forth all day, scarring the earth with long ditches. Why should anyone destroy such a pretty meadow like that?"

Later in the afternoon, they passed the same place again, and this time they saw the farmer sowing grains of wheat in the furrows.

"Now what's he doing?" they asked themselves. "He must be a madman. He's taking perfectly good wheat and tossing it into these ditches!"

"The country is no place for me," said one of the brothers. "The people here act as if they had no sense. I'm going home." And he went back to the city.

But the second brother stayed in the country, and a few weeks later saw a wonderful change. Fresh green shoots began to cover the field with lushness he had never imagined. He quickly wrote to his brother and told him to hurry back to see the miraculous growth.

So his brother returned from the city, and he too was amazed at the change. As the days passed they saw the green earth turn into a golden field of tall wheat. And now they understood the reason for the farmer's work.

Then the wheat grew ripe, and the farmer came with this scythe and began to cut it down. The brother who had returned from the city couldn't believe it. "What is this imbecile doing now?" he exclaimed. "All summer long he worked so hard to grow this beautiful wheat, and now he's destroying it with his own hands! He is a madman after all! I've had enough. I'm going back to the city.

But his brother had more patience. He stayed in the country and watched the farmer collect the wheat and take it to his granary. He saw how cleverly he separated the chaff, and how carefully he stored the rest. And he was filled with awe when he realized that by sowing a bag of seed, the farmer had harvested a whole field of grain. Only then did he truly understand that the farmer had a reason for everything he did.

"And this is how it is with God's works, too," he said. "We mortals see only the beginning of His plan. We cannot understand the full purpose and end of His creation. So we must have faith in His wisdom."

Jewish Folktale

THE RICHES OF LIFE

You are richer today than you were yesterday if you have laughed often, given something, forgiven more, made a new friend, or made stepping stones out of your stumbling blocks; if you have thought more in terms of "thyself" than "myself" or if you have managed to be cheerful even if you are weary. You are richer tonight than you were this morning, if you have taken time to trace the handiwork of God in the commonplace things of life, or if you have learned to count out things that really do not profit to your gain in faith and wisdom, or if you have been a little blinder to the faults of friends or foes. You are richer if a little child has smiled at you or if you have looked for the best in others and given the best in you.

Anon.

The pleasantest things in the world are pleasant thoughts; and the great art of life is to have as many of them as possible."

Montaigne

Tennyson and a fellow companion walked through a garden of "God's gift of roses." They were enhanced by the fragrance that attracted the keenness of scent in their nostrils and in their minds they listed the God-like beauty that surrounded them, which brought forth from the lips of Tennyson's companion these words, "What has the spirit of the Master done for you?" Tennyson, plucking the most beautiful rose the eye could behold, answered: "What the sunshine and dew from heaven has been to this rose, so has been the spirit of Christ to my life."

He who runs from God in the morning will scarcely find Him the rest of the day.

PATIENCE

" *How* poor are they who have not patience. What wound did ever heal but by degrees?" said Shakespeare. It is a difficult challenge to acquire patience. Yet indeed, it is one of life's most treasured virtues.

Patience involves an exercise of forbearance in depth. It takes patience to be a spouse, parent, friend, counselor and teacher. Many times just dealing with those you love takes more fortitude than we can muster. It was the Master himself who said, "In your patience, possess ye your souls." Luke 21:19.

We must learn to be quiet, humble, full of love, willing to submit to much frustration if we are to conquer being patient with family and others we communicate with each day. How peaceful life could be if we all could commit to silence when others verbally lose control of tempers. It takes much self-control if others momentarily wound our egos. If we could endure without complaint, many family situations could be handled with humor. It takes perseverance and patience to enjoy peace in the home.

A LESSON IN HUMANITY

*Y*ears ago, a 10-year-old boy approached the counter of a soda shop and climbed on to a stool . "What does an ice cream sundae cost?" he asked the waitress.

"Fifty cents," she answered.

The youngster reached deep in his pockets and pulled out an assortment of change, counting it carefully as the waitress grew impatient. She had "bigger" customers to wait on.

"Well, how much would just plain ice cream be?" the boy asked.

The waitress responded with noticeable irritation in her voice, "Thirty-five cents."

Again the boy slowly counted his money. "May I have some plain ice cream in a dish then, please?"

He gave the waitress the correct amount, and she brought him the ice cream.

Later, the waitress returned to clear the boy's dish and when she picked it up, she felt a lump in her throat. There on the counter the boy had left two nickels and five pennies. She realized that he had had enough money for the sundae, but sacrificed it so that he could leave her a tip.

Affirmation: "I will be patient with every child of God."

THE MILLER, HIS SON, AND THE DONKEY

A miller and his son were driving their donkey to a neighboring fair to sell him. They had not gone far when they met a group of girls returning from town laughing and talking together.

"Look there!" cried one of them. "Did you ever see such fools, to be trudging along the road on foot, when they ought to be riding!"

So the man put the boy on the donkey, and they went on

their way. Presently they came up to a group of old men in earnest debate. "There!" said one of them. "That proves exactly what I was saying. No one pays any respect to old age in these days. Look at that idle young rogue riding, while his poor old father has to walk. Get down, you lazy lout, and let the old man rest his weary limbs."

The miller made his son dismount, and got on the donkey's back in his place. And in this manner they proceeded along the way until they met a company of women and children.

"Why, shame on you, lazybones!" they cried. "How can you ride while that poor little lad can hardly keep up with you?" The good miller, wishing to please, took up his son to sit behind him.

But just as they reached the edge of the village a townsman called out to them: "I have a good mind to report you to the authorities for overloading that poor beast so shamelessly. You big hulking fellows should better be able to carry that donkey than the other way round."

So, alighting, the miller and his son tied the beast's legs together, and with a pole across their shoulders, carried the donkey over the bridge that led to the town. This was such an entertaining sight to the townsfolk that crowds came out to laugh at it. The poor animal, frightened by the uproar, began to struggle to free himself. In the midst of the turmoil, the donkey slipped off the pole and over the rail of the bridge into the water and was drowned.

Aesop's Fables

Try to please all and you end by pleasing none.

THE BEAUTY OF SILENCE

In a time of quiet devotional prayer, we close the door to outer distractions and remain silent for we have no other purpose at this time than to be in our communication with God. The silence we experience for even a few moments slows us down and soothes our emotions. In the silence, God is there. We close our eyes and let the silence embrace and stabilize us.

There are times when allowing the serenity of silence to improve our relationships with others is needed. Silence is needed when conversations take a turn toward controversial issues, such as, politics. Almost everyone has feelings of regret for not keeping silent when volatile feelings have been the result of freely giving our position on such a subject.

There are two good solutions: count to ten or twenty, or the surest way is to ask God to help you stay quiet. If we ask God for help we remain teachable, open, and receptive to his wishes.

When you realize you enjoy giving your opinion, try this affirmation instead. "I will remain silent and calm." If you are a vocal person and you do not know your audience, you may need to repeat this affirmation to yourself several times.

THE LION AND HIS THREE COUNSELORS

The King of Beasts was in an irritable mood. That morning his mate had told him that his breath was most unpleasant. After doing considerable roaring to prove that he was King he summoned his counselors. First he called the sheep.

"Friend sheep," he roared, opening wide his great mouth, "would you say that my breath smells unpleasant?"

Believing that the lion wanted an honest answer, the sheep gave it, and the King of Beasts bit off her head for a fool.

Then he called the wolf and asked him the same question. The wolf, catching sight of the carcass of the sheep, said: "Why, your majesty, you have a breath as sweet as blossoms in the spring-"

Before he could finish he had been torn to pieces for a flatterer.

At last the lion called the fox and put the question to him. The fox gave a hollow cough, then cleared his throat. "Your majesty," he whispered, "truly, I have such a cold in the head that I cannot smell at all."

Aesop's Fables

In dangerous times, men say nothing.

"GUILTY OR NOT GUILTY?"

She stood at the bar of justice,
A creature wan and wild,
In form too small for a woman,
In feature too old for a child.
For a look so worn and pathetic
Was stamped on her pale young face,
It seemed long years of suffering
Must have left that silent trace.

"Your name," said the judge, as he eyed her,
With kindly look, yet keen,
"Is -" "Mary Maguire, if you please, sir."

"And your age?" "I am turned fifteen."
"Well, Mary," – and then from a paper
He slowly and gravely read –
"You are charged here – I am sorry to say it –
With stealing three loaves of bread.

"You look not like an old offender,
And I hope that you can show
The charge to be false. Now, tell me,
Are you guilty of this, or no?"

17

Manna From Heaven

A passionate burst of weeping
Was at first her sole reply;
But she dried her tears in a moment,
And looked in the judge's eye.

"I will tell you just how it was, sir:
My father and mother are dead,
And my little brothers and sisters
Were hungry, and asked me for bread.
At first I earned it for them,
By working hard all day,
But somehow the times were hard, sir,
And the work all fell away.

"I could get no more employment;
The weather was bitter cold;
The young ones cried and shivered
(Little Johnnie's but four year old);
So what was I to do, sir?
I am guilty, but do not condemn;
I took – O! was it stealing? –
The bread to give to them."

Every man in the courtroom –
Graybeard and thoughtless youth –
Knew, as he looked upon her,
That the prisoner spoke the truth.
Out from their pockets came kerchiefs,
Out from their eyes sprung tears,
And out from old, faded wallets
Treasures hoarded for years.

The judge's face was a study,
The strangest you ever saw,
As he cleared his throat and murmured
Something about the law.
For one so learned in such matters,
So wise in dealing with men,

He seemed, on a simple question,
Sorely puzzled just then.

No one blamed him, or wondered
When at last these words they heard.
"The sentence of this young prisoner
Is for the present deferred."
And no one blamed him or wondered
When he went to her and smiled,
And tenderly led from the courtroom,
Himself, the "guilty" child!

Author Unknown

"The sufferings and trials that cross our pathway are the chisels that God uses to round our character into beauty."

Anon.

THE VIRTUE OF COMPASSION

ust as courage takes its stand by others in challenging situations, so compassion takes its stand with others in distress.

Compassion is a virtue that takes seriously the reality of other people's problems, heath issues, traumas suffered by others, emotional problems, as well as all of the external circumstances that may be a result of another's misfortune.

The seeds of compassion are planted among goodly men and women who are completely willing to help others in their time of need. We give freely to others so as to relieve their suffering and distress at a critical moment in their life.

It is so easy to give of our compassion to the elderly in respect for their contribution to our lives and to the nation as a whole. These beloved elders who have given their compassion and fulfilled their responsibilities in past decades deserve our respect and constant care. Let us as a nation and as individuals respect their wisdom, credit their endeavors, overlook their aging bodies, look into their eyes and see the young soul who is still smiling with love to each of us. Let us love and respect them back.

The dictionary describes compassion as follows: to feel pity or sorrow for the suffering or trouble of others, accompanied by the urge to help, to show deep sympathy.

It is said that the mark of a true follower of God consists in having pity and sympathy, showing and exhibiting mercy, tenderness and kindness.

The Lord, Jesus Christ, set the perfect example of seeking out and healing the sick.

"Finally, be ye all of one mind, having compassion one for another, love as brethren, be pitiful, be courteous."

1 Peter 3:8

LIFE'S SCARS

They say the world is round, and yet
I often think it square,
So many little hurts we get
From corners here and there.
But one great truth in life I've found,
While journeying to the West –
The only folks who really wound
Are those we love the best.

The man you thoroughly despise
Can rouse your wrath, 'tis true;
Annoyance in your heart will rise
At things mere strangers do;
But those are only passing ills;
This rule all lives will prove;
The rankling wound which aches and thrills
Is dealt by hands we love.

The choicest garb, the sweetest grace,
Are oft to strangers shown;
The careless men, the frowning face,
Are given to our own.
We flatter those we scarcely know,
We please the fleeting guest,
And deal full many a thoughtless blow
To those who love us best.

Love does not grow on every tree,
Nor true hearts yearly bloom.
Alas for those who only see
This cut across a tomb!
But, soon or late, the fact grows plain
To all through sorrow's test:
The only folks who give us pain
Are those we love the best.

Author Unknown

ST. NICKOLAS AND THE GOLDEN BARS

*L*ong ago there lived a husband and wife who had more money than they knew what to do with, but more than anything else they wanted a child. They prayed to God for many years to give them their heart's desire, and at last when a son was born, they were the happiest people in the world. They named him Nicholas.

They thought there was no one like their boy, and indeed, he was a kind and gentle child, and never gave them a moment's trouble. But while he was still a little boy, a terrible plague swept over the country, and his father and mother died, leaving him quite alone.

All the great riches which his parents possessed were left to Nicholas, and among other things he inherited three bars of gold. These were his greatest treasure, and he thought more of them than all his other riches.

Now in Nicholas's town there lived a nobleman with three daughters. They had once been very wealthy, but great misfortunes had overtaken the father, and now they were all so poor they scarcely had enough to live on. The nobleman tried as hard as he could to find work, but when people saw his soft hands, which had never known any kind of hard labor, they took him to be lazy, and turned him away.

At last a day came when there was not even enough bread to eat, and the daughters said to their father: "Let us go out into the streets and beg, or do anything to get a little money, so we won't starve."

But the father answered: "Not tonight. I cannot bear to think of it. Wait at least until tomorrow. Something may happen to save us from such disgrace."

Just as they were talking together, Nicholas happened to be passing, and since the window was open he heard all they said. It seemed terrible to think that this family should be so poor and actually in want of bread, and Nicholas tried to plan a way to help them. He knew they would be much too proud to take money from him, so he had to think of some other way. "I must ask God to show me how," he told himself.

So that night, before he climbed into bed, Nicholas prayed as hard as he could, and asked God to guide him. Suddenly he remembered the three golden bars, and at once an idea flashed into his head. He jumped up and took one of them, and quickly started out for the nobleman's house.

Just as he had hoped, Nicholas discovered that the same window was still open, and by standing on tiptoe, he could barely reach it. So he lifted the golden bar and slipped it through, and didn't wait to hear what became of it, in case anyone should see him.

Inside the house, the poor father sat worrying as his children slept. He wondered if there was any hope for them anywhere, and he prayed earnestly that heaven would send help. "Tomorrow I will knock on every door in the city until I find work," he told himself. "God will help us through these hard times."

Suddenly something fell at his feet. The nobleman looked down, and to his amazement and joy, he found it was a bar of pure gold.

"My child," he cried as he showed his eldest daughter the shining gold, "God has heard our prayers and has sent this from heaven! Now we will have enough to eat and some to spare. Call your sisters, and I will go and change this treasure."

The precious golden bar was soon sold to a bank, and it brought so much money, the family was able to live in comfort and have all they needed. And not only was there enough to live on, but so much was left over that the father gave his eldest daughter a large dowry, and very soon she was happily married.

When Nicholas saw how much happiness his golden bar had brought to the poor nobleman, he decided the second daughter should have a dowry too. So he went as before and found the little window again open, and was able to throw in the second bar as he had done before. This time the father was dreaming happily, and did not find the treasure until he waked the next morning. Soon afterward the second daughter had her dowry and was married too.

Now, the father began to think that it was a bit unusual, to say the least, that not one but two golden bars should fall from heaven, and he wondered if by any chance human hands had placed them in his room. The more he thought about it, the more mysterious it seemed, and he made up his mind to keep watch every night, in case another bar should be sent as a dowry for his third daughter.

And so when Nicholas went the third time and dropped the last bar through the little window, the father came quickly out, and before Nicholas had time to hide, caught him by the cloak.

"O Nicholas," he cried, "are you the one who has helped us in our need? Why did you hide?" And then he fell on his knees and began to kiss the hands that had helped him so graciously. But Nicholas asked him to stand up, and give thanks to God instead, and begged him not to tell anyone the story of the golden bars.

THE PARABLE OF THE PRODICAL SON

nd he said, A certain man had two sons: And the younger of them said to his father, "Father, give me the portion of goods that falleth to me." And he divided unto them his living.

And not many days after the younger son gathered all together, and took his journey into a far country, and there wasted his substance with riotous living. And when he had spent all, there arose a mighty famine in that land; and he began to be in want. And he went and joined himself to a citizen of that country; and he sent him into his fields to feed the swine. And he would fain have filled his belly with the husks that the swine did eat; and no man gave unto him.

And when he came to himself, he said, How many hired servants of my father's have bread enough and to spare, and I perish with hunger! I will arise and go to my father, and will say unto him, "Father, I have sinned against heaven and before thee, and am no more worthy to be called thy son: make me as one of thy hired servants."

And he arose, and came to his father. But when he was yet a great way off, his father saw him, and had compassion, and ran, and fell on his neck, and kissed him. And the son said unto him, 'Father, I have sinned against heaven, and in thy sight, and am no more worthy to be called your son.' But the father said to his servants, 'Bring forth the best robe, and put it on him; and put a ring on his hand, and shoes on his feet: and bring hither the fatted calf, and kill it; and let us eat, and be merry: for this my son was dead, and is alive again; he was lost , and is found.' And they began to be merry.

Now his elder son was in the field: and as he came and drew nigh to the house, he heard music and dancing. And he called one of the servants and asked what these things meant. And he said unto him, 'Thy brother is come; and thy father hath killed the fatted calf, because he hath received him safe and sound.' And he was angry, and would not go in: therefore came his father out, and entreated him. And he answering said to his father, 'Lo, these many years do I serve thee, neither transgressed I at any time thy commandment: and yet thou never gavest me a kid, that I might make merry with my friends: but as soon as this thy son was come, which hath devoured thy living with harlots, thou hast killed for him the fatted calf.'

And he said unto him, 'Son, thou are ever with me, and all that I have is thine. It was meet that we should make merry, and be glad: for this thy brother was dead, and is alive again; and was lost, and is found."

St. Luke 15:11-32

One of the wisest, most skilled teachers the world has ever known was Jesus Christ. He taught most of His sermons and lessons in parables and short stories, showing His respect for the humble, spiritual followers of all classes of followers.

A PSALM OF LIFE

Tell me not, in mournful numbers,
Life is but an empty dream! –
For the soul is dead that slumbers,
And things are not what they seem.
Life is real! Life is earnest!
And the grave is not its goal;

Manna From Heaven

Dust thou art, to dust returnest,
Was not spoken of the soul.

Not enjoyment, and not sorrow,
Is our destined end or way;
But to act, that each tomorrow
Find us farther than today.

Art is long, and Time is fleeting,
And our hearts, though stout and brave,
Still, like muffled drums, are beating
Funeral marches to the grave.

In the world's broad field of battle,
In the bivouac of Life,
Be not like dumb, driven cattle!
Be a hero in the strife!

Trust no Future, howe'er pleasant!
Let the dead Past bury its dead!
Act, - act in the living Present!
Heart within and God o'erhead!

Lives of great men all remind us
We can make our lives sublime,
And, departing, leave behind us
Footprints in the sands of time;

Footprints, that perhaps another,
Sailing o'er life's solemn main,
A forlorn and shipwrecked brother,
Seeing, shall take heart again.

Let us, then be up and doing.
With a heart for any fate;

Still achieving, still pursuing,
Learn to labor and to wait.

Henry Wadsworth Longfellow

"THE RETURN"

"Dark clouds blown by December winds,
Over the pasture, and fields, bare and cold.
Smoke curling up from the chimney top
Of a low roofed farm house gray and old.
And looking out on the wintry scene,
On withered meadow and narrow lane
Two old faces with love aglow,
Expectant, pressed to the window pane.

Gaily they nodded to passers by,
Neighbors On Christmas errands bent,
They waved a greeting and smiled to them;
On the dear old faces was sweet content.
God had answered at last their prayers,
Prayers that that longed seemed all in vain;
But after an absence of many years,
Their boy was coming home again.

He was only a lad when he went from home,
A willful boy, who would have his own way ;
To the lonely farm house he bade good-bye,
Leaving his mother to watch and pray.
Long years passed ere a letter came,
Telling of sorrow and broken pride;
Saying at last he was coming home,
He would be with them at Christmas tide.

Hand clasped in hand all day they sat,
Watching the road that stretched far away,

Manna From Heaven

Looking oft at a lock of hair and a pictured face
That once was young and gay;
Saying: Will he be changed-will he be old and grave,
Will he know us whose heads are white?
But we must wait, he will be with us before the night."

Over the landscape the twilight crept,
Veiling the face of the dying day, but still he came not.
And they sat and watched the meadow
And lane to their sight grew dim,
A figure appeared at the garden gate,
It was only a tramp but they welcomed him.

Gladly they gave of their Christmas cheer,
They heaped his arms till no more they'd hold
Bidding him enter and take a seat,
And there find shelter from the storm and cold.
For this is the Christmas –time they said
And our boy is coming home once more,
We have so much let us share with you,
Some of the blessings we have in store.
Standing outside, unkempt, ill clad.
With eyes of caverns of deepest woe;
He surveyed the old home, the home-like things,
The ancient fireplace, the warmth, the glow.

Poverty, shame, dissipation, and crime,
All of these stamped on his deep lined face;
He shook his head; for of such as he
At that pure hearthstone there is no place.
He turned away from the opened door,
Out through the garden gate he passed,
Out to the long white road once more;
That picture, that lock of hair;
Oh! the youth that I squandered long ago,

Let them remember me as I was,
'Tis better that they should never know.

Late in the window the lamplight burned,
The old folks waited, but all in vain;
Then remembering the tramp who had sought their door,
They prayed that his footsteps be led aright;
"Have pity on those, Dear God", they said,
"Whose boy is an outcast this Christmas night."

Anon.

The home is the temple of our shelter and rest.

HONESTY

Honesty is of upmost importance in today's world. Recently, we have all witnessed the fallout of dishonest sports heroes, clergy, including social issues of infidelity, child abuse, and financial ruin brought about by trusted people in the investment world. Nothing is more cruel than to see the savings of our seniors, who have saved for their retirement years, only to find their funds are worthless in their frail years.

I need not mention these items, we hear enough of such ills every night on the television, or from our newspapers. I shall just leave to all a constant reminder; honesty is best cultivated in the home by honest parents who explore life's experiences, and teach honesty to their children. Every soul is impeded when people are not honest with each other.

Honesty shows self respect and respect for others.

SOMEONE SEE'S YOU

*O*nce upon a time a man decided to sneak into his neighbor's fields and steal some wheat. "If I take just a little from each field, no one will notice," he told himself, "but it will all add up to a nice pile of wheat for me." So he waited for the darkest night, when thick clouds lay over the moon, and he crept out of his house. He took his youngest daughter with him.

"Daughter," he whispered, "you must stand guard, and call out if anyone sees me."

The man stole into the first field to begin reaping, and before long the child called out, "Father, someone sees you!"

The man looked all around, but he saw no one, so he gathered his stolen wheat and moved on to a second field.

"Father, someone sees you!" the child cried again.

The man stopped and looked all around, but once again he saw no one. He gathered more wheat, and moved to a third field.

A little while passed, and the daughter cried out, "Father, someone sees you!" Once more the man stopped his work and looked in every direction, but he saw no one at all, so he bundled his wheat and crept into the last field.

"Father, someone sees you!" the child called again.

The man stopped reaping, looked all around, and once again saw no one. "Why in the world do you keep saying someone sees me?" he angrily asked his daughter. "I've looked everywhere, and I don't see anyone. "Father," murmured the child, "Someone sees you from above."

A lesson in honesty for parents! Your children observe (and emulate) your actions.

STEADFASTNESS

A sincere character trait, admired by everyone, is steadfastness. It is a synonym for dependability, but in this case probably a more modern definition could include the action of goals. It stands for faithfulness, firmness in the right, and it means the determination in adhering to sound principles. Those who are steadfast are known to be unwavering in the face of temptations and obstacles.

Steadfastness is one of the primary essentials for accomplishment. Unless we have this quality we are uncertain, easily swayed, and do not possess the perseverance to follow through to the end and to accomplish things one sets out to do.

Steadfastness and convictions are closely interrelated. One cannot be steadfast unless he has strong convictions in which to adhere. Such examples are all around us. Many young men and women have such qualities, and in some cases seem to be born with extra talents and gifts to pursue their dreams. We have men and women who excel in sports, medicine, art, dance, engineering, electronics, and in the sciences. It takes many hours of steadfast training, arising in the morning before the world is awake, and total dedication to their goals.

Additionally, we have dedicated parents, mentors, coaches, family members who are willing to sacrifice, and additional help from academia, to support the person in their pursuits. Determination and practice, with goals in mind, make for champions in sports and creative pursuits. Additionally, adhering to rules of health, such as, exercise, good nutritional choices, cleanliness, refusing drugs, tobacco, and strong alcohol drinks make a difference in how our bodies handle the steadfastness of physical activity.

Let us continue in "steadfastness" in being good neighbors, in being kind and understanding, and in giving devoted service to others.

What becomes most important when life is viewed from a long perspective, is the assurance that one has never surrendered when the storms of life have beaten upon one's face; that we have always stood steadfast for what is right in any situation. That we have fought a "good fight" and won through steadfastness and firm convictions, then our actions may become a great character building opportunity.

COURAGE

We may wonder, if life never offered challenges, how would we then discover the depth of our courage and respondent skills? In truth, life experiences are replete with many challenges, and therefore, many opportunities for learning correct responses. In the Biblical story of David we read, "And David said to Solomon his son, Be Strong and of good courage and do it: fear not, nor be dismayed: for the Lord God, even my God, will be with thee: he will not fail thee, nor forsake thee, until thou hast finished all the work for the service of the house of the Lord."

1 Chronicles 28:20

With God we can face any situation with courage and poise. When we partner with God, we can act with certainty no matter what is going on around us. These realizations are a part of our conscious behavior, and provides opportunities for daily growth.

In response to natural disasters, such as floods, tornadoes, fires and earthquakes, which can randomly rob families of their very existence, a plan for quick, expedient and prayerful action is required. The same holds true if you are the victim of an accident. Because we have been created by God, we have access to the qualities of strength and courage once needed when adverse situations arise.

In response to man-made disasters, such as food and water shortages, power shortages, and a variety of other environmental problems, all of which will escalate yearly due to urbanization and continued population growth, a mutually accessible response plan is in order. We must be prepared with emergency supplies in a bag that we have access to and can be retrieved at a moment's notice.

Where might we begin if we find that we are affected by any of the aforementioned problems? Answer: take a full deep breath. Affirm, "I am courageous and strong." Repeat over and over many times. You will feel the courage fill your soul. Then do what is necessary to improve your situation, and seek safety.

Affirmations are important tools. They work subliminally and will re-orient your conscious and subconscious mind. The mind will soon accept them and they may work for you. However, practice makes perfect. Put your affirmation on a card and carry it with you. Refer to it several times a day for thirty days. If you do this faithfully, it will be there to give you courage when you need it.

Affirmation: "I am courageous and strong."

THE JOY OF FORGIVENESS

*E*veryone is worthy of forgiveness, not only because of something particular that was done, but because you are a creation of God. It is disconsolate when a person, after making a mistake, becomes so remorseful for their actions they fall back into the quagmire and repeat the mistakes again and again. Their reasoning must be loaded with guilt or fear, and their misguided thoughts exasperate into additional troubles. How much more reasonable is one who has faith. Faith helps them to surrender to the grace promised by a loving God.

The beauty of seeking and receiving forgiveness of mistakes, in time washes away our guilt, and we can let it go from our thoughts. Guilt can become a debilitating illness if left to fester. One has only to call upon God with a few simple words, "Please forgive me Lord, I will not do that again." God will forgive us and remember the act no more. There is an exception here; God does not expect you to commit the mistake again. So affirm to yourself over and over that you will keep your word. That is all that is expected of us.

We must forgive the actions of those who transgress against us. If we make an effort and eventually forget those who hurt us, we can enjoy these persons again and repair the broken friendship. This is so important when there are problems between family members. The proper repair of poor social relations are at stake here and thoughtful family members should act promptly to repair any misdeeds or misunderstandings.

There may come a time in our life when we are asked to forgive someone who has perpetrated a serious crime against a member of our family, or ourselves. Few are willing to forgive another, such as in the offence of murder. But it has been done. Special people have reached that plateau with enough faith.

Hoodlumism is born of idleness; it is useful energy gone to seed...the first step in the direction of crime. The hoodlum is very often a good boy who does not know what to do, and so he does wrong.

Elbert Hubbard

The little cares that fretted me,
I lost them yesterday
Among the fields above the sea,
Among the winds at play;
Among the lowing of the herds,
The rustling of the trees,

Among the singing of the birds,
The humming of the bees.

The foolish fears of what may happen
I cast them all away
Among the clover – scented grass,
Among the new-mown hay.
Among the husking of the corn
Where drowsy poppies nod,
Where ill thoughts die and good are born
Out in the fields of God.

Elizabeth Barrett Browning

KINDNESS BEGINS WITH ME

What does being kind really mean? We all know what kindness feels like and we enjoy the experience when it is given to us. The dictionary reports the meaning of kind as: sympathetic, friendly, gentle, tenderhearted, generous, in agreement with ones nature, and having essential character. On the other hand, kindness was measured as: a kind act or kindly treatment, feeling, affection and goodwill. I believe we would all enjoy being the recipient of any of those definitions.

When I was a small child my father never would allow us to bicker or fight and hitting one another was immediately forbidden. When a disagreement arose between us he would start to sing a hymn, "Cool Thou Feeling, Oh Thy Brother." If the quarrel did not stop my father would move to another hymnal. "Let Us Oft Speak Kind Words." If that song did not cure the quarrel, my father would leave the house and come back with a willow from a lilac tree. By the way, that stings pretty badly. After feeling that one time, we usually called it a draw. We finally learned to stop the quarrel before he got up from his chair.

Kindness is one habit everyone should practice. It is so sweet when we receive it from a friend or neighbor, who has been kind with our emotions. You understand your friend has a reverence for life. Kindness is love in motion, given and received in appreciation for each other. Kindness with little children builds their self-esteem. Kindness allows us to give comfort to the ill, the unhappy, and with those we love who have momentarily lost their way.

LET US OFT SPEAK KIND WORDS

Let us oft speak kind words to each other
At home or where're we may be.
Like the warbling of birds on the heather,
The tones will be welcome and free.
They'll gladden the heart that's repining,
Give courage and hope from above,
And where the dark clouds hide the shining,
Let in the bright sunlight of love.

Oh, the kind words we give shall in memory live
And sunshine forever impart.
Let us oft speak kind words to each other;
Kind words are sweet tones of the heart.

Like the sunbeams of morn on the mountains,
The soul they awake to good cheer;
Like the murmur of cool, pleasant fountains,
They fall in sweet cadences near.
Let's oft, then, in kindly toned voices,
Our mutual friendship renew,
Till heart meets with heart and rejoices
In friendship that ever is true.

Oh, the kind words we give shall in memory live
And sunshine forever impart.

Let us oft speak kind words to each other
Kind words are sweet tones of the heart.

Joseph L. Tounsend

THE LION AND THE MOUSE

One day a great lion lay fast asleep, a mouse ran about him in fun and then ran across his paw and awakened him. The great lion grabbed the mouse and was going to eat him, the little mouse cried, "Oh, please let me go sir, "someday I may be able to keep you from harm."

This made the great lion laugh and he declared, "Run on, you deserve to be free." Next day the lion fell in a snare by a rope tied to a tree. The little mouse heard the lion's great roar and he sounded so miserable. The little mouse ran to the great lion. Seeing that he was in trouble, the little mouse started chewing the ropes that held the lion prisoner. With his little sharp teeth, the mouse cut the ropes, and the lion came out of the snare.

"You laughed at me once and thought I was too small to help you. Because you were so kind and let me live, today I was able to return that kindness and save your life."

Application: No act of kindness, no matter how small, is ever wasted.

DEVOTION TO THE BEAUTIFUL

A kind philosopher went into the hills each day to study nature that he might be nearer unto God.

Then each evening on his return, he gathered the people of the village about him to impart unto them the lesson he had learned. As in all good things, there arises skepticisms; for one morning, before he departed, one of his potential friends asked him to bring him back a hawthorn twig. Another asked him to bring back a rose and a third asked him to bring him a lily. The kind philosopher assented to the requests of these three friends. So as the day wore on and evening let down her curtain, the three stood by to receive their gifts from nature. As they took them in their hands the first said: "Here is a dead leaf on my hawthorn twig." The second murmured: "Here is a thorn on my rose;" and the third cried out and said: "Yes, and here is some dirt on the root of my lily."

The kind philosopher took them back , took the dead leaf from the hawthorn twig and placed it in the first friends' hand. Likewise the thorn and the dirt from the rose and the lily. Then he said: "You have attracted what you first saw, I will keep the hawthorn twig, the rose, and the lily for the beauty I see in them." Those who grow most perfectly in life and in the service of the Lord, are the men and women who find only that which is good in others.

You cannot live a perfect day without doing something for someone who will never be able to repay you.

- John Wooden, College Basketball Coach

BEWARE OF WORDS THAT BETRAY YOU

A peasant of a small village spoke evil words against his neighbor. Meanwhile, the neighbor, learning of these ill words and grievance, sought an explanation from the peasant. Immediately, the peasant was humbled and with an attitude of penitence desired to make amends for the wrong he had done. He asked a presiding high priest what he could do to right this wrong with his neighbor. The High Priest, told him to take a sack and fill it with soft white feathers, then go to each house in the village and place a single feather on each threshold. The peasant did this and returned to announce that he had paid full penance for his wrong; but was told that his duty was not completed, that he must go and gather each single feather back into his sack. Of course, the peasant was very much dismayed, and replied, "Well the wind will have blown them away." So "of thy unspoken word, thou art master; thy spoken word is master of thee."

"If we were as ready to administer kindness as we are to inflict pain, or as patient to heal as we are quick to wound, then many unkind words would never have been spoken. Our eyes, being the windows of our soul surely our words and conduct must be the index to the soul."

Author unknown

When over the fair fame of friend or foe.
The shadows of disgrace may fall; instead
Of words of blame, or proof of thus and so,
Let something good be said.

"Forget not that no fellow-being yet
May stoop so low, but love will lift his head,
Even the cheek of shame with tears is wet,
If something good is said.

"No generous heart may vainly turn aside
In way of sympathy. No soul so dead,

But may awaken strong and glorified,
If something good is said.

"And so I charge you by the thorny crown
And by the cross on which the Savior bled,
And by your own soul's hope of fair renown,
Let something good be said.
—*James Whitcomb Riley*

APPRECIATION, A BEAUTIFUL WORD

few words of appreciation from one person to another can heal and transform the person who receives such a message. One caring person can make a positive difference in the life of another. Three little words ring out like a lovely melody, "I appreciate you." The amazing thing about letting others know how much we appreciate and acknowledge them, by doing so, we are also blessed and feel better about ourselves.

Try making an affirmation to look for someone special to honor. Giving each person a bouquet of flowers may not be feasible, but there are other ways to show appreciation. Sending a note and a message of thanks for their friendship, or just a quick telephone call takes very little time and effort. The receiver may feel that your attention is a great treasure of personal worth.

We may not be aware of an illness or a problem our friend may have. How we act in our relations with others makes a difference. Having appreciation comes close to compassion when we think about treating our neighbor as ourselves. We should treat no one with callous disregard for what they do toward us.

Children should be taught appreciation for what good deeds are done for them. They should be taught to write thank you notes. For example, many grandparents, on limited budgets, give expensive gifts to their grandchildren. Children should learn that when a gift is received, an expression of appreciation should be given promptly and sincerely. In many cases, the gift donor may not be present, in which case a telephone call or a written note would serve the same purpose, for an expression of appreciation.

TELL HIM SO

If you hear a kind word spoken
Of some worthy soul you know,
It may fill his heart with sunshine
If you only tell him so.

If a deed, however humble,
Helps you on your way to go,
See the one whose hand has helped you.,
Seek him out and tell him so!

If your heart is touched and tender
Toward a sinner, lost and low,
It might help him to do better
If you'd only tell him so!

Oh, my sisters, oh, my brothers,
As o'er life's rough path you go,
If God's love has saved and kept you,
Do not fail to tell men so!

Author Unknown

I SHALL NOT PASS THIS WAY AGAIN

Through this toilsome world, alas!
Once and only once I pass;
If a kindness I may show,
If a good deed I may do

41

To a suffering fellow man,
Let me do it while I can.
No delay, for it is plain
I shall not pass this way again

NOT EASILY DEFEATED

*O*ne day two adventurous frogs fell into a jar of cream. The top of the jar was quite a distance from the cream inside the jar where they were swimming. Both frogs tried to leap out, but there was nothing under them for support. One frog said, "If I am going to die I might as well get it over with." And into the cream he sank and drowned.

The other frog thought: "Well, if I am going out, at least I'm going down fighting." So using all his vigor he kept on trying, swimming around and trashing about until the cream started to change. Gradually he began to feel solid footing under him as his activity churned the cream into butter. Finally, after his legs got some solid traction, he leaped victoriously from the jar, the contents of which had now turned into solid butter.

Regardless of what confronts you always remember that those who overcome – are those who refused to fail.

THE JOY OF FRIENDSHIPS

*T*hrough the years we have been loved and comforted by loyal friends. Let us celebrate the wonder of friendship by giving some thought to what friendship really stands for; Friends are every day's hidden treasures, never to be thrown away or neglected – only loved, admired, and treated with respect.

Friends are a blessing adding fullness to our life, and they bring us sunshine and happiness to our every day experiences.

As friends they give us support and encouragement, they give us good advice – but never make decisions for us. They show us by their very loving presence whenever we experience sorrow. Friendships are a precious investment.

Friends are not necessarily members of our family and yet they are sometimes closer to us. However, the relationship is most special when members of your family are your closest friends as well.

Let us remember to say thank you often to our special friends. Tell friends how you feel about them. Let us remember each day that true friends accept each other. They do not act superior, or wound you with unkind words. They care, encourage, forgive, trust, give freedom, hold each other accountable, and love each other in a special bond.

NEW FRIENDS AND OLD FRIENDS

Make new friends, but keep the old;
Those are silver, these are gold.
New-made friendships, like new wine,
Age will mellow and refine.
Friendships that have stood the test-
Time and change-are surely best;
Brow may wrinkle, hair grow gray,
Friendships never knows decay,
For 'mid old friends, tried and true,
Once more we our youth renew,
But old friends, alas! may die,
New friends must their place supply,
Cherish friendship in your breast-
New is good, but keep the best;
Make new friends, but keep the old;
Those are silver, these are gold.

Joseph Parry

DAMON AND PYTHIAS

This beautiful story of friendship that has been told since the fourth century B.C. It sets the standard for a perfect friendship.

*D*amon and Pythias had been the best of friends since childhood. Each trusted the other like a brother, and each knew in his heart there was nothing he would not do for his friend. Eventually the time came for them to prove the depth of their devotion. It happened this way.

Dionysius, the ruler of Syracuse, grew annoyed when he heard about the kind of speeches Pythias was giving. The young scholar was telling the public that no man should have unlimited power over another, and that absolute tyrants were unjust kings. In a fit of rage, Dionysius summoned Pythias and his friend.

"Who do you think you are, spreading unrest among the people?" he demanded.

"I spread only the truth," Pythias answered. "There can be nothing wrong with that."

"And does your truth hold that kings have too much power and that their laws are not good for their subjects?"

"If a king has seized power without permission of the people, then that is what I say."

"This kind of talk is treason," Dionysius shouted. "You are conspiring to overthrow me. Retract what you've said, or face the consequences."

"I will retract nothing," Pythias answered.

"Then you will die. Do you have any last requests?"

"Yes. Let me go home just long enough to say goodbye to my wife and children and to put my household in order."

"I see you not only think I'm unjust, you think I'm stupid as well," Dionysius laughed scornfully. "If I let you leave Syracuse, I have no doubt I will never see you again."

44

"I will give you a pledge," Pythias said. "What kind of pledge could you possibly give to make me think you will ever return?" Dionysius demanded.

At that instant Damon, who had stood quietly beside his friend, stepped forward.

"I will be his pledge," he said. "Keep me here in Syracuse, as your prisoner, until Pythias returns. Our friendship is well known to you. You can be sure Pythias will return so long as you hold me."

Dionysius studied the two friends silently. "Very well," he said at last. "But if you are willing to take the place of your friend, you must be willing to accept his sentence if he breaks his promise. If Pythias does not return to Syracuse, you will die in his place."

"He will keep his word," Damon replied. "I have no doubt of that."

Pythias was allowed to go free for a time, and Damon was thrown into prison. After several days, when Pythias failed to reappear, Dionysius's curiosity got the better of him, and he went to the prison to see if Damon was yet sorry he had made such a bargain.

"Your time is almost up," the ruler of Syracuse sneered. "It will be useless to beg for mercy. You were a fool to rely on your friend's promise. Did you really think he would sacrifice his life for you or anyone else?"

"He has merely been delayed," Damon answered steadily. "The winds have kept him from sailing, or perhaps he has met with some accident on the road. But if it is humanly possible, he will be here on time. I am as confident of his virtue as I am of my own existence."

Dionysius was startled at the prisoner's confidence. "We shall soon see," he said, and left Damon in his cell.

The fatal day arrived. Damon was brought from prison and led before the executioner. Dionysius greeted him with a smug smile. "It seems your friend has not turned up," he laughed. "What do you think of him now?"

"He is my friend," Damon answered. "I trust him."

Even as he spoke, the doors flew open, and Pythias staggered into the room. He was pale and bruised and half speechless from exhaustion. He rushed to the arms of his friend.

"You are safe, praise the gods," he gasped. "It seemed as though the fates were conspiring against us. My ship was wrecked in a storm, and then bandits attacked me on the road. But I refused to give up hope, and at last I've made it back in time. I am ready to receive my sentence of death."

Dionysius heard his words with astonishment. His eyes and his heart were opened. It was impossible for him to resist the power of such constancy.

"The sentence is revoked," he declared. "I never believed that such faith and loyalty could exist in friendship. You have shown me how wrong I was, and it is only right that you be rewarded with your freedom. But I ask that in return you do me one great service."

"What service do you mean?" the friends asked.

"Teach me how to be part of so worthy a friendship."

FROM MY ARM-CHAIR

To the Children of Cambridge who presented to me on my seventy second (72) birthday, February 27, 1879, this chair made from wood of the village blacksmith's chestnut tree.

> Am I a king, that I should call my own
> This splendid ebon throne?
> Or by what reason, or what right divine,
> Can I proclaim it mine?
>
> Only, perhaps, by right divine of song
> It may to me belong;

Virtues

Only because the spreading chestnut tree
Of old was sung by me.

Well I remember it in all its prime,
When in the summer-time
The affluent foliage of its branches made
A cavern of cool shade.

There, by the blacksmith's forge, beside the street,
Its blossoms white and sweet.
Enticed the bees, until it seemed alive,
And murmured like a hive.

And when the winds of autumn, with a shout,
Tossed its great arms about,
The shining chestnuts, bursting from the sheath,
Dropped to the ground beneath.

And now some fragments of its branches bare,
Shaped as a stately chair,
Have by my hearthstone found a home at last,
And whisper of the past.

The Danish king could not in all his pride
Repel the ocean tide,
But, seated in this chair, I can in rhyme
Roll back the tide of Time.

I see again, as one in vision sees,
The blossoms and the bees,
And hear the children's voices shout and call,
And the brown chestnuts fall.

I see the smithy with its fires aglow,
I hear the bellows blow,
And the shrill hammers on the anvil beat
The iron white with heat!

And thus, dear children, have ye made for me
This day a jubilee,
And to my more than threescore years and ten
Brought back my youth again.

The heart hath its own memory, like the mind,
And in it are enshrined
The precious keepsakes, into which is wrought
The giver's loving thought.

Only your love and your remembrance could
Give life to this dead wood,
And make these branches, leafless now so long,
Blossom again in song.

Henry Wadsworth Longfellow

Mr. Longfellow had the above poem printed, and was accustomed to giving a copy to each child who visited him and sat in the chair.

Let each man learn to know himself
To gain that knowledge let him labor,
Improve those failings in himself
Which he condemns so in his neighbor.
How lenient our own faults we view,
And conscience's voice adeptly smother,
Yet, oh, how harshly we review
The self-same failings in another!

And if you meet an erring one
Whose deeds are blamable and thoughtless,
Consider, ere you cast the stone,
If you yourself are pure and faultless.
Oh, list to that small voice within,
Whose whisperings oft make men confounded,

And trumpet not another's sin;
You'd blush deep if your own were sounded.

And in self judgment if you find
Your deeds to others' are superior.
To you has Providence been kind,
As you should be to those inferior.
Example sheds a genial ray.
Of light which men are apt to borrow,
So first improve yourself today
And then improve your friends tomorrow.

Author Unknown

WHY FROG AND SNAKE NEVER PLAY TOGETHER

*O*nce upon a time, the child of the Frog was hopping along in the bush when he spied someone new lying across the path before him. This someone was long and slender, and his skin seemed to shine with all the colors of the rainbow.

"Hello there," called Frog-child.

"What are you doing lying here in the path?"

"Just warming myself in the sun," answered the someone new, twisting and turning and uncoiling himself.

"My name is Snake-child. What's yours?"

"I'm Frog-child. Would you like to play with me?

So Frog-child and Snake-child played together all morning long in the bush.

"Watch what I can do," said Frog-child, and he hopped high into the air.

"I'll teach you how, if you want," he offered.

So he taught Snake-child how to hop, and together they hopped up and down the path through the bush.

"Now watch what I can do," said Snake-child, and he crawled on his belly straight up the trunk of a tall tree, "I'll teach you if you want."

So he taught Frog-child how to slide on his belly and climb into trees.

After a while they both grew hungry and decided to go home for lunch, but they promised each other to meet again the next day.

"Thanks for teaching me how to hop," called Snake-child.

"Thanks for teaching me how to crawl up trees," called Frog-child.

Then they each went home.

"Look what I can do, Mother!" cried Frog-child crawling on his belly.

"Where did you learn to do that?" his mother asked.

"Snake-child taught me," he answered. "We played together in the bush this morning. He's my new friend."

"Don't you know the Snake family is a bad family?" his mother asked. "They have poison in their teeth. Don't ever let me catch you playing with one of them again. And don't let me see you crawling on your belly, either. It isn't proper."

Meanwhile, Snake-child went home and hopped Up and down for his mother to see.

"Who taught you to do that?" she asked.

"Frog-child did," he said. "He's my new friend."

"What foolishness," said his mother. "Don't you know we've been on bad terms with the Frog family for longer than anyone can remember? The next time you play with Frog-child, catch him and eat him up. And stop hopping. It isn't our custom."

So the next morning when Frog-child met Snake-child in the bush, he kept his distance.

"I'm afraid I can't go crawling with you today," he called, hopping back a hop or two.

Snake-child eyed him quietly, remembering what His mother had told him. "If he gets too close, I'll spring at him and eat him," he thought. But then he remembered how much fun they had had together, and how nice Frog-child had been to teach him to hop.

So he sighed sadly to himself and slid away into the bush.

And from that day onward, Frog-child and Snake-child never played together again. But they often sat alone in the sun, each thinking about their one day of friendship.

African Folktale

Have you ever wondered how many companionships we have missed because people are told they can't be friends with each other?

NEIGHBORS

Is some trait of your neighbor's distasteful to you?__
Forget it.
Is he getting more favors than you think his due?__
Forget it.

You have your own questions and problems to solve,
Your own goal to strive for and plans to evolve,
Don't waste your time airing his faults, but resolve__
To forget it.

Are you hurt by some careless or slighting remark?__
Forget it.
Does hate in your soul try to kindle a spark?__
Forget it.
Are you prone over wrong and injustice to brood?
Turn quickly your thoughts to the lovely and good;
And should aught that's impure ever seek to intrude__
Forget it.

Let not evil passions encumber your life__
Forget it.
Be it vanity, jealousy, anger, or strife__
Forget it.

For life's well supplied with most beautiful things,
And harmony sweet through each avenue rings,
If we learn to pass by what discordance may bring__
And forget it.

Author Unknown

THE BIRDS, THE BEASTS, AND THE BAT

*O nce upon a time war broke out between the birds and the
beasts of the earth. For along while the issue of the battle
was uncertain. The bat, taking advantage of the fact that he had*
certain characteristics of both, kept aloof and remained neutral.

The birds said, "Come with us." But he shook his head and
said, "I am a beast." Later some of the animals approached him
and asked him to join their side. "I am a bird," said he.

In due course, a peace was concluded between the embattled
birds and beasts. So the bat flew blithely up to the birds to join
them in their rejoicings. But the birds gave him the cold shoulder and flew away. And the beasts gave him exactly the same
treatment. Condemned by both sides and acknowledged by
neither, the unhappy bat was obliged to skulk away and live in
holes and corners, never caring to show his face except in the
dusk of twilight.

**Application: He winds up friendless who plays both sides
against the middle.**

Aesop's Fables

THE HEN AND THE FOX

A fox was out looking for a late supper. He came to a henhouse, and through the open door he could see a hen far up on the highest perch, safe out of his reach.

Here, thought the fox, was a case for diplomacy. Either that or go hungry! So he gave considerable thought to just how he should approach his intended supper.

"Hello, there, friend hen," said he in an anxious voice. "I haven't seen you about of late. Somebody told me that you have had a sick spell and I was sincerely worried over you. You look pale as a ghost. If you will just step down I'll take your pulse and look at your tongue. I'm afraid you are in for quite a siege."

"You never said a truer word, cousin fox," replied the hen. "It will have to be a siege, for I am in such a state that if I were to climb down to where you are, I'm afraid it would be the death of me."

LITTLE GIRLS WISER THAN MEN

*I*t was an early Easter. Sledding was only just over; snow still lay in the yards, and water ran in streams down the village street.

Two little girls from different houses happened to meet in a lane between two homesteads, where the dirty water after running through the farmyards had formed a large puddle. One girl was very small, the other a little bigger. Their mothers had dressed them both in new frocks. The little one wore a blue frock, the other a yellow print, and both had red kerchiefs on their heads. They had just come from church when they met, and first they showed each other their finery, and then they began to play. Soon the fancy took them to splash about in the water, and the smaller one was going to step into the puddle, shoes and all, when the elder checked her.

"Don't go in so, Malásha," said she. "Your mother will scold you. I will take off my shoes and stockings, and you take off yours."

They did so, and then, picking up their skirts, began walking toward each other through the puddle. The water came up to Malásha's ankles, and she said, "It is deep, Akoúlya. I'm afraid!"

"Come on," replied the other. "Don't be frightened. It won't get any deeper."

When they got near one another, Akoúlya said, "Mind, Malásha, don't splash. Walk carefully!"

She had hardly said this, when Malásha plumped down her foot so that the water splashed right on to Akoúlya's frock. The frock was splashed, and so were Akoúlya's eyes and nose. When she saw the stains on her frock, she was angry and ran after Malásha to strike her. Malásha was frightened, and seeing that she had got herself into trouble, she scrambled out of the puddle, and prepared to run home. Just then Akoúlya's mother happened to be passing, and seeing that her daughter's skirt was splashed, and her sleeves dirty, she said, "You naughty, dirty girl, what have you been doing!"

"Malásha did it on purpose," replied the girl.

At this Akoúlya's mother seized Malásha, and struck her on the back of her neck. Malásha began to howl so that she could be heard all down the street. Her mother came out.

"What are you beating my girl for?" said she, and began scolding her neighbor. One word led to another and they had an angry quarrel. The men came out, and a crowd collected in the street, every one shouting and no one listening. They all went on quarreling, till one gave another a push, and the affair had very nearly come to blows, when Akoúlya's old grandmother, stepping in among them, tried to calm them.

"What are you thinking of, friends? Is it right to behave so? On a day like this, too! It is a time for rejoicing, and not for such folly as this."

They would not listen to the old woman, and nearly knocked her off her feet. And she would not have been able to quiet the crowd, if it had not been for Akoúlya and Malásha themselves. While the women were abusing each other, Akoúlya had wiped the mud off her frock, and gone back to the puddle. She took a stone and began scraping away the earth in front of the puddle to make a channel through which the water could run out into the street. Presently Malásha joined her, and with a chip of wood helped her dig the channel. Just as the men were beginning to fight, the water from the little girls' channel ran streaming into the street toward the very place where the old woman was trying to pacify the men. The girls followed it, one running on each side of the little stream.

"Catch it, Malásha! Catch it!" shouted Akoúlya, while Malásha could not speak for laughing.

Highly delighted, and watching the chip float along on their stream, the little girls ran straight into the group of men; and the old woman, seeing them, said to the men:

"Are you not ashamed of yourselves? To go fighting on account of these lassies, when they themselves have forgotten all about it, and are playing happily together. Dear little souls! They are wiser than you!"

The men looked at the little girls, and were ashamed, and laughing at themselves, went back each to his own home.

"Except ye turn, and become as little children, ye shall in no wise enter into the kingdom of heaven."

All friendships have their tense moments. Learning to adjust and be forgiving can extend a friendship immeasurably.

Leo Tolstoy

THE LITTLE MATCH GIRL

*I*t was dreadfully cold; it was snowing fast, and was almost dark, as evening came on – the last evening of the year. In the cold and the darkness, there went along the street a poor little girl, bareheaded and with naked feet. When she left home she had slippers on, it is true; but they were much too large for her feet – slippers that her mother had used till then, and the poor little girl lost them in running across the street when two carriages were passing terribly fast. When she looked for them, one was not to be found, and a boy seized the other and ran away with it, saying he would use it for a cradle some day, when he had children of his own.

So on the little girl went with her bare feet that were red and blue with cold. In an old apron that she wore were bundles of matches and she carried a bundle also in her hand. No one had bought so much as a bunch all long day, and no one had given her even a penny.

Poor little girl! Shivering with cold and hunger she crept along, a perfect picture of misery.

The snowflakes fell on her long flaxen hair, which hung in pretty curls about her throat; but she thought not of her beauty nor of the cold. Lights gleamed in every window, and there came to her the savory smell of roast goose, for it was New Year's Eve. And it was this of which she thought.

In a corner formed by two houses, one of which project-ed beyond the other, she sat cowering down. She had drawn under her little feet, but still she grew colder and colder; yet she dared not go home, for she had sold no matches and could not bring a penny of money. Her father would certainly beat her; and, besides, it was cold enough at home, for they had only the house roof above them, and though the largest holes had been stopped with straw and rags, there were left many through which the cold wind could whistle.

And now her little hands were nearly frozen with cold. Alas!

A single match might do her good if she might only draw it from the bundle, rub it against the wall, and warm her fingers by it. So at last she drew one out. Whish! How it blazed and burned! It gave out a warm, bright flame like a little candle, as she held her hands over it. A wonderful little light it was. It really seemed to the little girl as if she sat before a great iron stove with polished brass feet and brass shovel and tongs. So blessedly it burned that the little maiden stretched out her feet to warm them also. How comfortable she was! But lo! The flame went out, the stove vanished, and nothing remained but the little burned match in her hand.

She rubbed another match against the wall. It burned brightly, and where the light fell upon the wall it became transparent like a veil, so that she could see through it into the room. A snow-white cloth was spread upon the table, on which was a beautiful china dinner service, while a roast goose, stuffed with apples and prunes, steamed famously and sent forth a most savory smell. And what was more delightful still, and wonderful, the goose jumped from the dish, with knife and fork still in its breast, and waddled along the floor straight to the little girl.

But the match went out then, and nothing was left to her but the thick, damp wall.

She lighted another match. And now she was under a most beautiful Christmas tree, larger and far more prettily trimmed than the one she had seen through the glass doors at the rich merchant's. Hundreds of wax tapers were burning on the green branches, and gay figures, such as she had seen in the shop windows, looked down upon her. The child stretched out her hands to them; then the match went out.

Still the lights of the Christmas tree rose higher and higher. She saw them now as stars in heaven, and one of them fell, forming a long trail of fire.

"Now someone is dying," murmured the child softly; for her grandmother, the only person who had loved her, and who was now dead, had told her that whenever a star falls a soul mounts up to God.

She struck yet another match against the wall, and again it was light; and in the brightness there appeared before her the dear old grandmother, bright and radiant, yet sweet and mild, and happy as she had never looked on earth.

"Oh, Grandmother," cried the child, 'take me with you. I know you will go away when the match burns out. You, too, will vanish, like the warm stove, the splendid New Year's feast, the beautiful Christmas tree." And lest her grandmother should disappear, she rubbed the whole bundle of matches against the wall.

And the matches burned with such a brilliant light that it became brighter than noonday. Her grandmother had never looked so grand and beautiful. She took the little girl in her arms, and both flew together, joyously and gloriously, mounting higher and higher, far above the earth; and for them there was neither hunger, nor cold, nor care – they were with God.

But in the corner, at the dawn of day, sat the poor girl, leaning against the wall, with red cheeks and smiling mouth – frozen to death on the last evening of the old year. Stiff and cold she sat, with the matches, one bundle of which was burned.

"She wanted to warm herself, poor little thing," people said. No one imagined what sweet visions she had had, or how gloriously she had gone with her grandmother to enter upon the joys of a new year.

Hans Christian Andersen

To feel another's anguish is the essence of compassion.

GO FORTH TO LIFE

Go forth to life, oh! child of Earth.
Still mindful of thy heavenly birth;
Thou are not here for ease or sin,
But manhood's noble crown to win.

Though passion's fires are in thy soul,
Thy spirit can their flames control;
Though tempters strong beset thy way,
Thy spirit is more strong than they.

Go on from innocence of youth
To manly pureness, manly truth;
God's angels still are near to save,
And God himself doth help the brave.

The forth to life, oh! child of Earth,
Be worthy of thy heavenly birth,
For noble service thou are here;
Thy brothers help, thy God revere!

Samuel Longfellow

FOR EVERYTHING THERE IS A SEASON

For everything there is a season, and a time for every purpose under the heaven:

A time to be born, and a time to die; a time to plant, an a time to pluck up that which is planted;

A time to kill, and a time to heal; a time to break down, and time to build up;

A time to weep, and a time to laugh; a time to mourn, and a time to dance;

A time to cast away stones, and a time to gather stones together; a time to embrace, and a time to refrain from embracing;

A time to get, and a time to lose; a time to keep, and a time to cast away;

A time to rend, and a time to sew, a time to keep silence, and a time to speak;

A time to love, and a time to hate; a time of war, and a time of peace.

From Ecclesiastes

SAY IT NOW

If you have a friend worth loving,
Love him. Yes, and let him know
That you love him, ere life's evening
Tinge his brow with sunset glow.
Why should good words ne'er be said
Of a friend – till he is dead?
If you hear a song that thrills you,
Sung by any child of song,
Praise it. Do not let the singer
Wait deserved praises long.
Why should one who thrills your heart
Lack the joy you may impart?

If you hear a prayer that moves you
By its humble, pleading tone,
Join it. Do not let the seeker
Bow before his God alone.
Why should not your bother share
The strength of "two or three" in prayer?

If you see the hot tears falling
From a brother's weeping eyes,
Share them. And by kindly sharing
Own our kinship in the skies.

Why should anyone be glad
When a brother's heart is sad?

If a silvery laugh goes rippling
Through the sunshine on his face,
Share it. 'Tis the wise man's saying –
For both grief and joy a place.
There's health and goodness in the mirth
In which an honest laugh has birth.

If your work is made more easy
By a friendly, helping hand,
Say so. Speak out brave and truly
Ere the darkness veil the land.
Should a brother workman dear
Falter for a word of cheer?
Scatter thus your seeds of kindness
All enriching as you go –
Leave them. Trust the Harvest Giver;
He will make each seed to grow.
So until the happy end
Your life shall never lack a friend.

Author Unknown

PREJUDICE

*P*rejudice borders on being an illness in ones character. Prejudice causes a person to judge another of different diversity, religious preference, age and health infirmities with disgust. This type of behavior is inappropriate. Additionally, such types of behavior can cause one to shun a victim needing our help and compassion.

We have been told in the scriptures that being prideful is also unacceptable behavior. Pride goes hand-in-hand with prejudice, for it makes us look at others and think we are so much better than they are, or so much richer or smarter.

God must feel pain when he observes one of his children treating another so shamelessly. Pride and prejudice encourages us to break the Second Commandment: "Love thy neighbor as thyself."

Cardinal to our accounts, in past history, of the seriousness of prejudice, we have only to turn to the mighty Roman Empire, where many of whom believe it was the most wicked. Ghastly were the accounts given of the activities in the great sports arenas at that time. It seems almost too surreal to believe; gladiators fought to their deaths before the cheering crowds, and Christians, of all ages, were fed to lions, in the name of entertainment. Imagine God's grief to such practices.

Ever more in the mind of Christians is the crucifixion of their Lord, Jesus Christ, for his ministry. People of every faith and condition have been inspired by Christ's compassionate words from the cross: "Father, forgive them; for they know not what they do." In the face of hatred, torture, and imminent death, He reiterated His message of love and reconciliation between God and humankind.

All religions and ethnic groups have suffered for their beliefs and acceptance. It began when the mass immigration of people came by ship from the British Isles, Europe, Sweden and Norway.

Catholics from Ireland and elsewhere were mistrusted, Lutherans were condemned, Baptists were criticized, and Mormons were hunted, driven and murdered. Our brothers and sisters of the Jewish faith were condemned and millions exterminated in Hitler's Germany. All these horrific condemnations are the result of religious prejudice and evil inner thoughts.

We have many accounts of persons who have died and gone to the Spirit World, beyond the veil of life into Paradise – the abode of the righteous after death. For unknown reasons some have been sent back and life has returned to their bodies. Some have asked about churches and have had interesting experiences.

According to the International Association for Near Death Studies, Betty J. Eadie, who wrote her exciting account of her experiences in "Embraced By the Light," remains the most detailed and spellbinding near death experience. You may contact Mrs. Eadie on her official website, Embraced By the Light. This is a synopsis of her remarks: "As our spiritual awareness grows, we must not condemn others who worship differently...After all, most of us will experience several religions in our search for truth. At each stop we may discover new truths, new opportunities. Then, if we have grown sufficiently, we may become restless again and open ourselves to yet greater truths." (The Ripple Effect, pp 115-116)

Mrs. Eadie was given the understanding that all religions were of God. People are at different stages of belief and different religions have more of God's gospel than others do.

To demonize another's religion is not what God wants us to do. It is not in God's plan for churches to write pamphlets to discredit other's beliefs. Most of the material is not true. You should investigate for yourself and not pass on to others information that may not be correct and cannot be verified.

Lee Nelson has compiled several volumes named, "Beyond The Veil". You learn from those who have seen the other side that there is no reason to fear death; that death is peaceful and sweet, and on both sides of the veil, we are watched over and cared for.

In God's eyes, religious prejudice, like any prejudice, should be avoided. Essentially, we should remove it, and replace prejudice with the Golden Rule.

Few men are worthy of experience. The majority let it corrupt them.

Joubert

WHEN LOVE IS SPECIAL

A universal wish for every girl and boy is to find that special person to love. Love is like a flower: it must be nourished and treated gently if it is to be an all-inclusive kind that lasts a lifetime. Love has many virtues, other than physical attraction, if it is special.

A wise man once remarked, "Love in youth is at its best and sweetest." I understand that love the second time around can be great, and is appreciated for its healing of broken hearts and mending of broken families.

Love is God's greatest blessing to mankind. As He has loved us we should love one another.

LOVE ME LITTLE, LOVE ME LONG

Love me little, love me long,
Is the burden of my song:
Love that is too hot and strong
Burneth soon to waste.
I am with little well content,
And a little from thee sent
Is enough, with true intent,
To be a steadfast friend.
Love me little, love me long,
Is the burden of my song.

Say thou lov'st me while thou live,
I to thee my love will give,
Never dreaming to deceive
While that life endures:
Nay, and after death in sooth,
I to thee will keep my truth,
As now when in my May of youth,
This my love assures.

Virtues

Love me little, love me long,
Is the burden of my song.

Constant love is moderate ever,
And it will through life persevere,
Give to me that with true endeavor.
I will it restore:
A suit of durance let it be,
For all weathers, that for me,
For the land or for the sea,
Lasting evermore.
Love me little, love me long,
Is the burden of my song.

-Unknown Author

CHAPTER TWO

Motivation and Change

YOUR SELF IMAGE

Self-image is an evaluation or conception of oneself. Additionally, self-image is the foundation upon which your personality, your behavior, your abilities, one's own identity and the very circumstances of one's life is built.

Every human being has a self-image. It can be a positive, or a negative one according to your personality. Important to the fact of self-image is the individuals mental and spiritual concept or picture of oneself. That is the real key to personality and behavior.

Self-image sets the boundaries for individual growth and accomplishment. An inadequate self-image can cause you to have a failure-type personality. Expand and change the self-image and you can develop into a positive, happy personality. Self-image psychology proves that "positive thinking" really works. Conversely, positive thinking will not work on someone with a damaged self-image.

In order to change, and one can change their self-image at any age, we need to know how self-image works. According to an abundance of scientific evidence and verified by many studies, the human brain and the nervous system operate to accomplish goals in the individual. Such efforts are a guidance system that works for one's success mechanism or against one's failure mechanism, depending on "you" the operator.

The scientific evidence is well presented in the writings of Maxwell Maltz, M.D., F.I.CS., in his renowned book called Psycho-Cybernetics. It is still in print in paperback editions, by Pocket Books, New York, N.Y.

We are not taught how to love – we must experience it. To build self-image in children, they should be told everyday by parents, "I love you". They should be reminded how proud parents are of them. You may not be proud of their actions, do tell them so "lovingly." Explain how much you want them to change. However, in your next breath, remind them that their behavior is inappropriate, that you expect them to make a change and that you love them, also do add, how proud you are to have them use your family name. Explain your love for them is now and forever. If you do not condone or support their misdeeds, you can call on God to help you. He will help show you the way to change your child's behavior, and will support your efforts. Remember, the older they become the more diffi-cult will be your task and your child or young adult may not listen to your counsel, so be prepared.

Parents of the older generations were raised in authoritative homes. Perhaps you were raised that way and, in turn, raised your children accordingly. An authoritative home atmosphere limits the participation of children when they wish to share their ideas. Some call such a home one in which a child is seen and not heard. Additionally, the authoritarian makes all the decisions and hands out the discipline. Children, in such a circumstance, do not have enough input on a personal level to grow and develop without fear. They grow inward, are shy, lack self-image and sometimes are afraid of mother and father. When children feel insecure in their family they become more introverted and lack self-esteem. They fear making mistakes and never learn properly that making mistakes teaches us how to learn and grow and become competitive to excel. If you have small children, teach them to have a great self-image and to like themselves.

It is so important to learn to like yourself as a valuable human being. To learn to like yourself, you need to know yourself. Since you spend so much time with yourself you should be satisfied with the way you handle life. There is little sense in living with yourself and being unhappy. Therefore, it is imperative that you have a great self-image.

Visualize how you use yourself. Mentally put yourself in trying situations or happy situations. Mentally solve all your weaknesses. This will give you strength to accept and stand behind your decisions in real life when you are called upon to make quick judgments. Learn to trust your judgment and feel confident.

Some great advice when it comes to accepting your self-image, "The soul is dyed with the color of your thoughts."

Marcus Aureluis

WISDOM

There are only two ways to live your life,
One is as though nothing is a miracle.
The other is as though,
Everything is a miracle

Albert Einstein

It takes years to become an "overnight" success.

> *Yogi Berra, Baseball great.*

AFFIRMATIONS WILL CHANGE YOUR LIFE

Affirmations are powerful tools in their use. They work subliminally, and are intended to reorient your conscious mind as well as your subconscious mind. Affirmations are a declaration of a revised, or improved approach to life. A new direction is commonly found in each affirmation.

Since affirmations go deep into your conscious and subconscious mind, they are repeated over and over until your mind develops an automatic reaction to them. Changes can occur as these affirmations penetrate deeply into your awareness. Affirmations seem to work more efficiently when used as a prayer.

How is an affirmation initiated? Write a forceful, positive statement for change upon a small card, and use it for reference regularly. Say the affirmation when you awaken in the morning, on your break at school or work, just before you retire for the evening, or at any other time of your choosing. If you are not comfortable using your affirmations as a prayer, just tell your subconscious what you want it to do and repeat the affirmations several times daily.

The wording in your affirmations should be carefully selected so as to not create unnecessary stumbling blocks. The statement should be all worded in the present tense, such as: I have, I am, or I do, etc.

Affirmation examples:

I have quit smoking.
I am losing weight.
I think well of myself.
I am proud of my accomplishments.

Motivation and Change

If you think you are beaten, you are,
If you think you dare not, you don't.
If you like to win, but you think you can't,
It is almost certain you won't.

If you think you'll lose, you're lost,
For out in the world we find,
Success begins with a person's will-
It's all in the state of mind.
If you think you are outclassed, you are,
You've got to think high to rise,
You've got to be sure of yourself before
You can ever win a prize.

Life's battles don't always go,
To the stronger or faster man,
But sooner or later the one who wins,
Is the one WHO THINKS HE CAN!

Author Unknown

Jesus warned us of putting new wine in old bottles, meaning you cannot put a patch on a serious problem. You must change your self-image in this case. Get a new mental picture of yourself. Team up with God to help you. Seek out motivational material. Use affirmation cards. Forgive yourself and others for hurts you are hanging onto. Be enthusiastic. Put yourself in the hands of God and pray often. He will guide you to green pastures and a happy life.

Put this affirmation on a card. Say it over and over daily for at least one month. It usually takes several weeks for change.

I love myself
I believe in myself
I respect my decisions
I am a child of God

When you are certain you have conquered the affirmation, and this new dimension is a part of your life, you are free to then choose another, or "move on."

The future is that time when, you'll wish you'd done, what you aren't doing now.

Anon.

THE RESOLUTION of MAHATMA GANDHI

Let the first act of every morning be to make the following resolve for the day.

I shall fear only God.
I shall not bear ill toward anyone.
I shall not submit to injustice from anyone.
I shall conquer untruth by truth.
And in resisting untruth, I shall put up with all suffering.

FINDING ENTHUSIASM DAILY

It seems impossible that we would find ourselves lacking in enthusiasm when God has made such a beautiful world for all of us to enjoy. But it happens – like sand dunes are formed – by a few particles of sand at a time. We get discouraged, doubtful, dejected, and become, at the end of our day, a little more negative or a little bit more pessimistic. It is most significant that we refuse to stay in a position of negative behavior very long. Not only do we find ourselves less enthusiastic or less optimistic, we may find our physical and emotional health affected accordingly. Stress, of this sort, may damage the immune system in our bodies, making us more prone to disease or feel tired or weary.

We must determine what is troubling our thoughts and begin right away to extract some changes. We may benefit from the words in Proverbs, "As a man thinketh so is he." We can actually become precisely what we imagine to be. Mirror your troubles constantly and you will shower yourself with added problems. When we stop negative thinking we begin to mend. Take note of your negative thinking and you will find your have some enthusiasm left. List those items also that make you feel happy and worthy.

Enthusiasm provides the vigor and vitality for life's adventure. It garners warmth, love, friendships, energy and happiness.

Webster's Dictionary describes enthusiasm as: to be inspired, be possessed of God, supernatural, and inspirational. If you are familiar with the study of how words are formed, or "root words", enthusiasm comes from two Greek words en and theos. En means in and theos means God, "full of God" is the meaning of enthusiasm. This brings us back to our faith in God. If we believe in God, love God, and pray to God daily, we should be enthusiastic. Use meditation to get rid of negative thought. Think of our beautiful country with its pristine valleys, magnificent oceans, breathtaking mountains and soaring peaks. Think of beautiful gardens and the faces of friends and loved ones. Read the scriptures and other uplifting materials. You may find walking or exercising reduces your tension also.

I love to train art students in the sources of color, and what to use to bring "zing" into their paintings. Look for beauty in Gods' world. Don't just ride in the car and ignore nature. Look for colors of different hue in the shadows, the sky, grasses and bushes, distant mountains, depth and sunshine colors in the water. Notice all these rare changes in nature such as sunsets: (please be a passenger in the automobile, bus or train, when you take this advice, for obvious reasons) you will be so enthusiastic at such simple pleasures you have ignored before. It is exciting to witness Mother Nature's palette of colors and God's creations.

Pick enthusiastic friends, they will be your example to guide you to higher standards for yourself. Enthusiastic people radiate and sparkle when they communicate with others. Enthusiastic people show how they feel and enjoy showing their outward feelings. There are personalities who are enthusiastic but hold their feelings inside of them. Share your enthusiasm by smiling at everyone you meet. Do not be offended if someone reminds you, in the meantime, that you do not appear to be very happy. Only a dear friend would be so helpful.

Seek out hobbies, music, and reading material that make you enthusiastic, or join group activities such as lectures, clubs, or church groups whose members you might enjoy. All of these activities can bring you joy.

Dale Carnegie, author of *How To Win Friends and Influence People,* said, "Act enthusiastic and you will become enthusiastic." It takes additional effort and time if you expect to change. We need to be realistic in our goals.

Continue to repeat your affirmations each day, every morning, noon and at night, and when you retire. It helps to repeat them several times during the day if you have the opportunity. Some examples are:

I am capable and enthusiastic.
I love change and new experiences.
I look for the best in a situation.
I remain positive always.
I am enthusiastic in all situations.

WISDOM FROM the AGES

Nobody grows old merely by living a number of years; people grow old by deserting their ideals. Years wrinkle the skin, but giving up enthusiasm wrinkles the soul. Worry, doubt, self-distrust, fear, and despair – these are the long years

that bow the head and turn the growing spirit back to dust. You are as young as your faith, and as old as your doubts; as young as your self-confidence, as old as your fears, as young as your hope; as old as your despair.
Zoroaster

Zoroaster: A teacher in the 6th century, who founded the Persian religion, Zoroastrianism, before Persians converted to Islam.

GOALS ARE IMPORTANT

Our aspirations in life are vital, and the tasks we have planned this day, this month, this year are very important. Goals seem to help us focus our energy in productive ways. Saving time for yourself is most important. We can set goals and make every effort to achieve them. We can use goals to increase the long-term effectiveness in our life.

Goals are best written down and read often. Goals are a form of commitments made in earnest. When we make these commitments, we are making a promise to ourselves. Keeping these promises gives us better self-control, regulates our time and improves our character in many ways. We are strengthened emotionally and spiritually. Rarely do we hear of goal-oriented persons arriving to obligations unprepared and late for appointments. Goals seem to be a built-in source for managing time and commitments.

Goals are advantageous in managing time when they are organized for a longer period of time. Daily goals help us get started and help us to arrive at the routine we have set for ourselves. However, they expedite greater advantages to organizing your time for longer periods.

For an example, if you have planned to start a fitness program and you will be managing your time for three days of exercise, then a weekly plan would accommodate you better than a daily goal. A weekly plan would be better if you are involved with family members and their activities.

Whatever time goal you desire, add activities that will bring you joy and uplifting things to do. If life is a chore, you may not accomplish some areas you wish to change or commit to doing.

"COUNCIL OF SEEDS"

Two little seeds awoke one day,
as seeds will do in the *month of May*,
But lo! And behold, they had clean forgot. If they were
carrots, or bean or whatnot;
At length they decided they must needs,
call a council of sixteen seeds;
Some said onions or beets; but no,
others said it couldn't be so;
Some said lettuce; and some said weeds;
then a sunflower spoke: "It may be so.
But the way to find out is just to grow."

Good advice from a child's rhyme but careful please, it must be your goal, and your dream, no one stands in your shoes, but you. Many are the souls that live lives of unhappiness and fretful jobs, fulfilling the dreams and goals of parents, spouses, and others.

Be selective, find your talent. Earn your living by doing what you are most suited for. Many a soul has spent a lifetime in employment and professions they did not enjoy. Life is to be enjoyed not endured. There are many cases where one is forced to work at jobs in times of recession and necessity, do not forget your dream and study, pray and put your life in God's hands. He will give you courage and find you an avenue to pursue your desire, as long as it is a worthy endeavor, and you have put forth the effort to succeed.

God is the silent partner in all great enterprises.

Abraham Lincoln

IT DEPENDS ON HOW YOU LOOK AT IT

Men give me some credit for genius. All the genius I have lies in this: When I have a subject in hand, I study it profoundly. Day and night it is before me. I explore it in all its bearings. My mind becomes pervaded with it. Then the effort which I make the people are pleased to call the fruit of genius. It is the fruit of labor and thought.

Alexander Hamilton

YOUR JOURNEY TO RECOVERY

*I*n time you will understand why today your journey seems a little hopeless. Just keep believing that everything will be okay. You may feel that you need help just to get through today, but you are stronger than you think.

Remember it is up to you to find the way to recovery. Believe in your heart you are already well and doing the best you can at the moment. Reach out and rely in your dreams and goals, and God will supply you with the strength and wisdom for healing to take place. It is a true fact that faith precedes the miracle. If you start each day with a prayer to your God, the door will be opened unto you. You, then in turn, should close each day with a prayer of gratitude to God for your blessings, for the privilege of life, and his wondrous care.

Your thoughts build your world around you. Whatever a person becomes in character he first believed in his heart. Sometimes you just have to be patient and brave. How else will you discover how really strong you are unless you find out in the face of worldly problems or health infirmities? We all grow in different stages and our bodies heal in different stages. Do not listen if others think you are not on their schedule. You are unique and not like anyone else.

Take your recovery time one day at a time. You will get through your situation triumphantly. Each day believe that recovery is in sight for you. Reconstruct your life and find peace within yourself. Read the Scriptures and gain its wisdom. For example, "Be still and know that I am God." Psalm 46:10. Try not to worry or be afraid. God is asking you to realize He is there to keep anxiety, fear, or loneliness away from you. Read the Scriptures to give you confidence in yourself and ask God to give you the blessings you stand in need of.

Learn to accept what has been given to you. Have love in your heart and a smile on your face. Think positive and smile through your tears. Your hope will come from within with the help of prayer. Faith can change any circumstance. Miracles happen every day to special people like you. Determine to trust the Lord and you will find comfort.

Someone is always with you. God is watching and caring for you. Friends give a strengthening hand. Find someone who will listen to your problems and help comfort you. Use affirmations to change your thoughts. Try not to think thoughts of your illness or heartache. Solutions will be found and you will be able to live life at its' fullest. Remember you have a Guardian Angel who loves you as much as God does.

Believe in your heart that you are a survivor. You will be blessed with the wisdom to heal your own self. You will be able to make decisions and solve your own problems with God's help.

Eventually you will be healed and you reminisce over your past experiences and look back over your trials and recall how you drew the strength to recover from your illness or heartache. You will take comfort from the fact you persevered and grew in the face of challenge. You can do it!

Good luck and may God bless you!

LEARN TO LET GO

*I*f you want to be healthy morally, mentally, and physical-ly, just let go. Let go of the little annoyances of everyday life, the irritations and the petty vexations that cross your path daily. Don't take them up, nurse them, pet them, and brood over them. They are not worthwhile. Let them go!

Learn to let go. As you value health of body and peace of mind, let go – just simply let go.

Author Unknown

Finish everyday and be done with it. You have done what you could. Some blunders and absurdities no doubt crept in; forget them as soon as you can. Tomorrow is a new day; begin it well and serenely, and with too high a spirit to be cumbered with your old nonsense. This day is all that is good and fair. It is too dear, with its' hopes and invitations to waste a moment on the yesterdays.

Ralph Waldo Emerson

PSALMS FOR COMFORT

*T*he Psalms are beautiful Hebrew poetry written to be sung. They were used in the acts of public worship in the ancient temples of Israel. They were written for different purposes, such as, for prayer and worship while others were written for the purpose of public worship.

The Psalms became the treasures of the people, having been written for over a thousand years. They contain deeply emotion-al language with dramatic exaggeration and figurative speech. They were part of the ordinary life of the Israelites and used by the people to respond to God with songs of praise.

The Psalms emphasize that the Lord should be the center of our lives. They reflect great trust in the Lord by the worshippers.

They foreshadow the great events in the mission of Jesus Christ.

The Psalms teach of the Lord and our trust in Him. The Psalms teach us about the mission of Jesus Christ.

The Psalms can provide comfort and inspiration, as well as increase our capacity for rejoicing and thanksgiving.

The sentiment expressed are at the heart of our beliefs and remind us of the reality of a divine, purposeful, powerful Creator, and that the Lord is in control and is good.

Two Psalms that give comfort are:

Be still and know that I am God.

Psalm 46:10

Create in me a clean heart, oh God, and renew a right spirit within me.

Psalm 51:10

HELP IN TIME OF NEED

Way of Salvation	John 14:6
	Act 16:31
	Romans 10:9
Comfort In Sorrow	2 Cor 1:3-5
Relief in Suffering	2 Cor 12:8-10
	Hebrews 12:3-13
Guidance in Times of Decision	James 1:5-6
	Proverbs 3:5-6
Protection in Danger	Psalm 91
	Psalm 121
In Times of Trouble	Psalm 46

Courage in Fear	Heb 3:5-6
	Ephes 6:10-18
Peace in Turmoil	Isaiah 26:3-4
	Phil 4:6-7
Rest in Weariness	Matt 11:28-29
	Psalm 23
Strength in Temptation	James 1:12-16
	1 Cor 10:26-31
Warning in Temptation	Gal 5: 19-21
	Heb 10:26-31

Quick Reference:

The Lord's Prayer	*Matthew 6*
The Ten Commandments	*Exodus 20*
Beatitudes	*Matthew 5*
The Lord is my Sheppard	*Psalm 23*
The Lord Seeth	*1 Sam 16:7*

I count him braver who overcomes his desire, than him who conquers his enemies; for the hardest victory is the victory over self.

Aristotle

Be merciful with yourself,
Forgive yourself,
This is a divine commandment.

Author Unknown

What we have done for ourselves alone – dies with us. What we have done for others and the world remains immortal.

Author unknown

RECOGNIZING INSPIRATION AND CREATIVITY

*H*ave you ever experienced a sudden change in your feelings regarding how you think and live? Suddenly you feel invigorated, excited, and the momentum grows and grows? You may get a sudden urge to improve your health and declare to yourself, right then and there, to go on a diet or otherwise improve your appearance. During these experiences you might consider a drastic job change or wish that you had taken a different avenue in your career.

Sometimes these feelings are intense and grow to the point that you must share the information with someone. When the female gender gets these feelings, quite regularly, she settles for a few hours in the "Magic Shop," otherwise known as the beauty shop. She may arrive home with a new hair cut or dye job. Sometimes we end up with our feelings being satisfied. If not, what do we do?

Where do these inspirational promptings come from? Sometimes from hidden desires to find work you are better suited for, or to follow your dreams to another profession. Sometimes your inspiration comes from other people who have set their goals, and are participating in jobs of their choice.

Everyone of us were born with talents which we do not pursue. Look for creative things to do that will improve your life and add some spice to it. This is especially important if you are retired with nothing to fill your hours but television. Check out your local area for Senior Centers and fun activities for Seniors. If your health is "testy" there are quiet things you can do with group participation.

If your real need is a job change or a change in your living conditions, turn to God in prayer for help. Have the faith to realize God knows the length of our stay in our earthly quarters. He knows our needs, our wants, and our desires.

If you are planning a job change move slowly and wisely. Ask for God's help in giving you the proper paths to follow. Do have a job to go to before you leave your present employment. This may take extra planning to set aside additional funds for emergencies. God will tell you where to find the help you need. Do not hurry this process it may take weeks.

Following creative pursuits can be very rewarding, even if it becomes only a hobby. Remember how we felt when we were young – we jumped right into new projects without asking, "how do we do this?"

Recently I received an aphorism in the mail, which I would like to share with you:

GIVE YOURSELF A CHANCE!

The most unfortunate thing that happens to a person who fears failure is that he limits himself by becoming afraid to try anything new.

Success takes hard work and God.

John Wooden, College Coach

MAINTAINING THE MAGIC OF OPTIMISM

*H*ow you think is very important. To be optimistic you must be confident, calm, and have the ability to handle any situation that comes along without falling to pieces. Additionally, not everyone has an optimistic nature, and will find themselves overwhelmed by the events of the day. This type of thinking generates many frustrations and makes us pessimistic.

Optimism is defined as: the belief that we live in the best of all worlds, the doctrine or belief that good will ultimately prevail over evil, the tendency to take the most helpful or cheerful view in all matters and expect the best outcome possible.

Optimism is the tendency to always view the positive side of any situation. It means reacting to problems with hope and courage, keeping in mind and analyzing every item in detail with the intention of improving the situation.

An optimistic person accepts a situation as it exists. The pessimistic viewpoint is directly opposite. This type of personality thinks nothing can be fixed and puts the blame on himself. He will then dwell on his incompetence of handling the whole situation.

An optimistic person has better mental and physical health than a pessimistic person and they live longer due to lack of stress. An optimistic person rarely suffers from depression or diseases of the immune system. An optimistic person is tough minded as well as a positive thinker.

If a problem is hard to overcome, try these options to be optimistic:

a) Reject failure thoughts, rather picture your successes in everything you accomplish.
b) Try to find pleasure in your job and other activities.
c) Choose companions who are optimistic.
d) List daily several nice things that happened to you today at work or in your world before you retire. Do this every single day until you are back on track.

GREEN THINKING

The little cabbage in the field was consulting its mother about life.

"Life," said mother, "is a gamble; you've got to withstand storms, drought, wind, animals – not to mention bugs, lice, mold, rot. But, if you don't give up you'll thrive and grow."

"Life certainly is a gamble," agreed the little cabbage, "but there's one thing you haven't quite made clear. When do I quit growing?"

"As in any other gamble," said the mother cabbage, "quit when you're a head!"

THE OPTIMIST

The optimist fell ten stories
At each window bar
He shouted to his friends:
"All right so Far."
Author Unknown

WE ARE UNIQUE PERSONALITIES

*W*e have a purpose to fulfill in life. We are heirs to God's Kingdom and we are heirs to all of God's blessings. Let us hold a sacred image of ourselves as a spiritual being with unlimited potential.

We know how important each one of His children is in God's world. As unique individuals and creations of God, we bring our own special blessings to those with whom we have daily associations.

If we focus on the experiences of positive, happy and spiritual activities happening to us each day – we will ensure that a positive momentum will be felt by everyone around us. We are encouraged by our contemporaries who are eager to join in friendship with us, and we experience great joy and love. Life is an exciting experience.

Beauty comes in many different shapes, colors and sizes and God treasures us all. We are as unique as each snowflake. Be proud of your uniqueness. Being one of a kind is indeed a blessing. Life would certainly be unusual if there were hundreds of us alike. We would feel much less special.

Our body is a sacred temple. Our minds hold the treasure of divine ideas. We must have a positive self-image as a spiritual being with unlimited potential. Scientists remind us that we only develop a small portion of our brain and rarely realize how much talent we have that goes undeveloped.

Give of yourself and to those around you. Vow to those around you: your service, your smile, your complete friendship. It is so easy and you will experience the blessing of the finer things in life, which includes love and friendship.

ONE AND ONLY YOU

Every single blade of grass,
And every flake of snow-
Is just a wee bit different …
There's no two alike, you know.

From something small, like grains of sand,
To each gigantic star,
All were made with THIS in mind;
To be just what they are!

How foolish then, to imitate-
How useless to pretend!
Since each of us comes from a MIND
Whose ideas never end.

There'll only be just ONE of ME
To show what I can do-
And you should likewise feel very proud,
There's only ONE of YOU.

That is where it all starts
With you, a wonderful
Unlimited human being.

John T. Moore

Motivation and Change

As the plant springs from the seed, so every act of man springs from the hiddenseeds of thought. Act is the blossom of thought, and joy and suffering are its fruits.

Man is always master of himself, even in his weakness and most abandoned state.

Man's mind is like a garden which may be intelligently culti-vated or allowed to run wild. If useless seeds are planted, then its kind will be yielded and useless weed-seeds, eventually, will take root and grow. As a gardener cultivates his plot, keeping it free from weeds, man must also tend carefully the garden of his mind, weeding out worthless, idle, and impure thought seeds; therefore, pursuing the path to perfection. Thought is the foun-tain of action; make the fountain pure and your life will be pure. If you would renew your body, then guard your mind."

James Allen

Whatever you can do, or dream you can begin it. Boldness has genius, power, and magic in it.

Goethe

TO CHANGE

1) Learn to know yourself.
2) Learn to truly esteem yourself.
3) Learn to let God run your life.
4) With God's help, fear nothing.

THE PAPAGO LEGEND

Early one morning against the dawn light, the sandals of the Healer came to the village of the Papago. The children had been loudly playing, and when the Lord of the Wind and Water, whom the Papago call E-see-cotl, was seen approaching,

87

the people were embarrassed and roundly rebuked the young ones.

"Nay," replied the Prophet to them in Papago. "Do not scold the little children, but instead let them come to me, for such is the will of my Father in Heaven."

Everyday after that, say the Papago, He met and talked with the children. The Prophet did not live among them but made His home on a distant mountain called Bavo-kee-vulik, which means the hourglass mountain, for at this time that was the shape of the mountain.

One day E-see-cotl, the Healer, wandered into a secret temple where a child was being sacrificed.

The eyes of the Master went red with anger. He snatched up the baby, healed its gashes, and calling it by name, gave it back its breathing.

The priesthood stared and their arms were frozen. They could not move, much as they would have liked to kill Him. Stepping outside where the people were gathered He told them of the secret ceremony which was against all of His teachings. The people were ashamed, but afraid of the priesthood.

That night, two priests determined to murder this saintly man who was winning the people. They stole out in the moonlight for Bavo-kee-vulick, slipping knives under their blankets.

The moon was still up, yet the dawn light was coming as they neared the hour glass mountain. In a part of His cave facing the Dawn Star, the Prophet was kneeling in prayer as the two blood-priests stole up the mountain. The Prophet arose and awaited their coming.

As they slipped into the cave with knives uplifted, the Lord of wind and Water stepped forth from the cave into the moon-light, and faced them in their hiding place in the cave's dark midnight.

"Why do you not step forth from the cave and kill me? I have no knife nor rod to strike thee. Yet you cannot, even though in the moonlight I stand revealed? Know you not that you cannot kill me until the tasks which were assigned by my Father to me upon this earth are finished?"

Suddenly the earth began to tremble. The roar became deafening, and rocks fell downward, dropping like rain about the Prophet. Now the earth shook as in a spasm, and with the roar of a hundred oceans, the mountain collapsed, leaving the Healer standing still on the rock in the moonlight. From within the mountain He heard two voices pleading Him to go to the village and tell the people how the mountain had entombed them.

As the dawn light came, E-see-cotl walked into the village. All the people stood staring in frightened awe at Bavo-kee-vulik and then at the Prophet.

"Where are the priests who came to see you when the Fire God shook the mountain?"

"They came with knives before the trembling. They are still within the mountain, and from a great distance, you can hear their voices. My Father has spoken in the earthquake. No more am I to live among you."

Walking away from them in the dawn light went white robed E-see-cotl, nor ever after did they see him.

Author Unknown

THE GOLDEN RULE

Given by the Prophet to the Shawnee Nation

"Do not kill or injure your neighbor, for it is not he that you injure; you injure yourself. Do good to him, thus adding to his days of happiness even as you then add to your own."

"Do not wrong or hate your neighbor; for it is not he you wrong; you wrong yourself. Rather love him, for The Great Spirit loves him, even as he loves you."

NATIVE TEN COMMANDMENTS

Treat the Earth and all that dwell thereon with respect.
Remain close to the Great Spirit
Show respect for our fellow beings.
Work together for the benefit of all mankind.
Give assistance and kindness wherever needed.
Do what you know to be right.
Look after the well-beings of mind and body.
Dedicate a share of your efforts for greater good.
Be truthful and honest at all times.
Take full responsibility for your actions.

CHEROKEE WISDOM

One evening an old Cherokee told his grandson about a battle that goes on inside people.

He said, "My son, the battle is between two "wolves" inside us all.

One is Evil. It is anger, envy, jealousy, sorrow, regret, greed, arrogance, self-pity, guilt, resentment, inferiority, lies, false pride, superiority, and ego.

The other is Good. It is joy, peace, love, hope, serenity, humility, kindness, benevolence, empathy, generosity, truth, compassion and faith."

The grandson thought about it for a minute and then asked his grandfather:

"Which wolf wins?"

The old Cherokee simply replied, "The one you feed."

APACHE BLESSING

May the sun bring you new energy by day,
May the moon softly restore you by night,
May the rain wash away your worries,
May the breeze blow new strength into your being,
May you walk gently through the world and know
it's lasting beauty, all the days of your life.

IT ALL DEPENDS ON HOW YOU LOOK AT IT.

A man pulled into a gas station on the outskirts of town. As he filled his tank, he remarked to the attendant, I've just accepted a job in town. I've never been to this part of the country. What are people like here?"

"What are people like where you came from?" the attendant asked.

"Not so nice," the man replied "In fact, they can be quite rude."

The attendant shook his head. "Well, I'm afraid you'll find the people in this town to be the same way."

Just then another car pulled into the station. "Excuse me," the driver called out. "I'm just moving to this area. Is it nice here?"

"Was it nice where you came from?" the attendant inquired.

"Oh, yes! I came from a great place. The people were friendly, and I hated to leave."

" Well, you'll find the same to be true of this town."

"Thanks!" yelled the driver as he pulled away.

"So what is this town like?" asked the first man, now irritated with the attendant's conflicting reports.

The attendant just shrugged his shoulders. "It's all a matter of perception. You'll find things to be just the way you think they are."

Author unknown

91

Manna From Heaven

I have never seen a monument erected to a pessimist.

Paul Harvey, Radio Personality

MAKING WISE DECISIONS

If youth are to make correct decisions we must counsel them with the facts and good information. It is the responsibility of adults to help youth understand the critical purpose of making correct decisions, and having vital knowledge to assist in making correct choices.

Satan sells his philosophy of life to young people before they are capable of realizing the outcome of their immature decisions. As a result, we have youthful drug addicts, alcoholics, sexual promiscuity, runaway youth, suicides, and gang activities, and even murders of young people who might have had the potential and ability to excel in life.

At times it may appear that we have no options in a matter, or that our choices are limited by circumstances. No matter what decision is to be made, we always have a choice. Choose how you will address a situation, and how to respond to the outcome. Touch on each option first before a final decision is made.

We, as adults, must teach our children to expect the consequences in the decisions they make. When they make mistakes restitution and repentance should follow. We are all spiritual beings and capable of solving many problems using a prayerful approach to the situation. We can release all concern about the outcome, and we can expect positive results.

"Let us choose what is right, let us determine among ourselves what is good."

Job 34:4

You know that the beginning is the most important part of any work, especially in the case of a young and tender child; for that is the time ones character is being formed and the desired impression is more readily taken . . . Shall we just carelessly allow children to hear any casual tales which may be devised by casual persons, and to receive into their minds ideas for the most part the very opposite of those which we should wish them to have when they are grown up?

We cannot . . . Anything received into the mind at that age is likely to become indelible and unalterable; and therefore it is most important that the tales which the young first hear should be models of virtuous thoughts. . .

Then will our youth dwell in a land of health, amid fair sights and sounds, and receive the good in everything; and beauty, the effluence of fair works, shall flow into the eye and ear, like a health-giving breeze from a purer region, and insensibly draw the soul from the earliest years into likeness and sympathy with the beauty of reason.

USING YOUR IMAGINATION

A camera can capture only images of what is evident in the physical world. With our imagination, we can use a spiritual vision to see a new world with endless possibilities.

Knowing that God's power is greater that any person or circumstance – we can envision the good possibility of a world of peace and love. We can imagine people everywhere embracing the God that life has to offer and we can visualize people cooperating hand in hand to create a better world for all. We can pray daily that all people in our universe may find change and experience a renewal of their spiritual awareness. If only everyone could envision the fact that they are children of God.

We all believe that the majority of people are inherently good, doing their best according to their awareness at the time. We need to pray that good people everywhere will extend tenderness, forgiveness and cooperation to others. That includes our immediate family, neighbors, our enemies in other countries, to our leaders in government, to ourselves, knowing we are all students in life trying to do our best. Sometimes we may forget that people make honest mistakes or are given incorrect information. We should be patient and understanding with those who are trying to do good.

You who are letting miserable misunderstandings run on from year to year, meaning to clear them you who are not keeping wretched quarrels alive because you cannot quite make up your mind that now is the day to sacrifice your pride and (settle) them: You who are passing men sullenly upon the street, not speaking to them out of some silly spite; you who are letting (someone's) heart ache for a word of appreciation or sympathy, which you mean to give him someday; If you only could know and see and feel, all of a sudden, the time is short, how it would break the spell! How you would go instantly and do the thing which you might never have another chance to do.

Phillips Brook

The world looks like a multiplication table or a mathematical equation, which, turn it how you will, balances itself. You cannot do wrong without suffering wrong...A man cannot speak but he judges himself...Every secret is told, every wrong redressed, in silence and certainty...The thief steals from himself. The swindler swindles himself...Men suffer all their life long, under the foolish superstition that they can be cheated. But it is...impossible for a man to be cheated by anyone but himself...What will you have? Quote God: pay for it and take it...Thou shalt be paid exactly for what thou hast done, no more, no less.

Ralph Waldo Emerson

MEDITATION

Recently I attended a small gathering of people quite unrelated to each other in lifestyle. I was able to determine my assessment of the others because we were given the opportunity to tell a little about ourselves. Not being judgmental, I sat quietly and listened with great interest about the lives of these strangers. I found out that many shared the same desire to find meditation and quietness in their lives. I also became aware that some people need to take time to slow down and take reasonable care of themselves. There were others who ran on stress for fuel, not unlike a car that runs on high octane gasoline.

Meditation can bring leadership into your life and give you the spiritual food to accomplish all that you wish to become. When I meditate, I love to communicate with nature. Through my art training I have learned to love the sea. In order to paint a seascape, you must learn the anatomy of a wave. You must learn to paint translucent water, how to use shadow, sunlight and atmosphere, to influence the effect of all the components that go into painting the sea. You must know where a wave came from and how it is formed. One must learn to think and get lost in what they are thinking about.

Music is a successful tool for meditation. A wonderful way to seek peaceful thoughts is within an atmosphere of beautiful music. Some of our most cherished moments are found within this blissful time when music is allowed to influence our thought patterns.

Body comfort and a conducive atmosphere are important features of a plan for meditation. Find a spot where you are comfortable and will not be disturbed. Take deep breaths, count to four, let the air out slowly with your lips poised as though you are drinking through a straw. Do not let anything break the rhythm of your breathing and calm your mind and think of the object, in detail, that you wish to concentrate on. Allow nothing else to enter your thoughts. You will arise feeling renewed. This method may be used to reduce blood pressure. Make a habit of meditation for stress.

AS A MAN THINKETH

art of man's mortal progress is to control one's thoughts and manage our conscious and subconscious levels of thinking. Thoughts are very powerful and the content of our thinking will affect the kind of future we will experience.

The thoughts that we are currently thinking will expand our desires and goals, or on the other hand, pull us down to a level where we focus on all the negative aspects of our lives. We can be successful and prosperous, or suddenly find ourselves desperately in need of change to survive.

Recently I cleaned out my office and discarded all the clutter I could find. As a result, it brightened the environment around where I spend my time and do my work. It is just as important to do an inner cleaning of the mind by releasing past hurts, negative thoughts and feelings, uncertainties and worry. Our creator meant for us to have joy and not to dwell on negative issues. When we harbor negative thoughts we encourage anxiety, sadness, depression, and not only do we suffer diseases and illness but it affects every condition and circumstance of our lives. If one continues to dwell in negative thought, he or she will never reach his or her potential for accomplishing any chosen goal.

James Allen has quoted from Proverbs 23:7, in saying, "For as he thinketh in his heart, so is he." By this statement, Mr. Allen goes on to say, " The aphorism, 'as a man thinketh in his heart so is he', not only embraces the whole of a man's being, but is so comprehensive as to reach out to every condition and circumstance of his life." I highly recommend his book, As A Man Thinketh.

A man is literally what he thinks, his character being the complete sum of all his thoughts.

We are sending out thoughts of greater or lesser vibration almost constantly. The matter of thought attraction is a serious one, and when we think about how our thoughts change our surroundings it is time to investigate the seriousness of thought attraction.

THOUGHTS ARE THINGS

I hold it true that thoughts are things;
They're endowed with bodies
and breath and wings:
And that we send them forth to fill
The world with good results, or ill.
That which we call our secret thought
Speeds forth to earth's remotest spot,
Leaving its blessings or its woes
Like tracks behind it as it goes.

We build our future, thought by thought,
For good or ill, yet know it not.
Yet so the universe was wrought.
Thought is another name for fate;
Choose then thy destiny and wait,
For love brings love and hate brings hate.

Henry Van Dyke

GET A TRANSFER

If you are on the Gloomy Line,
Get a transfer.
If you're inclined to fret and pine,

Manna From Heaven

Get a transfer.
Get off the track of doubt and gloom.
Get on the Sunshine track-there's-room-
Get a transfer.

If you're on the Worry Train,
Get a transfer.
You must not stay there and complain,
Get a transfer.
The Cheerful Cars are passing through,
And there's lots of room for you,
Get a transfer.

If you're on the Grouchy Track,
Get a transfer.
Just take a Happy special back,
Get a transfer.
Jump on the train and pull the rope,
That lands you at the station Hope-
Get a transfer.

Author Unknown

HOW TO BE HAPPY

Are you almost disgusted with life, little man?
I'll tell you a wonderful trick
That will bring you contentment, if anything can,
Do something for somebody quick!

Are you awfully tired with play, little girl?
Wearied, discouraged, and sick-
I'll tell you the loveliest game in the world,
Do something for somebody, quick!

Though it rains, like the rain of the flood, little man,
And the clouds are forbidding and thick,

You can make the sun shine in your soul, little man,
Do something for somebody, quick!

Though the stars are like brass overhead, little girl,
And the walks like a well-heated brick,
And our earthly affairs in a terrible whirl,
Do something for somebody, quick!

Author Unknown

LOSS OF A LOVED ONE

The most shattering experience that can befall a person is the death of a loved one. Grieving over such a loss, we may feel as though the ache in our heart will never ease. Even in the mist of pain or distress, we know that we are not alone. God is with us.

God constantly assures us that his love soothes and sustains us, and that he walks with us in our sorrow. We have the assurance and kind words of family and friends, and help and comforting words from our neighbors who care. We are never alone.

Our hearts can be soothed and our minds at peace knowing we shall see our loved one again and they have only stepped through the veil to God's Paradise. This can give us strength and courage to go forward with the duties that need to be taken care of.

You may feel that no words or formula can get you over the immediate, overwhelming pain when first it happens. God is there with you. Be strong and courageous. Do not be frightened or dismayed, for the Lord God is with you wherever you go or whatever you have to do. Do not be afraid to cry or pray your grief away. The nearer you get to God the more He will comfort you.

THE VILLAGE BLACKSMITH

Under a spreading chestnut tree
The village smithy stands;
The smith, a mighty man is he,
With large and sinewy hands;
And the muscles of his brawny arms
Are strong as iron bands.

His hair is crisp, and black, and long,
His face is like the tan;
His brow is wet with honest sweat,
He earns whate'er he can,
And he looks the whole world in the face,
For he owes not any man.
Week in, week out, from morn till night
You can hear his bellows blow;
You can hear him swing his heavy sledge,
With measured beat and slow,
Like a sexton ringing the village bell,
When the evening sun is low.

And children coming home from school
Look in at the open door;
They love to see the flaming forge,
And hear the bellows roar,
And catch the burning sparks that fly
Like chaff from a threshing floor.

He goes on Sunday to the church,
And sits among his boys;
He hears the parson pray and preach,
He hears his daughter's voice,
Singing in the village choir,
And it make his heart rejoice.

It sounds to him like her mother's voice,
Singing in Paradise!
He needs must think of her once more,
How in the grave she lies;
And with his hard, rough hand he wipes
A tear out of his eyes.

Toiling-rejoicing-sorrowing
Onward through life he goes;
Each morning sees some task begin,
Each evening sees it close;
Something attempted, something done,
Has earned a night's repose.

Thanks, thanks to thee, my worthy friend,
For the lesson thou hast taught!
Thus at the flaming forge of life
Our fortunes must be wrought;
Thus on its sounding anvil shaped
Each burning deed and thought!

Henry Wadsworth Longfellow

Dedicated to my brother, Norris Keith Miles, who died at sixteen years of age, from a high school sports accident. This was his favorite poem and he recited if from memory with great passion.

A CHILD'S DREAM, OF A STAR

They used to say to one another, sometimes, supposing all the children upon earth were to die, would the flowers, and the water, and the sky be sorry? They believed they would be sorry. For, said they, the buds are the children of the flowers, and the little playful streams that gambol down the hillsides are the children of the water; and the smallest bright specks playing at hide-and-seek in the sky all night, must surely be the children of the stars; and they would all be grieved to see their playmates, the children of men, no more.

There was one clear, shining star that used to come out in the sky before the rest, near the church spire, above the graves. It was larger and more beautiful, they thought, than all the others, and every night they watched for it, standing hand in hand at a window. Whoever saw it first, cried out, "I see the star!" And often they cried out both together, knowing so well when it would rise, and where. So they grew to be such friends with it, that, before lying down in their beds, they always looked out once again, to bid it good night; and when they were turning round to sleep, they used to say, "God bless the star!"

But while she was still very young, oh, very, very young, the sister drooped, and came to be so weak that she could no longer stand in the window at night; and then the child looked sadly out by himself, and when he saw the star, turned round and said to the patient pale face on the bed, "I see the star!" and then a smile would come upon the face, and a little weak voice used to say, "God bless my brother and the star!"

And so the time came, all too soon! When the child looked out alone, and when there was no face on the bed; and when there was a little grave among the graves, not there before; and when the star made long rays down toward him, as he saw it through his tears.

Now, these rays were so bright, and they seemed to make such a shining way from earth to heaven, that when the child went to his solitary bed, he dreamed about the star; and dreamed that, lying where he was, he saw a train of people taken up that sparkling road by angels. And the star, opening, showed him a great world of light, where many more such angels waited to receive them.

All these angels, who were waiting, turned their beaming

eyes upon the people who were carried up into the star; and some came out from the long rows in which they stood, and fell upon the people's necks, and kissed them tenderly and went away with them down avenues of light, and were so happy in their company, that lying in his bed he wept for joy.

But there were many angels who did not go with them, and among them one he knew. The patient face that once had lain upon the bed was glorified and radiant, but his heart found out his sister among all the host.

His sister's angel lingered near the entrance of the star, and said to the leader among those who had brought the people thither:

"Is my brother come?"

And he said, "No."

She was turning hopefully away when the child stretched out his arms, and cried, "Oh sister, I am here! Take me!" and then she turned her beaming eyes upon him, and it was night; and the star was shining into the room, making long rays down toward him as he saw it through his tears.

From that hour forth, the child looked out upon the star as on the home he was to go to, when his time should come; and he thought that he did not belong to the earth alone, but to the star too, because of his sister's angel gone before.

There was baby born to be a brother of the child; and while he was so little that he never yet had spoken a word, he stretched his tiny form out on his bed, and died.

Again the child dreamed of the opened star, and of the company of angels, and the train of people, and the rows of angels with their beaming eyes all turned upon those people's faces.

Said his sister's angel to the leader:

"Is my brother come?"

And he said, "Not that one, but another."

As the child beheld his brother's angel in her arms, he cried, "Oh, sister, I am here! Take me!" And she turned and smiled upon him, and star was shining.

He grew to be a young man, and was busy at his books when an old servant came to him and said:

"Thy mother is no more. I bring her blessing on her darling son!"

Again at night he saw the star, and all that former company. Said his sister's angel to the leader:

"Is my brother come?"

And he said, "Thy mother!"

A mighty cry of joy went forth through all the star, because the mother was reunited to her two children. And he stretched out his arms and cried, "Oh, mother, sister, and brother, I am here! Take me!" And they answered him, "Not yet," and the star was shining.

He grew to be a man, whose hair was turning gray, and he was sitting in his chair by the fireside, heavy with grief, and with his face bedewed by tears, when the star opened once again.

Said his sisters' angel to the leader, "Is my brother come?"

And he said, "Nay, but his maiden daughter."

And the man who had been the child saw his daughter, newly lost to him, a celestial creature among those three, and he said, "My daughter's head is on my sister's bosom, and her arm is around my mother's neck, and at her feet there is the baby of old time, and I can bear the parting from her, God be praised!"

And the star was shining.

Thus the child came to be an old man, and his once smooth face was wrinkled, and his steps were slow and feeble, and his back was bent. And one night as he lay upon his bed, his children standing round, he cried as he had cried so long ago:

"I see the star!"

They whispered to one another, "He is dying."

And he said, "I am. My age is falling from me like a garment, and I move toward the star as a child. And oh, my Father, now I thank Thee that is has so often opened, to receive those dear ones who await me!"

And the star was shining; and it shines upon his grave.

Motivation and Change

Charles Dickens

MEMORY

My childhoods' Home I see again
And sadden with the view;
And still, as memory crowds my brain,
There's pleasure in it, too.

O memory! thou midway world
'Twixt earth and paradise,
Where things decayed and loved ones lost
In dreamy shadows rise,

And freed from all that's earthly, vile,
Seem hallowed, pure and bright,
Like scenes in some enchanted isle
All bathed in liquid light.

As, leaving some grand waterfall,
We, lingering, list its roar_
So memory will hallow all
We've known but know no more.

Near twenty years have passed away
Since here I bid farewell
To woods and fields, and scenes of play,
And playmates loved so well.

Where many were, but few remain
Of old familiar things,
But seeing them to mind again
The lost and absent brings.

The friends, I left that parting day,
How changed; as time has sped!

Manna From Heaven

Young childhood grown, strong manhood gray;
And half of all are dead.
I hear the loved survivors tell,
How nought from death could save,
Still every sound appears a knell
And every spot a grave.

I range the fields with pensive tread,
And pace the hollow rooms,
And feel (companion of the dead)
I'm living in the tombs.
- Abraham Lincoln
(When thirty- seven years old.)

Faith is the greatest comfort in the loss of a loved one.

Don't grieve for me for now I'm free,
I'm following the path God has laid you see

I took His hand when I heard Him call,
I turned my back and left it all.

I could not stay another day
To laugh, to love, to work, to play.

Tasks left undone must stay that way.
I found that peace at the close of day.

If my parting left a void,
Then fill it with remember joy.

A friendship shared, a laugh, a kiss,
Oh yes, these things , I too will miss.

Be not burdened with times of sorrow,

I wish you the sunshine of tomorrow.

My life's been full, I've savored much.
Good friends, good times,
A loved ones touch.

Perhaps my time seemed all too brief,
Don't lengthen it now with undue grief.

Lift up your hearts and peace to thee,
God wanted me. He set me free.

Author Unkown

PEOPLE WHO RETURN FROM DEATH EXPERIENCES

How would you react to the wonderment of knowing that death is peaceful, beautiful, calm, and in many cases a pleasant experience? Death according to many unique accounts from persons who have briefly stepped through the veil to the other side in Paradise and returned, speak only of the beautiful surroundings.

Persons who report after death experiences no longer fear death. Many report they regret being returned to life from the peaceful surroundings of Heaven. Reports are given to physicians from their patients, in such a case, accounts of their ability to have actually seen relatives and spoken to them. Perhaps, God has given this experience for persons to change and the knowledge of repentance, enabling them to gain the desire to improve their lives. There have been reports of such experiences given to families where problems existed and forgiveness was needed to heal old wounds. The rewards can be wonderful and a great comfort in any cases.

MY JOURNEY TO THE VEIL AND MY RETURN TO LIFE

*M*ost persons discount the ancient belief that one can "return from the dead." Since the year 1976, medical professionals have begun to document hundreds of reports of after-life experiences by their patients. The accounts are very similar, however, some reports are more complicated and detailed. One of the most detailed reports came out of the University of Florida, by Dr. Michael B. Sbom, a cardiologist, and Sarah Kreutziger, a social worker and psychologist. I am unable to tell you how you may purchase this report.

My narration of my experience has been told only to a few. Because we live in a skeptical world I have been reluctant to share my spiritual experience with others. My journey to the "veil" of life is meant to be read and not discussed. My purpose in sharing my transcendence rests with the peace and comfort it might give to those who mourn. May I give peace without fear to those who face death in the immediate future, by sharing this fact: death is peaceful beyond measure, not to be feared but to be accepted with anticipation of rest and loss of pain.

My experience with the closeness of those who have passed on and those who face death was given to me at an early age. When I was five years old, my wonderful brother just 16 years old died. Just before he sank into a state of unconsciousness, he remarked, "Why is Grandma Miles at my bedside? She keeps asking me to come with her." My brother did not know that his Grandmother had just passed away on the 19th of January and it was January 21st. It was only a few short hours, that he crossed over the veil to the comfort of his God on high. My parents were devastated but comforted to know that Grandma, who died just days before, had taken him home through the veil.

In 1963, I was 23 years old, a wife, and mother of a 2 year old son, and the mother of a newborn son just 2 weeks old. My delivery from my pregnancy was difficult and mishandled. In the first few months of the pregnancy I was threatening to abort. My physician gave me some new drug on the market, to prevent the loss of my child. In the delivery I was undergoing an ordeal. The placenta, due to the drug, was grounded into my uterus like cement. The physician had a hard time removing it. During the night I began to hemorrhage and required surgery and blood transfusions. I was sent home too early. I was so ill, I did not know how I would be able to take care of my children. My wonderful mother became my caregiver. I knew something was terribly wrong and the physician told me to "suck it up" that I was being a baby. I continued to go downhill. My husband was due at his employment early one morning, the first time my mother had not stayed all night. She arrived to find me unconscious and hemorrhaging on the floor. My two little ones were screaming and my two year old was almost in shock, too young to know what to do.

The hospital was 20 miles away and while I was in the ambulance I heard the attendant say, "She is gone." At that moment I was filled with the most exhilarating feeling I had ever felt. I felt peaceful, restful, and happy. It was not very long until the ambulance arrived at the hospital. The hospital personnel came running out of the emergency exit with the gurney.

Suddenly, I was ejected into a position where I viewed my detached body from the height of several feet. I realized I was floating at the top of the ambulance. I looked down and it was evident to me that I was truly deceased but I was at peace. I remembered nothing of my life, until suddenly, I found myself in the emergency room looking down at myself as the hospital personnel were working on me.

Believe it or not there was some humor in all of this. I remember a well dressed woman sitting in a wheel chair and she was bloody from a wound all across the forehead and bleeding profusely. The nurses were trying to stop the bleeding. She had been in an automobile accident. She kept screaming, "Get her out of here I don't want her dying around me." At first they just told her, "Please be quiet, she can hear you." She kept on screaming the same old message, until the nurse taking care of me, pulled the curtain aside and said, " If you say anything more I am going to slap your face, shut up." In the meantime, back at the ceiling, I was watching them give me CPR, one young man picked me up and literally threw my back against the wall. I was wondering what they would do next, when all of a sudden I was taken in an instant to a dark tunnel. I found myself moving fast down the length of the tunnel. I was not walking, not floating, but moving rapidly, not unlike, a magnet drawing me forcefully. Only then, did I suffer any apprehension.

The light at the end of the tunnel looked to me to be a large hole in a cave. It was hard to determine in the darkness of the tunnel. The light grew brighter and brighter as I grew nearer to the end of the tunnel, It reminded me of looking at the sun directly without sun glasses. However, it was not a yellow light but a bluish white light that appeared clear and light in weight, is the only way I can describe it The light sent large rays of light out into the tunnel, as I came closer, making the reality of the blending of the darkened tunnel and lighted places, most mysterious.

Immediately, as I arrived some 50 feet from the tunnel, I became aware of a person waiting for me at the light. She was on the right side of me. Her dress was in the likeness of a monk, a hooded light brown habit with long sleeves and tied in the middle with a braided rope of the same material. She stood looking at me and smiled but did not approach me. She did not need to speak to me, for I was instantly made aware, that there would be no sound, that we were to exchange thoughts, by a non-verbal thought process. I was made aware that she, in all probability, was my sister, Trecca, who died about 15 years before I was born. She held out her hand, conversed with me through thought informing me that I was to come with her. I looked at her and declined. It was so strange that we knew what was being said to each other.

It was only at this instant, that I realized we were not alone, I did not see him but knew that he was a person of great authority, but he was somewhere in the area on my left side. His thoughts asked me why I desired not to stay. I defended my action, "I have two babies at home who need me, my husband is not a member of my church, I want my children to have a membership in that church and I want to be sure my children would be raised in that religion."

My answer came from an authority and I was aware of that. I could feel that he was someone special. I do not claim that he was the Lord, for I saw him not. His thought came with resounding force, "Let her return."

I flew at great speed back to the hospital, instantly my soul and body were united. I have never been in such painful circumstances, every cell in my body was crying out at the same time, I was almost overcome with the pain. I awakened crying in my misery. The nurse, who by the way, was crying also, said, "Oh look our little mother is back with us again, honey, you are hurting from the blood transfusion as it goes to your lungs." The non-verbal thought came to me as before, "One always suffers when the soul reunites with the body." When we go back _ we pay a great price of pain for the privilege.

I feel most grateful for I was given my life back again, to raise and enjoy my children, and to love and enjoy our grandchildren and great-grandchildren. I am so grateful that I was given the privilege of extending my life and seeing my desires and talents fulfilled. But, I am aware that I missed the beauty and comfort of the Heavens above, and I know the time will come when God shall call me home to give him an accounting of my love and service and I shall not be afraid.

I shall never forget my experience, I stood so close at the "invisible veil of life," in all its glory, and I cannot deny it.

Gwenith Miles Lewis

GOD BE WITH YOU TILL WE MEET AGAIN

God be with you till we meet again;
By his counsels guide, uphold you;
With his sheep securely fold you.
God be with you till we meet again.

God be with you till we meet again;
When life's perils thick confound you,
Put his arms un-failing round you.
God be with you till we meet again

God be with you till we meet again;
Keep love's banner floating o'er you
Smite death's threatening wave before you
God be with you till we meet again.

Jeremiah Rankin

CHAPTER THREE

God and Service

MY SHEEP KNOW MY VOICE

A youth of 20 years of age was asked to become a shepherd to the sheep of a wealthy Ranger. He had been chosen for this position because of his honesty and integrity. It didn't take long for the sheep to recognize their shepherd's voice and stop at his call. One day, a test came to the shepherd boy to prove his steadfastness. Along in the late afternoon a man dressed as a hunter came to the place where the shepherd was watching his sheep and asked a favor of him. "As you see, I am an elderly gentleman and it's vastly important for me to reach a cottage that's beyond that hill with this message before dark, and, as I am weary of travel, will you go? The shepherd stood puzzled and in deep thought, wondering what manner of man this was and what would be beyond the hill. But he explained that the sheep would not know his voice when he called them into their corral at dusk and they would wander away into the darkness and become a prey for the waiting bear or tiger. "I cannot leave them for they are trusted to my care." Still, the hunter, tried to persuade him to go, but to no avail, for the shepherd remembered he had been chosen because of his honesty and his promise to the Ranger was the that he could be depended on, and he would remain steadfast to his duty. At this the hunter unmasked and before the shepherd stood the Ranger who uttered these words: "Now I know of your faithfulness and surely your watch will not be in vain."

These tried and true old stories reflect the teachings of many years and many great men. Youth of today could benefit from their message.

MAY JOY FILL YOUR HEART

When we awake in the morning, we want our first thoughts to be filled with joy. Joy colors our world like the brilliant hues of a morning sunrise; one which promises us new hope and fulfillment of dreams for the coming day. Filling our thoughts from a pool of joy within, we bring joy to whatever we are doing each day. When we reflect on our happiest moments, they may be those times we were sharing our joy by serving others. The example of how a person views a glass as either half full or half empty reminds us that our outlook on life is up to each individual.

Each one of us should strive to not look back at yesterday, or at mistakes we have made. We learn from our mistakes and then forget them. There are times we are prone to fall into negative thinking when we find ourselves unable to find a solution to serious problems. We find ourselves in areas where others, at times, cannot provide us with a solution. Serious matters cannot readily be solved unless we involve God. Through his grace, we may find solutions and a light in the darkness.

Many experiences in life will bring us joy; a birth, a marriage, a note, or a phone call from a lost friend. True joy is knowing that your God loves you, and that he wants you to have a fulfilling and productive life. He created us to have joy!

God and Service

"Life is a place of service," Leo Tolstoy said, *"Joy can be real only if people look upon their life as a service, and have a definite object in life outside themselves and their personal happiness."*

DROP A PEBBLE IN THE WATER

Drop a pebble in the water:
just a splash and it is gone;
But there's half-a-hundred ripples
circling on and on and on,
Spreading, spreading from the center,
flowing on out to the sea.
And there is no way of telling
where the end is going to be.

Drop a pebble in the water:
in a minute you forget,
But there's little waves a-flowing,
and there's ripples circling yet,
And those little waves a-flowing
to a great big wave have grown;
You've disturbed a mighty river
just by dropping in a stone.

Drop an unkind word, or careless:
in a minute it is gone;
But there's half-a-hundred ripples
circling on and on and on.
They keep spreading, spreading,
spreading from the center as they go,
And there is no way to stop them,
once you've started them to flow.

Drop an unkind word, or careless:
in a minute you forget;

But there's little waves a-flowing,
and there's ripples circling yet,
And perhaps in some sad heart
a mighty wave of tears you've stirred,
And disturbed a life was happy
ere you dropped that unkind word.

Drop a word of cheer and kindness:
just a flash and it is gone;
But there's half-a-hundred ripples
circling on and on and on,
Bearing hope and joy and comfort
on each splashing, dashing wave
Till you wouldn't believe the volume
of the one kind word you gave.

Drop a word of cheer and kindness:
in a minute you forget;
But there's gladness still a-swelling,
and there's joy a-circling yet,
And you've rolled a wave of comfort
whose sweet music can be heard
Over miles and miles of water just
by dropping one kind word.

James W. Foley

TWENTY THIRD PSALM

The Lord is my shepherd; I shall not want.

He maketh me to lie down in green pastures: he leadeth me beside the still waters.

He restoreth my soul: he leadeth me in the paths or righteousness for his name's sake.

Yea, though I walk through the valley of the shadow of death, I will fear no evil: for thou art with me; thy rod and thy staff they comfort me.

Thou preparest a table before me in the presence of mine enemies: thou anointest my head with oil; my cup runneth over.

Surely goodness and mercy shall follow me all the days of my life; and I will dwell in the house of the Lord forever.

WHEN COMFORT IS NEEDED

We may find comfort in the gentle touch of a loved one. We can receive comfort from friendships and companionships of those around us, to gladden our hearts. However, God is our comfort and strength in times of trouble.

Perhaps moments ago we might have felt alone. God's wisdom is shown to us sometimes in good music, positive television shows, and in books we read.

In turn, we are grateful for opportunities to bring faith, hope, and love to others in times when such comfort is needed. The spirit of God, through our voice when we embrace others who need our comfort, is fulfilled in our touch and our duties of service.

When we are caught up in confusion because of some unexpected happening in our day, we can always turn to God. He gives us comfort and peace that surpasses all understanding. Let God's peace infuse you with the assurance that you will have a life filled with love and hope, regardless of what happens.

In the book of Job, in the Bible, we read the story of Job who suffered much but refused to utter any vocal complaint of his circumstances.

He inspires us to hold to our faith and know God is present in the situation and that he is restoring what can be done. Job refused to blame God, although he lost everything he owned plus his health. In the end of this period of testing from the Lord – Job regained his health and all of the material possessions were restored. Comforted he praised his Heavenly Father for His goodness.

All the world's a stage, and all men and women merely players; they have the exits and their entrances. And one man in time plays many parts.

Shakespeare

BUILDING BRIDGES FOR OTHERS

bridge becomes a passable pathway over an impassable natural obstacle. Individuals who willingly build such bridges have performed a service for current use, as well as use by future generations.

This ongoing service should be the cardinal act in our efforts to give service to others. Such an envoy is a remarkable example of love. Sharing your talents and volunteering your time for the benefit of others, is a gift of greater worth than any material gift one may give.

Another example, additionally given, is the sharing of your faith, which binds people together in ways that cannot be duplicated. Many people shy away from this gift of sharing thoughts of your faith. It is a misconception if they believe you are saying, in so many ways, to change religions. What the true gift of sharing your faith with others means, you share the love of God. This can build solid friendships and relationships.

God and Service

This poem is an excellent example of concern and caring for the younger generation.

THE BRIDGE BUILDER

An old man, going a lone highway,
Came, at the evening, cold and gray,
To a chasm, vast, and deep, and wide,
Through which was flowing a sullen tide.
The old man crossed in the twilight dim;
The sullen stream had no fears for him;
But he turned, when safe on the other side,
And built a bridge to span the tide.
"Old man," said a fellow pilgrim, near,
"You are wasting strength with building here;
Your journey will end with the ending day;
You never again must pass this way;
You have crossed the chasm, deep and wide –
Why build you the bridge at the eventide?"

The builder lifted his old gray head:
"Good friend, in the path I have come," he said,
"There followeth after me today
A youth, whose feet must pass this way.
This chasm, that has been naught to me,
To that fair-haired youth may a pitfall be.
He, too, must cross in the twilight dim;
Good friend, I am building the bridge for *him*."

Will Allen Dromgoole

UNAWARES

They said: "The Master is coming to honor the town today,
And none can tell at what house or home the
Master will choose to stay;"
And I thought while my heart beat wildly,
what if He should come to mine,
How would I strive to entertain
and honor the Guest Divine.

And straight I turned to toiling to make
my house more neat, I swept, polished,
and garnished and decked it with blossoms sweet.
I was troubles for fear the Master might come
ere my work was done,
And I hastened and worked the faster
and watched the hurrying sun.

But right in the midst of my duties,
a woman came to my door,
She had come to tell me her sorrows
and my comfort and aid to implore;
And I said: "I cannot listen nor help you any today,
I have greater things to attend to."
And the pleader turned away.

But soon there came another; a cripple, thin.
Pale, and gray, And said:
"Oh, let me stop and rest a while in your house, I pray!
I have traveled far since morning, I am hungry
and faint and weak; My heart is full of misery
and comfort and help I seek".

And I cried: "I am grieved and sorry,
but I can't help you today.
I look for a great and noble guest;
and the cripple went away.

God and Service

And the day wore onward swiftly,
and my task was nearly done,
A prayer was offered in my heart
that the Master to me might come.
And I thought I would spring to meet Him
and serve Him with utmost care,
When a little child stood by me with
a face so sweet and fair,
So sweet, but with marks of tear-drops;
and his clothes were tattered and old.
A finger bruised and bleeding and
his little bare feet were cold.

And I said: "I'm sorry for you,
you are sorely in need of care.
But I cannot stop to give it,
you must hasten elsewhere."
And at the words a shadow swept
o'er his blue veined brow;
"Someone will feed and clothe you, dear;
but I'm too busy now."

At last the day was ended and
my toil was over and done,
My house was swept an garnished and
I watched in the dark alone.
Watched, but no foot-fall sounded,
no one paused at my gate,
No one entered my cottage door;
I could only pray and wait.
I waited till night had deepened and
the Master had not come-
He has entered some other door and
gladdened some other home.
My labor has been for nothing and I bowed
my head and I wept,
My heart was sore with longing;

Yet, in spite of it all, I slept.
Then the Master stood before me
and His face was grave and fair;
"Three times today I came to your door
and I craved your pity and care;
Three times you sent me onward,
unhelped and uncomforted-
And the blessing you might have had
is lost and your chance to serve has fled."

"Oh, Lord, dear Lord, forgive me,
how could I know it was Thee?"
My soul was shamed and bowed
in the depths of humility.
And He said: "The sin in pardoned,
but the blessing is lost to thee;
For comforting not the least of Mine,
you have failed to comfort Me."

Author unknown

The most exhausting thing in life is being insincere.

Anne Morrow Lindberg

GOD GIVES US DIVINE ORDER

*W*e are living in an ever-changing world. Perhaps even the environment we grew up in has changed so drastically we no longer recognize it. No matter how much everything around has changed, one thing remains the same: God is with us and bringing his divine order and peace into our life. Our faith in God must be so absolute, and our trust in God's love must be so strong we cannot depart from it.

The story of Joseph's betrayal by his brothers reveal how divine order can turn a seeming disaster into a blessing. Even though Joseph's own brothers plotted to cause him harm, divine order prevailed and he was saved and exalted to rule over them, and he was given the opportunity to save them from famine.

God's will for us has a divine order also. So let us not panic when events seem out of order. We must know in our heart that God will bring order from disorder. Faith on your part must be exercised.

There are times when we may be ill or a loved one has a frightening illness, or there are times when we have needs and meeting those needs seem to take an eternity to resolve. Then we must remain patient and calm and remember God is present and divine order is at work. We can and will receive of God's will through prayer.

God does work in mysterious ways and does wonderful works through people and events that affect us and our loved ones. If we live accordingly with faith in God, if the outcome is sad and devastating, God's order is unfolding and all of these events are part of a plan. We can take comfort in knowing all of the events we experience are part of a larger plan.

From our limited human point of view, we may imagine that the world would be better without the appearance of disorders, when in fact; some measure of chaos is inherent in life. Without a hint of unpredictability, only boredom and sameness would prevail.

When we come to the plateau of awareness that we were sent to earth to progress in God's universe, we are able to understand the apparent chaos in the universe is based upon the divine laws of progression

IN GOD WE TRUST

From the early, learned man to the youngest child, there exists this common trust in God.

The story is told of a little girl's first visit to the dentist's office to have a tooth extracted (probably occurring many years in the past before medication was available). The dentist, realizing how frightened the child was, said: "Here child, is a fifty-cent piece. You hold it in your hand, and after we are through you may have it." The little girl did not flinch through the operation. Afterward, the dentist said, "You were so brave."

"Yes," she answered, "for the coin you gave me had written on it 'In God We Trust' and that is what I did."

THE SERMON TO THE BIRDS

Very kind and loving was St. Francis – kind and loving not only to men but to all living things. He spoke of the birds as his little brothers of the air, and he could never bear to see them harmed.

At Christmastime he scattered crumbs of bread under the trees, so that the tiny creatures could feast and be happy.

Once when a boy gave him a pair of doves which he had snared, St. Francis had a nest made for them, and the mother bird laid her eggs in it.

By and by, the eggs hatched, and a nest full of young doves grew up. They were so tame that they sat on the shoulders of St. Francis and ate from his hand.

And many other stories are told of this man's great love and pity for the timid creatures which lived in the fields and woods.

One day as he was walking among the trees the birds saw him and flew down to greet him. They sang their sweetest songs to show how much they loved him. Then, when they saw that he was about to speak, they nestled softly in the grass and listened.

"O little birds," he said, "I love you, for you are my brothers and sisters of the air. Let me tell you something, my little brothers, my little sisters: You ought always to love God and praise him."

"For think what He has given you. He has given you wings with which to fly through the air. He has given you clothing both warm and beautiful. He has given you the air in which to move and have homes."

"And this of this, O little brothers: you sow not, neither do your reap, for God feeds you. He gives you the rivers and the brooks from which to drink. He gives you the mountains and the valleys where you may rest. He gives you the trees in which to build your nests."

"You toil not, neither do you spin, yet God takes care of you and your little ones. It must be, then, that He loves you. So, do not be ungrateful, but sing His praises and thank Him for his goodness toward you."

Then the saint stopped speaking and looked around him. All the birds sprang up joyfully. They spread their wings and opened their mouths to show that they understood his words.

And when he blessed them, all began to sing; and the whole forest was filled with sweetness and joy because of their wonderful melodies.

St. Francis, founder of the Franciscan Order of the Roman Catholic Church, is known for his love of peace and his respect for all living things. St. Francis lived a simple life of poverty.

THE BEATITUDES

Blessed are the poor in spirit: for theirs is the kingdom of heaven.

Blessed are they that mourn: for they shall be comforted.

Blessed are the meek: for they shall inherit the earth.

Blessed are they which do hunger and thirst after righteousness: for they shall be filled.

Blessed are the merciful: for they shall obtain mercy.

Blessed are the pure in heart: for they shall see God.

Blessed are the peacemakers: for they shall be called the children of God.

Blessed are they which are persecuted for righteousness' sake: for theirs is the kingdom of heaven.

Blessed are ye, when men shall revile you, and persecute you, and say all manner of evil against you falsely for my sake.

Rejoice, and be exceeding glad: for great is your reward in heaven: for so persecuted they the prophets which were before you.

I AM WITH THEE

There are times when we feel that life is a race, and as hard as we try, we cannot keep up. We may experience situations in which others, or even ourselves, doubt our capabilities. There is a way, however, to overcome such thoughts and feelings. We can use circumstances as examples to remind us of the importance of bringing any doubt and fear to our God in prayer. As we pray, we can allow our hearts to be filled with joy and our minds with resources and solutions. As we emerge from prayer with God, we can be inspired and renewed. With confidence, we can think about the options that come to us in prayer. We can recognize that God is the ultimate source of all positive affirmations and solutions.

The good news that we receive with an open mind and heart is that we are never stuck in one job, one place, or one situation. With God as our guide, we have choices. Divine wisdom guides us in choosing positive life-affirming alternatives that invite us to use our talents and abilities in new ways. As we explore, we become aware of, and refreshed by, the diversity of life. What may have seemed unusual is revealed to be a blessed alternative. God's way is our way.

The wisdom that created the universe is available to guide us in our own life's decision. So what holds us back from letting God guide our life? One answer may be that we are not certain if God is there guiding our decisions. How can we be sure?

Because God is love, love is the greatest of all mortal blessings. He wants us to be loved and to love others as our self. Through love, we can let go in sweet surrender, and then wonderful and miraculous things begin to happen. Nothing beyond that point can limit us in achieving something important to us. All things are possible and we can relax and enjoy each day in confidence.

We are most of us very lonely in this world; you who have any who love you, cling to them and thank God.

Author Unknown

To be honest, to be kind;
To earn a little and to spend a little less;
To make upon the whole a family happier for his presence;
To renounce when that shall be necessary
and not to be embittered;
To keep a few friends, but those without capitulation. –

Above all, on the same grim conditions,
to keep friends with himself –
Here is a task for all that a man has
of fortitude and delicacy.

Robert Louis Stevenson

LET THIS BE YOUR FINEST YEAR

*R*alph Waldo Emerson suggested that we should recognize within our heart that every year can be the best year we have ever lived. And Plato said we should take charge of our lives for you can do what you will with it.

We should practice the art of forgetting. Man is what he remembers, but man is also what he forgets. One of the healthiest things a person can do is become a master of forgetting. If we take the "T" off the word <u>forget</u> – it spells "forge". Forge ahead and start anew!

We should expect great things and put our life in God's hands. Have high hopes, have great dreams and have great beliefs. Have visions and believe in them. Believe life is good and it is going to be better, and the best is yet to come. Then you are likely to exceed your expectations for God's gifts.

Our physical body responds to our thoughts, our emotions, and conditions in our environment. How we feel and act impacts our experiences of life. At the depths of our souls, however, we are spiritual in nature.

Should our world seem busy and complex, we can turn within to rediscover the serenity of our soul. In meditation and prayer, our awareness of God is heightened. We are regenerated spiritually, which is beyond what a simple physical rest, emotional comfort, or mental calm can bring us.

To the depths of our beings, our awareness of God sustains us. Living from the serenity of our soul, we are renewed.

God and Service

God is our refuge and strength,
A very present help in trouble,
Therefore will not we fear,
Though the mountains be carried
Into the mists of the sea.

Psalm 46:10

THE TEN COMMANDMENTS

Beginning with Adam, the Lord has always revealed His governing principles to his people.

*M*oses received the Ten Commandments twice from God. Both times they were written on tablets of stone by the finger of God. On both instances the same principles and standards of moral conduct were given unto the people.

The Lord expects us to keep the Sabbath Day holy, as a day of rest and learning.

Thou shalt have no other gods before me.

Thou shalt not make unto thee any graven image, or any likeness of anything that is in heaven above, or that is in the earth beneath, or that is in the water under the earth: thou shalt not bow down thyself to them, nor serve them: for I, the Lord thy God am a jealous God, visiting the iniquity of the fathers upon the children unto the third and fourth generation of them that hate me; and showing mercy unto thousands of them that love me, and keep my commandments.

I.   Thou shalt not take the name of the Lord thy God in vain: for the Lord will not hold him guiltless that taketh his name in vain.

II. Remember the Sabbath day, to keep it holy. Six days shalt thou labor, and do all thy work: but the seventh day is the Sabbath of the Lord thy God: in it thou shalt not do any work, thou, nor thy son, nor thy daughter, thy manservant, nor thy maid-servant, nor thy cattle, nor thy stranger that is within thy gates: for in six days the Lord made heaven and earth, the sea, and all that in them is, and rested the seventh day: wherefore the Lord blessed the Sabbath day, and hallowed it.

III. Honor thy father and thy mother: that thy days may be long upon the land which the Lord thy God giveth thee.

IV. Thou shalt not kill.

V. Thou shalt not commit adultery.

VI. Thou shalt not steal.

VII. Thou shalt not bear false witness against thy neighbor.

X. Thou shalt not covet thy neighbor's house, thou shalt not covet thy neighbor's wife, nor his manservant, nor his maid-servant, nor his ox, nor his ass, nor anything that is thy neighbor's.

THE AWESOME POWER OF PRAYER

*B*ack in the eighteenth century a poet and lyricist, by the name of James Montgomery, penned the immortal text later to be used in the hymn known as "Prayer Is The Soul's Sincere Desire." Mr. Montgomery has expressed the key to sincere prayer; it comes directly from the soul. The first lines of the text read as follows: "Prayer is the soul's sincere desire, uttered or unexpressed. The motion of a hidden fire that trembles in the breast." When sincere prayer is exercised there is no limit to what can happen in your life or in the life of one who benefits from your well-worded prayer.

God and Service

People who are unaccustomed to praying need not worry if praying for the first time. If their prayer consists of the virtues of new faith, gratitude and sincerity your prayer will be heard. One hears stories frequently of first prayers being so powerful and sincere the prayer has changed the course of a person's life from that moment the prayer was spoken. Never be afraid to pray for God loves the person who is humbled enough to change and seek His help.

If your prayers are hurried and lack thought or if your prayer is child like in nature it would be well to give your prayer some serious thought. If your prayer is a memorized statement or a scripted short thought, change your prayer to your own words and use prayer verbiage, which shows respect to God, with such words a Thee and Thou.

Have you heard a defeated person say, "I can't pray?" Or they might remark, "My prayers don't go anywhere or God does not answer my prayers." Remind them to be humble and ask God in simple words to hear his /her prayer; tell them to try an attitude of change and go into a quiet room with the purpose of kneeling down before God and say an optimistic prayer for God's help. They will find they are now in an attitude of prayer.

Several times in my life I have had God purposely show me He has protected me. I believe that is because I talk to God when we are alone together. I ask his advice and constantly thank him for my blessings. I feel comfortable talking with God about little things and serious problems. Several of my encounters where God has helped me have been when I was driving the car. I shall share one example with you.

My husband was due in on an early flight at an airport a distance from our home. It had been raining most of the day and night before and this morning it was pouring. The streets and roads were covered with water but I had no choice but drive and be on time. I was anxious because the freeways were crowded with the morning commute and most of the drivers were rushing and paying no attention to the dreadful weather conditions. I purposely talked with God and explained my fears. I asked him over and over to protect me and I sang songs to keep my spirits up. On arrival at the airport, the gutters on the both sides of the street were running with almost a foot of water and the streets began to flood. My husband ran from the airport and opened the door on the passenger side. He sat down in the seat and said, "go ahead and drive." I rarely drive when we are together and I did not want the responsibility but I started the car and accepted my unwanted assignment.

Driving along the crowded freeway the rain was making the roadway hard to see ahead of me. Suddenly, a car engine fell off a truck in front of me and I was driving in an inner lane. Moments before a car was to the right of me and I had no place to go. I do not know who's hands rested on mine, but God does. The two of us made a sharp turn to the right around the engine and the car to my right dropped back allowing me room to enter his lane and pull back into my own.

This is what prayer will do for you if you call upon God to protect you. His goodness and mercy will abide with you over and over in times of trouble and harm.

I will never forget the two warm, steady hands that guided mine in the direction I needed to move the car. I will never forget the peace I felt and the joy that filled my soul.

God hears and answers prayers and reminds us, "Be still and know that I am God."

PRAYER IS THE SOULS SINCERE DESIRE

Prayer is the soul's sincere desire.
Uttered or unexpressed.
The motion of hidden fire
That trembles in the breast.

God and Service

Prayer is the burden of a sigh,
The falling of a tear.
The upward glancing of the eye
When none but god is near.
Prayer is the simplest form of speech
That infant lips can try;
Prayer, the sublimest strains that reach
The Majesty on High.

Prayer is the Christians vital breath,
The Christians native air,
His watchword at the gates of death;
He enters heav'n with prayer.

Prayer is the contrite sinner's voice,
Returning to his ways.
While angels in their songs rejoice
And cry, "Behold he prays!"

The Saints in prayer appear as one
In word and deed and mind,
While with the Father and the Son
Their fellowship they find.

Nor prayer is made on earth alone,
The Holy Spirit pleads,
And Jesus at the Father's throne.
For sinners intercedes.

O thou by whom we come to God,
The Life, the Truth, the Way!
The path of prayer thyself hast trod;
Lord teach us how to pray.

James Montgomery

THE BOY IN THE ORGAN LOFT

*D*r. Moffit, a missionary from Africa, arrived to preach a sermon in a church in Scotland. It was a frigid cold day and the wind was blowing. It was a day to stay indoors. He had come to appeal for men to go to Africa as missionaries. When Moffit looked over the small congregation, he saw a number of women, but to his consternation only one male in the entire church and a boy pumping the organ in the loft. At first, Dr. Moffit felt he should change his sermon, but then decided to go ahead with the one he had planned. Its text – Proverbs 8:4: "Unto you, O men, I call: and my voice is to the sons of man."

"The boy listened intently, drinking in words that thrilled him, words which prove that we never really know how what we say may affect other people. When he grew up and obtained his degree in medicine, it was the boy who remembered Dr. Moffit's plea and gave a lifetime of unselfish devotion to Africa and to Christianity. His name was David Livingston."

LOOK FORWARD EACH NEW DAY

*W*e *can remember, with gratitude, our memories of the past. We sometimes are amazed at how the years have rushed by, and we can reflect on all the experiences we have shared with others, as well as the joy and love we were fortunate enough to receive in return.*

How wise we are to spend time in prayer before we start our new day. If we are facing health challenges, God is our ultimate physician. We can ask for guidance in choosing medical professionals, who then would be responsible to seek out the best course of treatment. If we are seeking employment opportunities, we can allow God to help us secure our preferred job source. God can assist us in making correct decisions.

There is a healing preparation going on in each new adventure, when we pray to be divinely guided, we then are ready for a positive change.

TRY SMILING

When the weather suits you not,
Try smiling.
When your coffee isn't hot
Try smiling.
When your neighbors don't do right,
Or your relatives all fight,
Sure 'tis hard, but then you might
Try smiling.

Doesn't change the things, of course –
Just smiling.
But it cannot make them worse –
Just smiling.
And it seems to help your case,
Brightens up a gloomy place,
Then it sort o' rests your face –
Just smiling.

Author Unknown

THE HONEST DISCIPLES

Once a Rabbi decided to test the honesty of his disciples, so he called them together and posed a question.

"What would you do if you were walking along and found a purse full of money lying in the road?" he asked.

"I'd return it to its owner," said one disciple.

"His answer comes so quickly, I must wonder if he really means it," the Rabbi thought.

"I'd keep the money if nobody saw me find it," said another.

"He has a frank tongue, but a wicked heart," the Rabbi told himself.

"Well, Rabbi," said a third disciple, "to be honest, I believe I'd be tempted to keep it. So I would pray to God that He give me the strength to resist such temptation and do the right thing."

"Aha!" thought the Rabbi. "Here is the man I would trust."

The Jewish folk tales remind us that faith is often the path to other virtues.

HANUKKAH HYMN

Rock of Ages, let our song
Praise Thy saving power;
Thou, amidst the raging foes,
Wast our sheltering tower.
Furious, they assailed us,
But Thine arm availed us,
And Thy word
Broke their sword
When our own strength failed us.

Kindling new the holy lamps,
Priest approved in suffering,
Purified the nation's shrine,
Brought to God their offering.
And His courts surrounding,
Hear, in joy abounding,
Happy throngs
Singing songs
With a mighty sounding.

Children of the martyr race,
Whether free or fettered,

Wake the echoes of the songs
Where ye may be scattered.
Yours the message cheering
That the time is nearing
Which will see
All men free,
Tyrants disappearing.

This Hanukkah hymn commemorates the rededication of the Temple in Jerusalem.

THE LIGHT OF GOD

The first day of winter marks the longest time of darkness for the year. Yet with each new day that follows that longest night, the light of day grows a little longer until spring ends. Although, the appearance of light seems to lessen during the winter season, the sun itself continues to shine.

The light of God is always shining in our souls as well. Prayer infuses us with energy and instills within us the absolute assurance that we are in tune with God.

How may we keep the light of God directing our vision toward a fuller understanding of what is true and eternal? Daily prayer is a vital tool. Prayer builds our faith and this changes us inwardly and outwardly. Have you ever noticed how those who do not hide their faith in God seem to radiate from the inside out? They are more attuned to the peace that being in God's light of understanding brings to every individual. They show the very essence of confidence, energy and joy in expression.

"O send out thy light and thy truth: let them lead me; let them bring me unto thy holy hill and to thy tabernacles."

Psalm 43:3

The little I have seen of the world teaches me to look upon the errors of others in sorrow, not in anger. When I take the history of one poor heart that has sinned and suffered, and think of the struggles and temptations it has passed through, the brief pulsations of joy, the feverish inquietude of hope and fear. The pressure of want, the desertion of friends, I would fain leave in the erring soul of my fellow-man with Him came from whose hands.

Henry Wadsworth Longfellow

GRATITUDE

It is very important that we thank God for our many blessings. Many times our prayers to God are in the nature of our needs and wants, rather than our gratitude to God for his many blessings.

Our prayerful thoughts are turned inward to our weaknesses and to our need for forgiveness. All of these experiences we need to talk to God about, but first we should express our gratitude for the many blessings we have been privileged to enjoy.

We can accomplish this opportunity easier if we became humble and took time to consider our faith. It helps before we pray if we take a few moments to reflect on God's goodness to us. Counting our blessings each day will help to get in the proper attitude to receive the Holy Spirit, then we will be ready to begin our prayer, and to tell God what we are grateful for.

God does so much for us and we find ourselves realizing we do not do that much for any other person. This opens the way for us to ask God to send us the opportunity for service to others. The Lord knows where our service is needed before we do.

Faith is strong; we may ask God for the wrong things. God may not answer our prayers for He will not shower us with blessings that we should not have. God knows us and understands what is best for us to have to grow and learn.

God and Service

Every evening when I said my good night prayer, I had the tendency to ask my father in Heaven to send more business for my real estate office. I had so many things I wanted to do for my family. He answered my prayer in the strangest way. It did not happen that I received more money – it came as an answer one evening for me to help someone else.

In my real estate business I was privileged to serve four couples who came from the same professional organization.

One evening after my prayers, I climbed into bed only to suddenly feel wide awake. A still small voice said to me to contact one of the above couples and thank him for his recommending me to the other couples he associated with. I was also requested that I should send him a check. Months had gone by and this felt like a strange request. I did not sleep well and later received this same nagging advice. In the morning I sent him a thank you note plus a check.

One week later the husband thanked me for my note and check. He reported that my check was an answer to prayer. Their daughter was in need of dental care and their dentist had requested a down payment. The couple had used their savings to purchase their home and their savings were now depleted. The couple had prayed to God that He would send help to them. When my thank you note came to them with the enclosed check, they were stunned. My check was for the same amount needed for the down payment.

I learned a great lesson – sacrifice is needed sometimes to build our faith. Having received more business would not have increased my faith in God's goodness, but the joy of knowing the Lord had chosen me to help this couple was a faith building blessing. I humbly thank Him for such a great experience.

ANDROCLES AND THE LION

*O*nce there was a slave named Androcles who was cruelly treated by his master. When the opportunity came he escaped to the forest. In his wanderings he came upon a lion. His first instinct was to turn about and flee. Then he noticed that the lion seemed to be in great distress and was moaning and whimpering piteously.

As the slave came near, the lion put out his paw, which was swollen and bleeding. A large thorn had penetrated one of the lion's toes, and this was the cause of all the animal's discomfort. Quickly Androcles pulled out the thorn and bound up the wounded paw. To show his gratitude the lion licked the man's hand like a dog, and then he led him to his cave for a shelter. Every day, after his wound had healed, he would go hunting in the forest and return with fresh meat for his master's refreshment.

But one day, when Androcles and the lion went out together, they were both captured and taken to the city to be used in the circus. The slave was to be thrown to the lion, after the animal had been kept without food for several days to make him more ferocious.

The Emperor and all his court came to the arena to view the spectacle. The despairing slave was unchained and led out into the amphitheater before the Emperor's box. Then the lion was let loose, and rushed bounding and roaring toward his victim. But as soon as he came near Androcles he recognized his friend. To the surprise of the audience, the lion seemed to fawn upon the slave whom they had expected to see torn to shreds by the savage beast. Pleased by this unusual spectacle the Emperor summoned Androcles to him, and the slave told him the whole story. Thereupon the slave was pardoned and freed, and the lion set loose to return to his native forest.

Application: Gratitude is a quality not limited to man.

THERE WILL BE CROSSROADS IN YOUR LIFE

There will be many crossroads in our life, some of which will be unforeseen and troublesome.

When we ask for God's guidance, it should not be a single occurrence. We need to develop the habit of going to God in prayer, time and time again. Only then will we be prepared when the unforeseen events are forced upon us.

Each time we become humble and reconnect with God's presence in prayer, we are ready to accept His solution to our problem. We can give thanks to God for helping us to remain calm even when we are faced with stressful situations.

When we open our mind and heart to God's loving direction, that guidance may come in the midst of prayer or a growing conviction in our heart and mind of a plan of action. We may question, at times, whether we are making the right decision. Yet if we remain silent and let God speak to our hearts, we will feel His unmistakable presence and loving assurance that we are making the correct decision.

There may be additional problems in our daily life, when it would seem to be in our best interest to ignore a situation or relationship, and just move on. We can find comfort, strength, and guidance when we thank our Heavenly Father for what has been and what is yet to be. We can see that the very resources we require are always present and accessible to us. Whatever need is given, we can be ready to receive. Just know that asking God to do what is best for us we will experience blessed serenity.

God will provide for us and we can be a channel through which divine ideas and expressions of our talents can bring about this inspiration and realization of our deep spiritual worth. We can handle life's problems. We need to relax and stop struggling. I carry in my wallet an affirmation, which reads: "Lord help me to remember that nothing is going to happen to me today that you and I can't handle."

I believe that God is revealing the way that is best for us. We can clear our minds of any preconceived ideas and open it to the revelation that God is here to guide us.

"O send out your light and your truth; let them lead me."

Psalm 43:3

Dear Lord! Please help my life to be
So patient, kind and true
That when at last my race is run
I can cross my "Patch of Blue."

And then one day – when I tried to look
I found I could not see.
In my despair I cried aloud,
"O God – it cannot be
That I must nevermore enjoy
This precious, precious view,
That I must learn to do without
My little "Patch of Blue.'"

I know not what's in store for me
Of sorrow, joy or pain;
I do not know when I can see
My bit of sky again.
But I'm sure God's love and mercy
Will lead me safely thro',
And in my very heart of hearts
He can put a "Patch of Blue."
Oh! Friend o' mine! Are you shut in?

Does your life seem hard to bear?
Does your heart grow sick with longing
For the joys you once could share?
"I'll go with you," saith the Master,
And his promises are true;
So we're sure that in His blessed arms
We'll find our "Patch of Blue."

Selected

THE TOUCH OF THE MASTER'S HAND

'Twas battered and scarred, and the auctioneer
Thought it scarcely worth his while
To waste much time on the old violin,
But held it up with a smile:
"What am I bidden, good folks," he cried,
"Who'll start the bidding for me?"
"A dollar, a dollar"; then, "Two!" "Only two?
Two dollars, and who'll make it three?
Three dollars, once; three dollars, twice;
Going for three – But no,
From the room, far back, a gray haired man
Came forward and picked up the bow;
Then, wiping the dust from the old violin,
And tightening the loose strings,
He played a melody pure and sweet
As a caroling angel sings.

The music ceased, and the auctioneer,
With a voice that was quiet and low,
Said: "What am I bid for the old violin?"
And he held it up with the bow.
"A thousand dollars, and who'll make it two?

Two thousand! And who'll make it three?
Three thousand, once, three thousand, twice,
And going and gone," said he.
The people cheered, but some of them cried,
"We do not quite understand
What changed its worth.," Swift came the reply:
"The touch of the master's hand."

And many a man with life out of tune,
And battered and scarred with sin,
Is auctioned cheap to the thoughtless crowd,
Much like the old violin.
A "mess of pottage," a glass of wine;
A game – and he travels on.
He is "going" once, and "going" twice,
He's "going" and almost "gone."
But the Master comes, and the foolish crowd
Never can quite understand
The worth of a soul and the change that's wrought
By the touch of the Master's hand.

Myra Brooks Welch

The story is told of a vessel stranded off the coast of South America whose Captain signaled to a passing ship to share their water with his passengers as they were suffering from thirst. The passing ship signaled back telling him to let down his bucket into the water in which they were floundering, because they were in the mouth of the Amazon River and the water was fresh.

God helps those that help themselves first. Then he joins the situation. It is the same with Faith. Faith without works is dead.

God and Service

LOVE OF HOME AND FAMILY

*W*e are commanded to love one another likewise. When we love as Jesus recommends we put our own personal concerns behind us and fulfill the concerns of others. One exceptional example of that kind of love is the unconditional love of parents for their children. God has an infinite love for us and if we love him back we will keep his commandments. If we stumble and fall and forget to keep his commandments or willfully defy them, God suffers as any parent or guardian would suffer – obedience to God's laws brings comfort and happiness. In the home, obedience to rule brings comfort and happiness.

The pure rule of love is easily transferred to relative or neighbors. If we love our neighbor and other acquaintances we love God also. This scripture from the bible clarifies this type of love. "Love *worketh no ill to his neighbor: therefore love is the fulfilling of the law."*

Romans 13:10

*W*hy would parents be unforgiving to the children they brought into the world and loved and cared for so tenderly? Many parents' hearts get broken if their child commits a serious crime. But the chain of love still remains as does the love of God. Not returning the love is the sin of omission.

Children should show love and respect to parents even if their parenting skills were not perfected, it was probably not their fault. If your parents lacked parenting skills look to the grandparents and the grandparents before them. Life was hard in generations before us. I heard a psychologist remark on television that generations back all the families would be considered nonfunctional by today's standards. So "lighten up" and forget your parents mistakes. Their love is forever just as God's love is for you also.

Speak not ill of your family members or take sides against them. God sees us as a family unit. We should guard against

145

tearing each other down or their children. We sometimes do not realize it but if there is love and trust in the family, there will be peace in the family, if there is peace in the family there will be peace in the town or city, if there is peace in the town or city, there will be peace in the state, if there is peace in the state, there will be peace in the nation, if there is peace in the nation, there will be peace in the world. It all starts in the home.

If your family is not close to each family member, plan to change the problems now. If you speak ill of one another stop the practice now – today. God will bless you for your change. Remember "Thumper" in the Disney movie. His great line goes like this – "if you can't say nothing nice, don't say nothing at all." Good advice for all of us.

LOVE ONE ANOTHER

What did the Lord really have in mind when He commanded us to love one another?

He said, "A new commandment I give unto you. That ye love one another; as I have loved you, that ye also love one another." John 13:34. He also added if we keep that commandment men shall know we are His disciples (followers,) if we have Love one for another.

As we reach out to understand this literal love God has for us, let us remember He created you and I, and forever reaches down through His Son and blesses us with truth, comfort, wisdom, hope, peace, faith, kindness and perfect love.

A Pharisee, a lawyer by profession, asked Jesus, "Master, which is the greatest commandment in the law?" Jesus answered, "Thou shalt love the Lord thy God with all thy soul, and with all thy mind." This is the first and great commandment, and the second is like unto it, "Thou shalt love thy neighbor as thy self."

On these two commandments hang all the laws and the prophets." Matthew 22:36-40.

If we, as God's children of the world, could truly understand the virtue to love one another there would be no quarreling, wars, contention, pride, no restricting of philosophies, no language barriers, there would be eternal peace among men. Only God's plan can be instituted to benefit all men.

Practicing and adopting God's plan and using His guidance we should know that God's love is supreme. We could show love to each other regardless of race, color and religion. If we would make God's love paramount in our lives, we would not judge, segregate, judge men on their appearances or measure them by their possessions.

Would it not be a wonderful thing to have the "greed and wants" missing and eliminated from our households and the contention that money matters affect the peace and love in our homes?

If we, as God's children, could truly understand the virtue to love one another we would be astounded at its complexity and impact. For God so loved the world , that He gave his only begotten Son that whosoever believeth in Him should not perish, but have eternal life. John 3:16 God allowed His Son to suffer a death of crucifixion. Why? God has a plan of salvation for all His children. We were sent here on earth, with our free agency, to do our best and to keep His commandments.

He has given us an elegant "road map." This road map is His list of commandments He has given us. Let us call them His "truths." These truths are the rules we should obey. By obeying these truths and building our faith in His works, we may return to Him and live in the Heavens above.

Our Heavenly Father gave us helps along the way. He gave us repentance and forgiveness when we make mistakes. When we sin or make mistakes of commission or omission He is there to comfort us. If we promise, in prayer, to stop the sin, and do not repeat it – we are forgiven. Miracles happen when we are truly repentant. Men and women have many times been forgiven instantly by the power and humbleness of their prayers. God takes into consideration why we sin and repeat it. We can be healed by His mercy and kindness and love for us.

Does God expect us to be perfect? No He does not. Throughout our mortal life He expects us to do our best and to overcome our imperfections. He teaches us that the sooner we repent and overcome our weaknesses the more we can help and love others with humble service.

In I Samuel 16:7, in the Holy Bible we read, "The Lord seeth not as man seeth, the Lord looketh on the heart." Is that not beautiful? What a friend we have in Jesus and God.

Only God can judge His people. He knows our spirits. He knows our troubles. He knows our strengths. He knows our weaknesses. Be merciful with yourself. Forgive yourself for this is God's divine commandment.

There would be peace in the world if we could learn to love our enemies and let go of hate, anger, and disgust. All these things destroy our spirits. But the Lord does not want us to overlook the problem if we need to protect our self, families and country.

LOVE AT HOME

There is beauty all around
When there's love at home.
There is joy in every sound
When there's love at home.
Peace and plenty here abide,
Smiling sweet on every side.
Time doth softly, sweetly glide
When there's love at home.
In the cottage there is joy

When there's love at home.
Hate and envy ne'er annoy
When there's love at home.
Roses bloom beneath our feet;
All the earth's a garden sweet,
Making life a bliss complete
When there's love at home.

Kindly heaven smiles above
When there's love at home.
All the world is filled with love
When there's love at home.
Sweeter sings the brooklet by;
Brighter beams the azure sky.
Oh, there's One who smiles on high
When there's love at home

Text and Music by John Hugh McNaughton

THE SIN of OMISSION

The bit of heart some counsel
You were hurried too much to say;
The loving touch of the hand, dear,
The gentle, winning tone
Which you had no time nor thought for
With troubles enough of your own.

Those little acts of kindness
So easily out of mind,
Those chances to be angels
Which we poor mortals find –

They come in night and silence,
Each sad, reproachful wraith,
When hope is faint and flagging,

And a chill has fallen on faith.
For life is all too short, dear,
And sorrow is all too great,
To suffer our slow compassion
That tarries until too late;
And it isn't the thing you do, dear,
It's the thing you leave undone
Which gives you a bit of a heartache
At the setting of the sun.

Margaret E. Sangster

"WHEN DO I DIE?"

The violent grinding of brakes suddenly applied, and the harsh sound of skidding wheels gradually died away as the big car came to a stop. Eddie quickly picked himself up from the dusty pavement where he had been thrown and looked wildly around.

Agnes? Where was the little sister he had been holding by the hand when they had started to cross the street? The next moment he saw her under the big car that had run them down. Her eyes were closed, and a dark stain spread slowly over her little white face.

With one bound the boy was under the car trying to lift the girl.

"You'd better not try, son," said a man gently. "Someone has gone to call an ambulance."

"She's not . . . dead, is she, mister?" Eddie begged in a husky voice.

The man stopped and felt the limp little pulse. "No, my boy," he said slowly.

A policeman came up, dispersed the gathering crowd, and carried the unconscious girl into a nearby drugstore. Eddies' folded coat made a pillow for her head until the ambulance arrived. He was permitted to ride in the conveyance with her to the hospital. Something about the sturdy, shabbily dressed boy who could not be more than ten years old, and his devotion to his little sister, strangely touched the hearts of the hardened hospital apprentices.

"We must operate at once," said the surgeon after a brief preliminary examination. "She has been injured internally and has lost a great deal of blood." He turned to Eddie, who, inarticulate with grief, stood dumbly by. "Where do you live?"

Eddie told him that their father was dead and their mother did day work – but he did not know where.

"We can't wait to find her," said the surgeon, "because by that time it might be too late."

Eddie waited in the sitting room while the surgeons worked over Agnes. After what seemed an eternity a nurse sought him out.

"Eddie," she said kindly, "your little sister is very bad, and the doctor wants to make a transfusion. Do you know what that is?" Eddie shook his head. "She has lost so much blood she cannot live unless someone gives her his. Will you do it for her?"

Eddies' wan face grew paler, and he gripped the knobs of the chair so hard that his knuckles became white. For a moment he hesitated; then gulping back his tears, he nodded his head and stood up.

"That's a good lad," said the nurse.

She patted his hand and led the way to the elevators which whisked them to the operating room. . . No one spoke to Eddie except the nurse who directed him in a low voice on how to prepare for the ordeal. The boy bit his quivering lip and silently obeyed.

"Are you ready?" asked a man swathed in white from head to foot, turning from the table over which he had been bending. For the first time Eddie noticed who it was lying there so still. Little Agnes! And he was going to make her well.

He stepped forward quickly.

Two hours later the surgeon looked up with a smile into the faces of the young interns and nurses who were engrossed in watching the great man's work.

"Fine," he said, "I think she'll pull through."

After the transfusion Eddie had been told to lie quietly on a cot in the corner of the room. In the excitement of the delicate operation, he had been entirely forgotten.

"It was wonderful, doctor!" exclaimed one of the young interns. "A miracle!" Nothing, he felt in his enthusiastic recognition of the marvels of surgery, could be greater than the miracles of science.

"I am well satisfied," said the surgeon with conscious pride.

There was a tug at his sleeve, but he did not notice. In a little while there was another tug – this time more convincing – and the great surgeon glanced down to see a ragged, pale-faced boy looking steadily up into his face.

"Say, doctor," said a husky voice, "when do I die?"

The interns laughed and the great surgeon smiled. "Why, what do you mean?"

"I thought . . . when they took a guy's blood . . . he . . . he . . . died."

The smiles faded from the lips of the doctors and nurses, and the young intern who had thought there was nothing greater than the marvels of science caught his breath suddenly.

Author Unknown

I LOVE YOU

*S*usan was a perceptive student. There was something about her that gave one the feeling that she had a deep understanding of the basic principles of the gospel of Jesus Christ. There was a wisdom in her remarks as there was in her behavior.

In order to stimulate the students in one of my classes to

think, reflect, and evaluate, I had asked them, "What do you understand by the statement, "I love you?" After the class in which this assignment was given, Susan asked if she could see me. She indicated that she had recently had an experience she thought would be interesting to me. Indeed it was!

"Perhaps I should begin," she said, "by telling you about my relationship with both my mother and my father. It has always been easy for me to talk with my mother. Ever since I was a child I have been able to go to her with my problems. I have always confided in her and have felt free to ask her about questions that disturbed me. I have shared both my failures and successes with her. Needless to say, there has been a close bond of friendship and love between us.

But the relationship with my father has been quite different. He is a man with a very strong personality in the sense that he is intelligent, skilled in decision-making, has great knowledge, and is very successful in business. He has also been an authoritarian. On numerous occasions he has simply announced decisions to me, and I soon learned that I was not to question these decisions. Because I did not feel relaxed and free in my relationship with him I was unable to share my innermost thoughts and feelings, or my problems, with him. Neither did he share his with me. All during these years I never really was sure how he felt about me, but I had the general impression that he more or less took me for granted. I somehow perceived that he felt my principal task was to obey his decisions concerning me.

Never once during the first seventeen years of my life did he ever say to me, 'I love you.' I must confess that in my teen years, I gradually began to develop mixed feeling concerning him. On the one hand I did appreciate his accomplishments, and I was grateful for the things he had done for me and the other members of our family. I should assure you, however, that these feelings resulted from my sense of feeling that it was my duty to appreciate him in these ways. It would not be correct for me to say that I spontaneously felt gratitude. On the other hand, I was beginning to develop a deep feeling of resentment toward him. As I grew older, I resented his arbitrary decision-making. I was often upset over the fact that he hardly recognized any of my achievements. Only when my mother would draw his attention to something I had done would he, even in a grudging way, make any comment about it.

When I was I my seventeenth year and a senior in high school, I was suddenly stricken with an infection. The doctors did everything they could to diagnose the source of the infection, but their first attempts were completely unsuccessful. I was getting steadily worse. I seemed to sense that this was a very serious situation and confided my feeling to my parents.

I was immediately administered to and additional specialists were called in on the case. After one of these consultations, the doctors left my hospital room to discuss their finding with my parents. They met in an adjoining room. They closed the door separating the two rooms, but the lock did not catch properly, and it opened just a small crack so that I was able to hear what was said. The gist of what the physician in charge stated was that they had done everything they could, but that I had a rare type of infection and none of the drugs they had thus far used on me were having the desired effect.

'I am deeply saddened to have to tell you this,' said the doctor, 'but unless we can find some other drug and locate the source of the infection your daughter will not be alive very long!' This really did not come as a surprise to me because I had realized the seriousness of my illness.

The doctors left and some minutes passed before the door to my room opened, and my father came to my bedside. I was so ill that I could not see him as clearly as normally, but he came close to me and as he took my hand, he said, 'I love you.' Tears were streaming down his face. 'Would it be possible,' he continued, 'for you to forgive me for the way I have treated you these many years? You see, I was reared in a home in which my own father was much like I am, and I became conditioned to behaving as he did. I know I haven't shared my life with you, and I have prevented you from sharing yours with me; but if you will give me another chance, I promise you that I will change.'

The resentment I had built up during the previous years immediately left me. I was filled with an exquisite joy, thankfulness and peace from within. I forgave him. 'I forgive you with all my heart,' I said, 'and I want you to know that I will treasure this experience this afternoon as much as any in my entire lifetime. I do love you, Dad, and I'll always love you.'

As a result of the blessing of our Heavenly Father and the skill of the medical profession, I did recover from the infection; and I want you to know that this was the beginning of a new relationship between my father and me. He began to ask my opinions on various questions. He was now sensitive to my feelings. He began to share with me some of his own experiences, and for the first time in our lives we would talk alone for a considerable length of time.

I recently was married, and the night before my wedding he said to me, 'One of the deep regrets of my life is that I was so blind during the first seventeen years of your life, but I want to tell you how deeply I appreciate your forgiveness. During the last four years we have been able to achieve a wonderful relationship. Beyond this I want you to know that this has affected not only my relationship with you, but my relationships with many other people. I began to look at myself and the manner in which I had treated the members of our professional organization. I saw that I had left much to be desired. You might be interested in knowing that several of the members have since commented to me that I am a changed person. Needless to say, they feel that the change has been all for the good. There is a new morale in our organization because I now see each member as an important individual rather than just someone to carry out my decisions.

Author Unknown

THE HOUSE BY THE SIDE OF THE ROAD

There are hermit souls that live withdrawn
In the peace of their self-content;
There are souls, like stars, that swell apart,
In a fellow less firmament;
There are pioneer souls that blaze their paths
Where highways never ran;
But let me live by the side of the road
And be a friend to man.

Let me live in a house by the side of the road,
Where the race of men go by –
The men who are good and the men who are bad,
As good and as bad as I.
I would not sit in the scorner's seat,
Or hurl the cynic's ban;
Let me live in a house by the side of the road
And be a friend to man.

I see from my house by the side of the road,
By the side of the highway of life,
The men who press with the ardor of hope,
The men who are faint with the strife.
But I turn not away from their smiles nor their tears –
Both parts of an infinite plan;
Let me live in my house by the side of the road
And be a friend to man.

Let me live in my house by the side of the road
Where the race of men go by-
They are good, they are bad, they are weak, they are strong.
Wise, foolish – so am I.
Then why should I sit in the scorner's seat
Or hurl the cynic's ban? –
Let me live in my house by the side of the road
And be a friend to man.

Sam Walter Foss

CROWDED WAYS OF LIFE

[Written in reply to *The House by the Side of the Road*, by Sam Walter Foss.]

'Tis only a half truth the poet has sung
Of the "house by the side of the way."
Our Master had neither a house nor a home,
But He walked with the crowd day by day.
And I think, when I read of the poet's desire,
That a house by the road would be good;
But service is found in its tenderest form
When we walk with the crowd in the road.

So I say, Let me walk with the men in the road,
Let me seek out the burdens that crush,
Let me speak a kind word of good cheer to the weak
Who are falling behind in the rush.
There are wounds to be healed, there are breaks we must mend,
There's a cup of cold water to give;
And the man in the road by the side of his friend
Is the man who has learned to live.

Then tell me no more of the house by the road;
There is only one place I can live-

It's there with the men who are toiling along,
Who are needing the cheer I can give.
It is pleasant to live in the house by the way
And be a friend, as the poet has said;
But the Master is bidding us: "Bear ye their load,
For your rest waiteth yonder ahead."

I could not remain in the house by the road
And watch as the toilers go on,
Their faces beclouded with pain and with sin,
So burdened their strength nearly gone.
I'll go to their side, I'll speak in good cheer,
I'll help them to carry their load;
And I'll smile at the man in the house by the way,
As I walk with the crowd in the road.

Out there in the road that goes by the house,
Where the poet is singing his song,
I'll walk and I'll work 'midst the heat of the day,
And I'll help falling brothers along-
Too busy to live in the house by the way,
Too happy for such an abode.
And my heart sings its praise to the Master of all,
Who is helping me serve in the road.

Walter S. Gresham

CHRISTMAS

Are you willing to forget what you have done for other people, and to remember what other people have done for you; and to think what you owe to the world; to put your rights in the background, and your duties in the middle distance, and your chances to do a little more than your duty in the foreground; to see that your fellowman are just as real as you are; and try to look behind their faces to their hearts, hungry for joy; to own. That probably the only good reason for your existence is not to close your book of complaints against the management of the universe, and are you willing to do these things even for a day? Then you can keep Christmas.

Are you willing to stoop down and consider the needs and the desires of little children; to remember the weakness and loneliness of people who are growing old; to stop asking how much your friends love you, and ask yourself whether you love them enough; to bear in mind the things that other people have to bear on their hearts; to try to understand what those who live in the same house with you really want, without waiting for them to tell you; to trim you're your lamp so that it will give more light and less smoke, and to carry it in front so that your shadow will fall behind you; to make a grave for your ugly thoughts and a garden for your kindly feelings, with the gate open - are you willing to do these things even for a day? Then you can keep Christmas.

Are you willing to believe that love is the strongest thing in the world – stronger than evil, stronger than death, and that the blessed life which began in Bethlehem nineteen hundred years ago is the image and Brightness of the Eternal Love? Then you can keep Christmas.

And if you keep it for a day, why not always? But you can never keep it again.

Henry Van Dyke

159

CONSCIENCE

I sat alone with my conscience
In a place where time had ceased,
And we talked of my former living
In the land where the years increased;
And I felt I should have to answer
The question it put to me,
And to face the answer and questions
Through all eternity.

The ghosts of forgotten actions
Came floating before my sight,
And things that I thought were dead things
Were alive with terrible might.
And the vision of all my past life
Was an awful thing to face,
Alone with my conscience sitting
In that solemnly silent place.

And I thought of a faraway warning,
Of a sorrow that was to be mine,
In a land that was then the future,
But now is the present time.
And I thought of my former thinking
Of the judgment day to be;
But sitting alone with my conscience
Seemed judgment enough for me.

And I wondered if there was a future
To this land beyond the grave;
But no one gave me an answer,
And no one came to save.
Then I felt that the future was present,
And the present would never go by,

For it was but the thought of my past life
Growing into eternity.

Then I woke from my timely dreaming,
And the vision passed away,
And I knew that the far-off seeming
Was a warning of yesterday;
And I pray that I may not forget it,
In this land before the grave,
That I may not cry in the future
And no one come to save.

And so I have learned a lesson
Which I ought to have known before,
And which, though I learned it dreaming,
I hope to forget no more.
So I sit along with my conscience
In the place where the years increase,
And I try to remember the future
In the land where time will cease.

And I know of the future Judgment,
How dreadful soe'er it be,
That to sit alone with my conscience
Will be judgment enough for me.
Charles William Stubbs

GOSSIP

omeone wisely penned this aphorism, "gossip seems to travel over the sour grapevine." We can smile at a humorous suggestion, but gossip is a very serious offense, and serves no beneficial purpose.

First, one commits to tale bearing, which usually amounts to nothing but scandal. Many times the accounts given and passed on to others are frequently false or exaggerated. In most cases, it is given directly to discredit another. If the truth were known, the person starting the gossip does so to pass on his or her own hidden agenda against another. What starts out to be revenge at another can turn into serious offenses for all who listen and pass on the information.

Bearing false witness and meddling in the affairs of others is serious enough to qualify to be punishable by law. Many persons have been imprisoned as a result of gossip and false witness.

Listening to and participating in the spread of gossip is an area where each individual can effectively stop this cancerous action, by himself or herself taking positive action to stop the further spread of such derogatory comments. The commandment of, "Love thy neighbor as thyself," is the key to resolving this problem.

Gossip is the knife of the party!

THE EAGLE THE WILDCAT, AND THE SOW

An Eagle chose the top branches of an old oak tree for her nest and hatched her young there. A wildcat had selected the hollow trunk of the same tree for her den where she would raise her little ones. And down among the roots of the old oak a sow had burrowed a hole where she planned to raise her piglets in comfort.

For some time all three families lived peaceably in the old oak, until the wildcat took the notion to start gossiping about her neighbors.

"Neighbor," she whispered to the eagle, "as you know I have the highest respect for that old sow down below. But if she keeps rooting under this tree the whole thing will come crashing down someday. That's probably what she has in mind so she can feed our babies to her litter."

Needless to say, the mother eagle was worried. She was so disturbed that she did not dare to leave her nest to go in search of food. Meanwhile, the gossiping wildcat visited the sow.

"Mrs. Sow," she whispered, "I'm no gossip, as you know, but if I were you I wouldn't leave home today. I overheard that eagle upstairs telling her children they were going to have pork for supper."

So the eagle stayed in her nest and the sow remained with her little pigs. But the wildcat sneaked off every night and got all the food for her kittens, while her neighbors lived in distrust of each other.

It is possible that both families would have starved to death had not the wildcat made the mistake of getting caught in a hunter's snare, and the sow and the eagle became reunited in caring for the abandoned kittens.

Application: Gossips are to be seen and not heard.

THE MAN IN THE GLASS

When you get what you want in your struggle for self,
And the world makes you king for a day,
Just go to the mirror and look at yourself,
And see what the man has to say.

For it isn't your father or mother or wife
Whose judgment upon you must pass.
The fellow whose verdict counts most in your life,
Is the one staring back from the glass.

You may be like Jack Horner and chisel a plum
And think you're a wonderful guy,
But the man in the glass, he says you're a bum
If you can't look him straight in the eye.

He's the fellow to please, never mind all the rest,
For he's with you clear to the end,
And you've passed your most dangerous, difficult test
If the man in the glass is your friend.

You may fool the whole world down the pathway of years
And get pats on the back as you pass.
But your final reward will be heartache and tears,
If you've cheated the man in the glass.

Author Unidentified

JUDGMENT

Should you feel inclined to censure
Faults you may in others view,
Ask your own heart, ere you venture,
If that has not failings too.

Let not friendly vows be broken'
Rather strive a friend to gain;
Many a word in anger spoken
Finds its passage home again.

Do not, then, in idle pleasure,
Trifle with a brother's fame;
Guard it as a valued treasure,
Sacred as your own good name.

Do not form opinions blindly.
Hastiness to trouble tends;
Those of whom we thought unkindly,
Oft become our warmest friends.

Author Unknown

God and Service

*E*very motion of the constantly shifting bodies in the world, is timed to the occasion for some definite, foreordered end. The flowers blossom in obedience to the same law that marks the course of constellations... Nature is one, and to me the greatest delight of observation and study is to discover new unities in this all-embracing and eternal harmony... Men, with only a book of knowledge... have seized upon evolution as an escape from the idea of a GOD. 'Evolution!' – a wonderful, mouth-filling word... Just say 'evolution' and you have explained every phenomenon of Nature, and explained away GOD. It sounds big and wise. Evolution, they say, brought the earth through its glacial periods, caused the snow blanket to recede, and the flower carpet to follow it, raised the forests of the world, developed animal life from the jelly-fish to the thinking man. But what caused evolution? There they stick. To my mind, it is inconceivable that a plan that has worked out... the development of beauty, that has made very microscopic particle of mater perform its function in harmony with every other in the universe – that such a plan is the blind product of an unthinking abstraction. No; somewhere, before evolution was, was an Intelligence... You may call that Intelligence what you please; I cannot see why so many people object to call it GOD.

John Muir

GOD'S HEALING POWER

*T*he Lord, Jesus Christ, in his mortal ministry, went among the children of men working mighty miracles. We are filled with wonder by the accounts of the healing power of Christ. We do not need to understand why or how one is healed. All we need to know is the power of God is the same yesterday, today, and forever. Healings come to a person by faith and by the will of God. The heavens are never closed – they are just as open today as they were in the time of Christ. All one has to do is ask God, in faith, and miracles can happen.

Early in the history of the scriptures, we have seen the name, "The Elders". In many cases in the Bible, this means the men of the elderly generation. Additionally, the men holding authority in the governing positions in the church were referred to as Elders. In some religions, this visionary person may be referred to as a Priest, Rabbi, Minister, or Prophet. They are persons called upon to administer to the sick and the needy of the church.

Healing takes place by the faith of the person receiving the blessing, as well as by the faith of those giving the blessing. The key here is the faith in God held by the participants. You can rely on that healing. Faith in God is the requirement in coping with illness. It is tangible evidence of God at work in the world, using earthly hands to accomplish the healing purposes by those holding the authority to administer His ordinances.

When you believe in God's healing power, you put yourself in contact with the peace and confidence of God's goodness and mercy. Life will take its course, you will suffer illness – and ultimately death cannot be escaped. It will be at this time God may not heal you but he will heal your soul and give you peace more durable than you can comprehend.

Affirm to God: "Divine energy flows throughout my body. I am whole and well." Commit this affirmation to memory or write it on a card. Say it many times each day. You will be filled with a feeling of well being through your verbal activity with God.

BRIGHTLY BEAMS OUR FATHER'S MERCY

Brightly beams our Father's mercy
From his lighthouse evermore,
But to us he gives the keeping
Of the lights along the shore
Let the lower lights be burning
Send a gleam across the wave
Some poor fainting, struggling seaman
You may rescue, you may save.

Dark the night of sin has settled;
Loud the angry billows roar.
Eager eyes are watching, longing,
For the lights along the shore.
Let the lower lights be burning,
Send a gleam across the wave
Some poor fainting, struggling seaman
You may rescue, you may save.

Trim your feeble lamp, my brother;
Some poor sailor, tempest-tossed,
Try now to make the harbor,
In the darkness may be lost.
Let the lower lights be burning;
Send a gleam across the wave
Some poor fainting, struggling seaman
You may rescue, you may save.

Jewish Folktale

CHAPTER FOUR

Families are Forever

A TRIBUTE TO FATHERS

$\mathcal{M}$emories and intense emotional perceptions are brought to mind when we think of our fathers. There are those among us fortunate enough to honor their parent in person. Others are privileged to have affectionate memories. Nothing is more refreshing than to hear a son freely speak of his affection for his dad. The male gender, at times, are reticent to discuss emotional issues. Devout expression spoken of the parents is more priceless than jewels of any kind.

A father is a man who loves his family with unconditional love. Blessed are the children whose father is the rock of their security. Unconditional love is constant through good times and bad times; through the failures or successes of each of his children. Such a father will stand behind his children during heartache or transgression.

Fatherhood is not tied to wealth, inheritance, or intelligence. Fatherhood comes from the heart and soul. Fatherhood bears the grim responsibility of the discipline in a family. If youth believe he is strict, chances are he does not want his children to make the mistakes of his youth. Dads are very wise about such things.

Responsible fathers who mold their sons' lives through the example they set, are a blessing to young boys. Blessed are such fathers who teach with love and tenderness. We give our praise to such a man. Scouting, Indian Guides, etc., Are activities fathers and sons can participate in together.

Let us honor the man who trains young boys to be strong youth and great citizens. I am referring to the adult Scout leaders who serve tirelessly in behalf of their youth. These great men teach principles of good citizenship, honesty, and service to others.

The greatest profession is Parenting.

John Wooden, College coach

SUCCESS

You can use most any measure,
When you're speaking of success.

You can measure it in fancy home,
Expensive car or dress.

But the measure of your real success,
Is the one you cannot spend.

It's the way your kids describe you,
When they're talking to a friend.

Martin Buxbaum

TO ANY DADDY

There are little eyes upon you,
And they're watching night and day;
There are little ears that quickly
Take in every word you say;

Families are Forever

There are little hands all eager
To do anything you do;
And a little boy who's dreaming
Of the day he'll be like you.

You're the little fellow's idol;
You're the wisest of the wise.
In his little mind, about you
No suspicions ever rise;
He believes in you devoutly,
Holds that all you say and do,
He will say and do, in your way,
When he's grown up like you.

There's a wide-eyed little fellow,
Who believes you're always right;
And his ears are always open,
And he watches day and night;
You are setting an example
Every day, in all you do,
For the little boy who's waiting
To grow up to be like you.

BIGGER THINGS TO DO

I used to think it mattered, used to think I had to be
Forever at the business of acquiring nothing
but earthly wealth for me.
Then I gave myself to labor, and I bent my back to toil,
And to make myself the richer, oft I burned the midnight oil,
Till one day a little fellow seemed to look
me through and through,
And asked if making money was the only thing men do.
It was just a youngster's question, but it struck me like a blow,

He had heard me talk my business, and he had
seen me come and go.
He had watched me night and morning either
happy or dismayed,
Elated or disgruntled, by investments I had made.
And he'd come to the conclusion,
I could see beyond a doubt,
That money was the only thing his daddy thought about.

I know I choked a little as I took him on my knee,
And I turned away a moment so a tear he would not see.
Then I hugged him somewhat tighter than it was my wont to do,
And I told him "more important than all else on earth, is you."
There's a bigger thing than money and there's a much fairer joy.
That's wrapped up in the future of a certain little boy.

I couldn't quite explain it, for he couldn't understand,
But I know he caught the pressure of his daddy's rugged hand.
And I know we both grew closer as I held him on my knee,
And I tried to draw a picture of the man I hoped he'd be,
But what's more I learned a lesson one that
caused my eyes to swim,
And I vowed to God that evening that I'd
spend more time with him.

Anon.

ONLY A DAD

Only a dad with a tired face,
Coming home from the daily race,
Bringing little of gold or fame
To show how well he has played the game;
But glad in his heart that his own rejoice
To see him come and to hear his voice.

Only a dad with a brood of four,
One of ten million men or more
Plodding along in the daily strife,
Bearing the whips and the scorns of life,
With never a whimper of pain or hate,
For the sake of those who are at home await.

Only a dad, neither rich nor proud,
Merely one of the surging crowd,
Toiling, striving from day to day,
Facing whatever may come his way,
Silent whenever the harsh condemn,
And bearing it all for the love of them.

Only a dad but he give his all,
To smooth the way for his children small,
Doing with courage stern and grim
The deeds that his father did for him.
This is the line that for him I pen:
Only a dad, but the best of men.

Edgar A. Guest

THE GAME OF LIFE

There was a blind father who always attended the base-ball games in which his son was a noted pitcher, just to hear his boy praised for his good work. It seemed to him that his worth of living was increased with this delight. But on the day of an important game, the boy's father died. Still, the heart-broken lad was urged not to desert his team. So he went in the game and at first his work was very poor and the opposing team was winning. But, all of a sudden, the boys face brightened and he began throwing the most faultless ball of his career, which brought victory to his team. When he was asked why the sudden change, he said: "Well, guys, the thought came to me that this was the first game my father ever saw me play and I had to make good."

This story I dedicate to the memory of our outstanding grandson. 21 year old, James Patrick Wernke, a Left-handed pitcher, who left a legacy of memories to all his many baseball friends, fans, and his family. One will never forget his winning smile and pitching ability. He lost his life trying to rescue his beloved pal, Kealie, a labrador retriever, from a rain swollen creek on December 12, 2009, in Fullerton, California.

THE CHILDREN'S HOUR

Between the dark and the daylight,
When the night is beginning to lower,
Comes a pause in the day's occupations,
That is known as the Children's Hour.

I hear in the chamber above me
The patter of little feet,
The sound of a door that is opened,
And voices soft and sweet.

From my study I see in the lamplight,
Descending the broad hall stair,
Grave Alice, and laughing Allegra,
And Edith with golden hair.

A whisper, and then a silence:
Yet I know by their merry eyes
They are plotting and planning together
To take me by surprise.

Henry Wadsworth Longfellow

Families are Forever

Letter In Memorial

Dear Dad,

I am writing this to you, though you have been dead thirty years…
I feel I must say some things to you, things I didn't know when I was a boy in your house…
It's only now after passing through the long hard school years, only now, when my own hair is gray, that I understand how you felt.
I must have been a… trial to you… I believed my own petty wisdom…
Most of all, I want to confess my worst sin against you. It was the feeling I had that you 'did not understand.'
When I look back over it now, I know that you did understand. You understood me better than I did myself…
And how patient you were with me! How full of long-suffering, and kindness!
And how pathetic, it now comes home to me, were your efforts to get close to me…
What was it held me aloof? I don't know. But it is tragic – that wall that rises between a boy and his father…
I wish you were here now, across the table from me, just for an hour, so that I could tell you how there's no wall anymore;
I understand you now, Dad, till I am over [there], and I believe you'll be the first one to take me by the hand and help me…
I know that [among] the richest, most priceless things on earth, and the thing least understood, is that mighty love and tenderness and craving to help, which a father feels toward his boy. For I have a boy of my own…
Up there somewhere in the Silence, hear me, dad, and believe me.

Author Unknown

THE JOY OF MOTHERHOOD

*S*ince the dawn of creation no aspect of a woman's life is as special as the important role of being a mother. As such, she then becomes the nurturer of her children - - - an opportunity without comparison! This is a built-in circumstance of motherhood.

For years we have heard religious leaders and wise men make the claim, "Mother is the heart of the home." Such remarks carry with them no negative reflection upon the importance of father in the home, and his responsibility as a provider, or his influence upon the family.

God instructed Adam and Eve to multiply and replenish the earth, and to have dominion over it, Genesis 1:28. Marriage is ordained of God and we need to strengthen these bonds, not destroy their purpose.

More than any other individual, Mother occupies the center position in a child's life. Mother has a far greater influence on her children from birth until they start their formal studies in education and adjust to leaving the security of the home.

An infant has a bond with mother. It is her touch, her voice, her smile, her loving care that the infant depends upon. Breast feeding is a great bonding tool for both mother and child. The power of a mother's touch is very sweet and is so needed today. When a child is injured, frustrated, sad, scared or fearful, the power of her touch, her kiss, a hug or her calming voice has a great impact on a child's security and self esteem.

When a child learns to walk and is still in the transition of learning to balance, it is the toddlers trust in Mother and father that allows him to let go of a stationary object and walk to parents for a great hug.

It is at the knee of Mother that a child learns to say his or her first prayers to a loving Heavenly Father. It is the responsibility of both parents to teach a child of God and to give them spiritual security. Children adjust to problems such as death, with spiritual values, and without them suffer emotionally.

Mothers teach their children patience, sharing, responsibility, truth, honesty, kindness and love. Mothers teach children to be unselfish and to be respectful of others. Mothers teach children many skills for social development such as manners. Mothers teach children to develop skills and talents such as music. She also accepts the responsibility to see they practice and perfect their talents and skills. Many times these efforts seem futile.

A child's intelligence is guided by mother's gentle encouragement. For example, reading is one of the most enjoyable experiences that mothers and children can enjoy together.

Mother is the first teacher to her children when it comes to the social relationships a child must learn. She starts with the toddler, and the words "thank you" and "please". She teaches them to share and get along with others. Many times mothers have a more difficult time teaching their children. There is a saying that the child learns what his environment teaches. A mother tries to keep peace in the home and to give the child security in a home where the environment is explosive or seemingly full of anxiety. God must truly love a mother when she must protect her children from all the physical and emotional situations in the homes of today. Single mothers need our love and prayers when they try to salvage their children's lives and bring positive interactions where strife abounds, especially in abuse situations and divorce. Every child brought into this world deserves a home where he is secure and can build his self worth.

A mother teaches by example as well as by precepts. Mothers should teach cultural refinement in the home. Teach children to love music and good books. She should teach her children good grammar and good literature and poetry. Her integrity with her children and acquaintances should be paramount. If a mother possesses bad habits and fowl speech, even in moderation, her child will emulate the same bad habits, possibly in excess.

Mothers influence their children to become the best they can and give them advice and the benefit of their wisdom. Young adults sometimes do not listen. Mothers may not realize that a young adult has a brain that is still learning. For a female her brain is not fully developed until 25 years of age. For a male the age is 27. Give these children room to grow. They are under more pressure than you are as a parent. Keep your loving relationship open and you will be rewarded.

Motherhood is wonderful and fulfilling. Remember to thank God everyday for such joy.

"God could not be everywhere and so He gave us Mothers.

Author Unknown

A TRIBUTE TO MOTHER

*M*y mother was the most beautiful woman I ever saw. All I am I owe to my mother. I attribute all my success in life to the moral, intellectual, and physical education I received from her.

George Washington

There never was a woman like her. She was gentle as a dove and brave as a lioness… The memory of my mother and her teachings were, after all, the only capital I had to start life, and on that capital I made my way.

Andrew Jackson

I remember my mother's prayers and they have always followed me. They have clung to me all my life.

Abraham Lincoln

Her heart was the abode of heavenly purity. She had no feelings but of kindness and beneficence... She had known, but her sorrow was silent... If there is existence and retribution beyond the grave, my mother is happy.

John Quincy Adams

The love of a mother is never exhausted. It never changes – it never tires – it endures through all, in good repute, in bad repute, in the face of the world's condemnation, a mother's love still lives on.

Washington Irving

In the world of former President Herbert Hoover: "After we have determined every scientific fact, after we have erected every public safeguard, after we have constructed every edifice for education or training or hospitalization or play, yet all these things are but a tithe of the physical, moral, and spiritual gifts which motherhood gives and home confers. None of these things carry that affection, that devotion of soul, which is the greatest endowment from mothers."

Beautiful are the tributes to mothers made by these great men of our country. They herald the teachings of mothers who taught faith, truth, and honesty. They were born to distinctive women with great incentives to make their sons men of stature and leaders of destiny.

TWO TEMPLES

A Builder builded a temple,
He wrought it with grace and skill;
Pillars and groins and arches
All fashioned to work his will.
Men said, as they saw its beauty,

"It shall never know decay;
Great is thy skill, O Builder!
Thy fame shall endure for aye."

A Mother builded a temple
With love and infinite care,
Planning each arch with patience,
Laying each stone with prayer,
None praised her unceasing efforts,
None knew of her wondrous plan,
For the temple of Mother builded
Was unseen by the eyes of man.

Gone is the Builder's temple,
Crumpled into the dust;
Low lies each stately pillar,
Food for consuming rust.
But the temple the Mother builded
Will last while the ages roll,
For that beautiful unseen temple
Was a child's immortal soul.

Hattie Vose Hall

Quotations From Great Men

*O*ne reason for a child's walking in wrong ways would be in his not knowing which way to walk. One reason for his going his own way would be if his parents did not unitedly know which way they want him to go. Agreement between parents on fundamentals, basic beliefs, is among the foremost essentials for a solid family, for the solid teaching of children. And in this there must be sincerity, because children will surely detect the signs of insincerity in any partnership of parents. They will feel the tensions and the differences even when they can't say why they are so.

Division between parents is unfair and confusing and weakens the foundations of the family. Those to whom a child should look for guidance, must be united in the guidance they give. Blessed are those whose parents have achieved a partnership, a solid working of a team of two.

Richard L. Evans

The educations of a child begins in infancy. At six months old it can answer smile by smile, and impatience with impatience. It can observe, enjoy, and suffer. Do you suppose it makes no difference to it that the order of the house is perfect and quiet, the faces of its father and mother full of peace, their soft voices familiar to its ear, and even those of strangers, loving; or that is tossed from arm to arm [in a]... reckless... household, or in the confusion of a happy one? The moral disposition is, I doubt not, greatly determined in those first speechless years.

John Ruskin

Would you have your son obedient to you when past a child; be sure then to... imprint it in his infancy; ... so shall you have... obedient... whilst he is a child, and your affectionate friend when he is a man... For the time must come, when [he] will be past the rod and correction;... and he that is good, a virtuous, and able man, must be made so within. And therefore what he is to receive from education, what is to sway and influence his life, must be something... woven into the very principles of his nature... The little, or almost insensible impressions on our tender infancies, have very important and lasting consequences.

John Locke

THE PARENT'S PRAYER

"Teach me to understand my children, to listen patiently to what they have to say, and to answer all the questions kindly. Keep me from interrupting them, talking back to them, and contradicting them. Make me as courteous to them as I would have them be to me. Give me the courage to confess my sins against my children and to ask them for forgiveness, when I know that I have done them a wrong."

"May I not vainly hurt the feelings of my children. Forbid that I should laugh at their mistakes or resort to shame and ridicule as punishment. Let me not tempt my child to lie and to steal. So guide me hour by hour that I may demonstrate by all I say and do that honesty produces happiness."

"Reduce, I pray, the meanness in me. May I cease to nag; and when I am out of sorts, help me to hold my tongue."

"Blind me to the little errors of my children and help me see the good things that they do. Give me a ready word for honest praise."

"Help me to grow up with my children, to treat them as would those of their own age; but let me not exact of them the judgment and conventions of adults. Allow me not to rob them of the opportunity to wait upon themselves, to think, to choose, and to make decisions."

"Forbid that I should ever punish them for my selfish satisfaction. May I grant them all their wishes that are reasonable, and have the courage always to withhold a privilege which I know will do them harm."

"Make me so fair and just, so considerate and companionable to my children, that they will have genuine esteem for me. Fit me to be the loved and imitated."

"With all Thy Gifts, O great Master, give me calm, poise and self-control."

Author Unknown

PARENTING SKILLS

A Parent's Prayer contains every thoughtful wish a parent could request. Fortunately, our present generation is able to accrue an abundance of information and support in their role as a parent. Available are lectures, books, tapes, and magazine articles, which may provide many avenues to improve parenting skills.

Bringing a child into the world is nothing short of a miracle. Infants are from the moment of birth just minutes from the arms of a loving Heavenly Father, and are already in possession of their soul.

Fortunately, for couples who are having problems conceiving, a child may be available through the adoption process. To receive an adoptive child is a miraculous gift from God, a triumph over one if life's saddest problems. There is nothing that brings a greater joy to a family than to nurture, with affection, a child who needs your love and care. An adoptive mother is sometimes better prepared physically in the care of a new baby. I speak from experience on this point.

There is no greater foundation of a happy home than the blessing of the children who make such an immeasurable difference.

GOOD AND BAD CHILDREN

Children, you are very little,
And your bones are very brittle;
If you would grow great and stately,
You must try to walk sedately.

You must still be bright and quiet,
And content with simple diet;
And remain, through all bewildering,
Innocent and honest children.

Manna From Heaven

Happy hearts and happy faces,
Happy play in grassy places –
That was how, in ancient ages,
Children grew to kings and sages.

But the unkind and the unruly,
And the sort who eat unduly,
They must never hope for glory –
Theirs is quite a different story!

Cruel children, crying babies,
All grow up as geese and gabies,
Hated, as their age increases,
By their nephews and their nieces.
Robert Louis Stevenson

THE PERFECT DINNER TABLE

This poem is about a time of day families need to spend together. The dinner hour should be more than eating. It should be about teaching, listening, and loving.

A tablecloth that's slightly soiled
Where greasy little hands have toiled;
The napkins kept in silver rings,
And only ordinary things
From which to eat, a simple fare,
And just the wife and kiddies there,
And while I serve, the clatter glad
Of little girl and little lad
Who have so very much to say
About the happenings of the day.

Four big round eyes that dance with glee,
Forever flashing joys at me,

Families are Forever

Two little tongues that race and run
To tell of troubles and of fun;
The mother with a patient smile
Who knows that she must wait awhile
Before she'll get a chance to say
What she's discovered through the day.
She steps aside for girl and lad
Who have so much to tell their dad.

Our manners may not be the best;
Perhaps our elbows often rest
Upon the table, and at times
That very worst of dinner crimes,
That very shameful act and rude
Of speaking ere you've downed your food,
Too frequently, I fear, is done,
So fast the little voices run.
Yet why should table manners stay
Those tongues that have so much to say?

Edgar Guest

CAN'T

Can't is the worst word that's written or spoken;
Doing more harm here than slander and lies;
On it is many a strong spirit broken
And with it many a good purpose dies.
It springs from the lips of the thoughtless each morning
And robs us of courage we need through the day:
It rings in our ears like a timely sent warning
And laughs when we falter and fall by the way.

Can't is the father of feeble endeavor,
The parent of terror and halfhearted work;

Manna From Heaven

It weakens the efforts of artisans clever,
And makes of the toiler an indolent shirk.
It poisons the soul of the man with a vision,
It stifles in infancy many a plan;
It greets honest toiling with open derision
And mocks at the hopes and the dreams of a man.

Can't is a word none should speak without blushing;
To utter it should be a symbol of shame;
Ambition and courage it daily is crushing;
It blights a man's purpose and shortens his aim.
Despise it with all of your hatred of error;
Refuse it the lodgment it seeks in your brain;
Arm against it as a creature of terror,
And all that you dream of you someday shall gain.

Edgar Guest

Any parent will tell you there is no such word as can't.

TWO PICTURES

Two pictures hung on the dingy wall
Of a grand old Florentine hall –

One of a child of beauty rare,
With a cherub face and golden hair;
The lovely look of whose radiant eyes
Filled the soul with thoughts of Paradise.

The other was a visage vile
Marked with the lines of lust and guile,
A loathsome being, whose features fell
Brought to the soul weird thoughts of hell.

Side by side in their frames of gold,

Families are Forever

Dingy and dusty and cracked and old,
This is the solemn tale they told:

A youthful painter found one day,
In the streets of Rome, a child at play,
And, moved by the beauty it bore,
The heavenly look that its features wore,

On a canvas, radiant and grand,
He painted its face with a master hand.

Year after year on his wall it hung;
T'was ever joyful and always young -
Driving away all thoughts of gloom
While the painter toiled in his dingy room.

Like an angel of light it met his gaze,
Bringing him dreams of his boyhood days,
Filling his soul with a sense of praise.

His raven ringlets grew thin and gray,
His young ambition all passed away;
Yet he looked for years in many a place,
To find a contrast to that sweet face.

Through haunts of vice in the night he stayed
To find some ruin that crime had made.
At last in a prison cell he caught
A glimpse of the hideous fiend he sought.

On a canvas weird and wild but grand,
He painted the face with a master hand.

His task was done; 'twas a work sublime-
An angel of joy and fiend of crime-
A lesson of life from the wrecks of time.

O Crime: with ruin thy road is strewn;
The brightest beauty the world has known
Thy power has wasted, till in the mind
No trace of its presence is left behind.

The loathsome wretch in the dungeon low,
With a face of a fiend and a look of woe,
Ruined by revels of crime and sin,
A pitiful wreck of what might have been,
Hated and shunned, and without a home,
Was the child that played in the streets of Rome.

Author Unknown

GRANDPARENTS AND CHILDHOOD

To a grandparent, a child represents a second chance at being a perfect parent. Grand-parenting is the best of times. We adore these cherubic, little folk with a very special feeling. We are not, in most cases, the authoritarian, and we cherish every moment of time we have in the presence of our grandchildren.

Love given by grandparents is one of life's more precious gifts. Grandparents have time to indulge, comfort, share, and listen to grandchildren. No matter what they do, or don't do, grandparents affect the emotional well being of their grandchildren. The purity of this feeling is love. Those who see their grandparents irregularly, or not at all, may feel deprived and abandoned.

Contrasts between parents and grandparents are legion. Parents are often times prone to play 'the heavy'. They are constantly given the task of discipline and must commit to the round-the-clock schedules for family members.

When both parents are employed, life can become hectic and debilitating for younger children. It is so important that younger children be left in the care of those they do not fear and they must feel secure and be treated fairly. Self-esteem is so important before six years of age.

During these modern times, the stability of families seems to be threatened. Divorce, illness, neglectful parents, accounts of child abuse, job security, and other vicissitudes in families make the love and stability of grandparents paramount. Having stable grandparents is a blessing to both parents and grandchildren and will result in a strong family relationship.

Grandparents, when they have good health, are becoming caregivers to their grandchildren. Parents of single moms and working parents are called upon more and more to be second parents. This is a blessing for all children. All grandparents have raised their own teenagers and have learned more patience in the handling of teens' feelings than parents have. They are better disciplinarians and commit to trying all the options that are available. Family relations are so much more solvent when grandparents are active with their grandchildren.

Grandparents enjoy their grandchildren's accomplishments and have time for baseball games, dance recitals and other pursuits of grandchildren. These activities can become fun outings.

Let us not forget that grandparents love to spoil their grandchildren. They break the rules for, 'no cookies before dinner', and many others as well. None of this rule breaking will corrupt their grandchildren. That is one reason that grandparents are so special!

MY GRANDMA

Yesterday I visited
One of the my most
Favorite people of all;
I didn't even have to call.

Manna From Heaven

And you should have
Seen her face,
Happiness
All over the place.

She kissed me on the cheek
Then said, with a wink,
"You must have some
Magic Power
To know that
I would need you
At this very hour."

In the kitchen
We worked away
Peeling apples for a pie.
And I felt my spirits fly
As Grandma sang her songs.
That's when I always long
To have her near.

Just about that time
She whispered in my ear.
"What wonderful thing
Did I do
To deserve a child
As dear as you."

Then she sprinkled
Sugar and Cinnamon
On an apple slice.
Popping it into my mouth
She said, "You're my
Favorite kind of spice."

Tasting all the sweetness
All the happiness we share,
I closed my eyes that minute
And said a silent prayer,

"Oh, thank you, thank you,
Dear Father up above,
For giving me a grandma
Who fills my life with love."

Joy Saunders Lundberg

MY GRANDPA

Today we went walking
My Grandpa and me.
Hand in hand
Into a wonderland
To see what we could see.

A baby squirrel scampered by
And led us to its home,
A giant tree
So strong and free
With branches stretched out wide
As if to say,
"Come, I'll provide
A warm safe place to be."
Like Grandpa
Whose big strong arms
Reach out and comfort me.

There on a fallen leaf
We watched a caterpillar crawl;
Not in any hurry at all

Manna From Heaven

To reach its destiny,
Happy just to be…
Like Grandpa and me.

Suddenly a lovely sound
Came floating down.
Then we saw a robin fly,
And I could not deny
There is no sweeter song,
Unless it's Grandpa whistling
As we walk along.

On down the hill
We found a pond
That glistened in the sun.
We picked a flower at its edge
And counted petals
One by one.

"A flower," Grandpa said,
"Is one of God's
Most excellent creations."
Then in the corner of his eye
I saw a tiny drop of dew.
"And another one,
My child," he said,
"Is you."

I threw my arms around him
And under a bright blue sky
I knew that I
Could never ever find
Any other Grandpa
Even half as great as mine.

Joy Saunders Lundberg

GRANDMOTHER'S OLD ARMCHAIR

My grandmother, she, at the age of eighty-three,
One day in May was taken ill and died;
And after she was dead the will of course was read
By a lawyer as we all stood side by side.
To my brother, it was found, she had left a hundred pound,
The same unto my sister, I declare;
But when it came to me the lawyer said, "I see
She has left to you her old armchair."

How they tittered, how they chaffed,
How my brother and sister laughed,
When they heard the lawyer declare
Granny'd only left to me her old armchair.

I thought it hardly fair, still I said I did not care,
And in the evening took the chair away.
My brother at me laughed, the lawyer at me chaffed,
And said, "It will come useful, John, some day
When you settle down in life,
Find some girl to be your wife,
You'll find it very handy, I declare;
On a cold and frosty night,
When the fire is burning bright.
You can sit in your old armchair."

What the lawyer said was true,
For in a year or two,
Strange to say, I settled down in married life.
I first a girl did court and then the ring I bought,
Took her to the church, and then she was my wife.
Now the dear girl and me
Are happy as can be,

And when my work is over, I declare,
I ne'er abroad would roam,
But each night I'd stay at home,
And be seated in my old armchair.

One night the chair fell down.
When I picked it up, I found
The seat had fallen out upon the floor,
And there before my eyes
I saw to my surprise,
A lot of notes, then thousand pounds or more.
When my brother heard of this,
The poor fellow, I confess,
Went nearly wild with rage and tore his hair.
But I only laughed at him,
And I said unto him: "Jim,
Don't you wish you had the old armchair?"

No more they tittered, no more they chaffed,
No more my brother and my sister laughed,
When they heard the lawyer declare
Granny'd only left to me her old armchair.

Author Unknown

SOMEBODY'S MOTHER

The woman was old and ragged and gray
And bent with the chill of the Winter's day.

The street was wet with a recent snow
And the woman's feet were aged and slow.

She stood at the crossing and waited long,
Alone, uncared for, amid the throng

Families are Forever

Of human beings who passed her by
Nor heeded the glance of her anxious eye.

Down the street, with laughter and shout,
Glad in the freedom of "school let out,"

Came the boys like a flock of sheep,
Hailing the snow piled white and deep.

Past the woman so old and gray
Hastened the children in their way.

Nor offered a helping hand to her –
So meek, so timid, afraid to stir

Lest the carriage wheels or the horses' feet
Should crowd her down in the slippery street.

At last came one of the merry troop,
The happiest lad of all the group;

He paused beside her and whispered low,
"I'll help you cross, if you wish to go."

Her aged hand on his strong young arm
She placed, and so, without hurt or harm,

He guided the trembling feet along,
Proud that his own were firm and strong.

Then back again to his friends he went,
His young heart happy and well content.

"She's somebody's mother, boys, you know,
For all she's aged and poor and slow,

"And I hope some fellow will lend a hand
To help my mother, you understand,

Manna From Heaven

"If ever she's poor and old and gray,
When her own dear boy is far away."

And 'somebody's mother' bowed low her head
In her home that night, and the prayer she said

Was, "God be kind to the noble boy,
Who is somebody's son, and pride and joy!"

Mary Dow Brine

Lately I have thought a lot about 'listening,' said Hannie Struve. "How often you hear a little child complain… 'you're not listening!'" And how easily the mother replies, 'What do you want?' and mostly the child does not really 'want' anything, only to communicate.

Take time to listen – to children, young people, others! Sometimes they are reluctant to seek counsel because they receive impatient replies.

"Why do we parents so often say, 'I'm busy now,'" asked Robert M. Neal. "Why do we… not realize that a child is like a sunbeam, here for a moment and then gone somewhere else."

Talking – listening – patience, willingness to learn enough before jumping to quick conclusions: Sometimes in just letting them talk and using us for listening, they will come soberly, safely to their own conclusions. But when two people both talk at once, when they cut each other short, or when they don't talk at all, there aren't' likely to be any satisfactory solutions.

Yes, it takes time to listen, but it takes more time to correct mistakes once they have been made. With too many misjudging, too many making mistakes, with too few taking time to listen, counsel cannot seem as satisfactory as it should.

"The key is communication," reported a Time essay. " 'Can't you see I'm busy?'… ought to be banned. 'Listen' ought to be [implanted] over every parent's heart."

If only we could feel we have been heard! If only we would listen when we should!

Richard L. Evans

TEACHING CHARACTER AWARENESS TO CHILDREN

Teaching children good character traits should be commenced, as soon as, they are capable of understanding the principles of good behavior. "Please" and "thank you," in addition, to basic sharing are understood by toddlers. If children are shown love and kindness, they learn quickly. Children love to learn and they can learn good character by reading stories and poems, and by listening to good music, and playing games.

So often, we observe small children running to–and- fro in stores and restaurants. Many of such spirited children are involved in accidents, which are serious. Parents need to teach guidelines in using caution and consideration of others, before going to school. Children need loving discipline and careful supervision.

There are so many materials available to help parents. A keyboard is very inexpensive and children or parents can play the melody of a song with one finger. There are such fun songs to sing. Go to the public library for such items and help.

There are so many stories that teach moral behavior. I especially like Aesop's Fables. They are fun and stimulate children's imagination. Following are some favorable stories that teach character traits to youth.

I see a mind all new and unstained
And a heart and a conscience untouched,
And a body that holds an untouched soul
Is given to be trained.

Oh Lord, give me the strength to measure the mind.
And read what the intellect holds,
To judge it aright, and develop its might
Till its power completely unfolds.

Author Unknown

CHILDREN LEARN WHAT THEY LIVE

If a child lives with criticism
He learns to condemn.
If a child lives with hostility
He leans to fight.
If a child lives with ridicule
He learns to be shy.
If a child lives with shame
He learns to feel guilty.
If a child lives with tolerance
He learns to be patient.
If a child lives with encouragement
He learns confidence.
If a child lives with praise
He learns to appreciate.
If a child lives with fairness
He learns justice.
If a child lives with security
He learns to have faith.
If a child lives with approval
He learns to like himself.
If a child lives with acceptance and friendship
He learns to find love in the world.

AESOP'S FABLES

Sometime between the year 500 and 600 BC, there lived a Greek slave named Aesop, who gained his freedom by entertaining the Nobles at Court with his amusing stories. Aesop's fables have been enjoyed throughout the centuries mainly because the fables have been instructive, as well as, amusing. Most of the characters in Aesop's fables are animals who talk and act like human beings.

Generations of children have enjoyed untold pleasures from hearing the stories of wit and wisdom. Two favorite stories are the Lion and the Mouse, and The Tortoise and the Hare. Another favorite is the Ant and the Grasshopper, which illustrated the value of hard work and preparation for the future. The fables illustrate the failings and virtues of human nature in a simple humorous way. Each fable ends with a proverb that sums the fables moral and advice.

No one knows how many of the stories attributed to Aesop were actually composed by him. Some of the fables originated from more ancient sources, and Aesop may have been responsible for telling them and making them become popular. Since then many writers have told the stories over and over and added or omitted a phrase or two and also expanded their meaning. The tales have never lost their original charm or simplicity.

THE BOY WHO CRIED WOLF

There was a Sheppard boy who kept his flock of lambs on a small hill above a small village. The boy became very tired of spending his days alone upon the hill, so he decided to play a trick on the men of the village. He ran to the top of the hill and with all the voice he could muster yelled, "Help! Help! Come quick, the wolves are killing my sheep."

The kind villagers left their work and ran up the hill. "Where are the wolves?" they cried. The boy started laughing, "There are no wolves."

Several days later, he went closer to the village and cried out in the same manner. The villagers again came running up the hill, only to find there were no wolves in the flock.

Then one day the wolves did attack the fold of sheep and the boy ran to the top of the hill and yelled as loud as he could, "Help! Help! There is a wolf in my flock."

The villagers heard him and they thought it was another mean trick. No one paid any attention to him or went out of their way to help him. The Sheppard boy lost all his sheep.

That is the kind of thing that can happen to people who falsify – even when they do tell the truth they will not be believed.

Aesop's Fables

THE MONKEY AND THE DOLPHIN

It was an old custom among sailors to take with them on their voyages, monkeys and other pets to amuse them while they were at sea. So it happened that on a certain voyage a sailor took with him a monkey as a companion on board ship.

Off the coast of Sunium, the famous promontory of Attica, the ship was caught in a violent storm and was wrecked. All on board were thrown into the water and had to swim for land as best they could. And among them was the monkey.

A dolphin saw him struggling in the waves, and taking him for a man, went to his assistance. As they were nearing the shore just opposite Piraeus, the harbor of Athens, the dolphin spoke. "Are you an Athenian?" he asked.

"Yes, indeed," replied the monkey, as he spat out a mouthful of seawater. "I belong to one of the first families of the city."

"Then, of course, you know Piraeus," said the dolphin.

"Oh, yes," said the monkey, who thought Piraeus must be the name of some distinguished citizen, "he is one of my very dearest friends."

Disgusted by so obvious a falsehood, the dolphin dived to the bottom of the sea and left the monkey to his fate.

Those who pretend to be what they aren't usually find themselves in deep water.

Aesop's Fables

THE FOX AND THE BRAMBLE

The hounds were in full cry in pursuit of the wily fox and were gaining on him rapidly. Turning suddenly from his course, the fox dived through a hedge that was full of sharp thorns.

"Those dogs will never follow me through these brambles," said the fox to himself.

Just then he stepped on one of the thorns.

"That was a dirty trick," he snarled. "What kind of bramble are you? Here I come to you for help, but you only stab me for my pains."

"Wait a minute, friend fox," replied the bramble. "I'm the one who should be angry. You came running to me for help with your tail between your legs. I didn't ask you to come this way, did I? You know I had thorns, and you were perfectly willing to have the dogs wounded by them. Now that you, yourself, got caught on one of them you complain. Next time I hope the hounds catch you!"

All that the fox could do was lick his smarting paw.

Application: To the selfish, all are selfish.

Aesop's Fables

THE WIND AND THE SUN

A dispute once arose between the wind and the sun over which was the stronger of the two. There seemed to be no way of settling the issue. But suddenly they saw a traveler coming down the road.

"This is our chance," said the sun, "to prove who is right. Whichever of us can make that man take off his coat shall be the stronger. And just to show you how sure I am, I'll let you have the first chance."

So the sun hid behind a cloud, and the wind blew an icy blast. But the harder he blew the more closely did the traveler wrap his coat around him. At last the wind had to give up in disgust. Then the sun came out from behind the cloud and began to shine down upon the traveler with all his power.

The traveler felt the sun's genial warmth, and as he grew warmer and warmer he began to loosen his coat. Finally he was forced to take it off altogether and to sit down in the shade of a tree and fan himself. So the sun was right, after all!

Application: Persuasion is better than force

Aesop's Fables

THE TRUMPETER TAKEN PRISONER

*D*uring a battle, a trumpeter very rashly ventured too near the enemy and was taken prisoner.

"Spare me, good sirs, I beseech you," he begged of his captors. "Do not put me to death. I do not fight. I have never taken a life. I do not even carry any weapon, except this harmless trumpet, which I blow now and then."

"All the more reason why you should die," replied the captors. "While you, yourself, have not the spirit to fight, you stir up the others to do battle and to take the lives of our comrades."

Application: He who incites to strife is worse than he who takes part in it.

THE CAT AND THE RAT

A Cat, grown feeble with age, and no longer able to hunt for mice as she was wont to do, sat in the sun and bethought herself how she might entice them within reach of her paws.

The idea came to her that if she would suspend herself by the hind legs from a peg in the closet wall, the mice, believing her to be dead, no longer would be afraid of her. So, at great pains and with the assistance of a torn pillowcase she was able to carry out her plan.

But before the mice could approach within range of the inno-cent-looking paws a wise old gaffer-mouse whispered to his friends: "Keep your distance, my friends. Many a bag have I seen in my day, but never one with a cat's head at the bottom of it."

Then turning to the uncomfortable feline, he said: "Hang there, good madam, as long as you please, but I would not trust myself within reach of you though you were stuffed with straw."

Application: He who is once deceived is doubly cautious.

THE BOASTING TRAVELER

A young man who had been traveling in foreign parts returned to his home city where he bragged and boasted to all who would listen of the great feats he had accom-plished in the places he had visited.

"Why, when I was in Rhodes," he shouted, thumping his chest, "I made the most extraordinary leap the people of that place ever had seen. I have witnesses to prove it, too."

In time his hearers became weary of the traveler's boasts, and one of them said: "These exploits of yours in Rhodes may all be true, but you can save yourself much breath by doing one of those marvelous leaps right now instead of merely talking about it."

Application: He who does a thing well does not need to boast.

THE GOOSE WITH THE GOLDEN EGG

A farmer went to the nest of his goose to see whether she had laid an egg. To his surprise he found, instead of an ordinary goose egg, an egg of solid gold. Seizing the golden egg he rushed to the house in great excitement to show it to his wife.

Every day thereafter the goose laid an egg of pure gold. But as the farmer grew rich he grew greedy. And thinking that if he killed the goose he could have all her treasure at once, he cut her open only to find – nothing at all.

Application: The greedy who want more lose all.

THE HARE WITH MANY FRIENDS

T here was once a hare who had so many friends in the forest and the field that she truly felt herself to be the most popular member of the animal kingdom. One day she heard the hounds approaching.

"Why should a popular creature like me have to run for her life every time she hears a dog?" said she to herself. So she went to the horse, and asked him to carry her away from the hounds on his back.

"There is nothing I would rather do, friend hare," said the horse, "but, unfortunately, right now I have some important work to do for my master. However, a popular creature like you should have no difficulty in getting someone to help you."

Then the hare went to the bull and asked him whether he would be kind enough to ward off the hounds with his horns.

"My dear friend," replied the bull, "you know how I feel about you, and how glad I always am to be of service. But at this very moment I have an appointment with a lady. Why don't you ask our mutual friend the goat?"

But the goat was busy too, and so was the ram, and so were the calf and the pig and the ass. Each assured the hare of his undying friendship and anxiety to aid her in her trouble, but each had some excuse which prevented him from performing the service. By this time the hounds were quite near, so the hare took to her heels and luckily escaped.

Application: He who has many friends has no friends.

THE FARMER AND THE NIGHTINGALE

After a hard day's work a farmer went early to bed. But he could not go to sleep because of the melodious singing of a nightingale all through the summer night. So pleased was he by the birds song that the next night he set a trap for it and captured it.

"Ah, my beauty," said he, "now that I have caught you, you shall hang in a cage and sing for me every night."

"But we nightingales never sing in a cage," replied the bird. "If you imprison me I shall sicken and die and you shall never hear my song again."

"Then I'll put you in a pie and eat you," said the farmer. "I always have heard that nightingale pie is a dainty morsel."

"Please do not kill me," begged the nightingale. "If you will set me free I'll tell you three great truths that will be worth far more to you than my poor body."

So the farmer set him loose, and he flew up to a branch of a tree.

"Hold on," said the farmer, "what are the three great truths you promised me?"

The nightingale trilled a few happy notes and said, "Never believe a captive's promise. Keep what you have. And never sorrow over what is lost forever." Then the songbird flew away.

Application: A bird in the cage is worth two on a branch.

THE HARE AND THE TORTOISE

A hare was continually poking fun at a tortoise because of the slowness of his pace. The tortoise tried not to be annoyed by the jeers of the hare, but one day in the presence of the other animals he was goaded into challenging the hare to a foot race.

"Why, this is a joke," said the hare. "You know that I can run circles around you."

"Enough of your boasting," said the tortoise. "Let's get on with the race."

So the course was set by the animals, and the fox was chosen as judge. He gave a sharp bark and the race was on. Almost before you could say "scat" the hare was out of sight. The tortoise plodded along his usual unhurried pace.

After a time the hare stopped to wait for the tortoise to come along. He waited for a long, long time until he began to get sleepy. "I'll just take a quick nap here in this soft grass, and then in the cool of the day I'll finish the race." So he lay down and closed his eyes.

Meanwhile, the tortoise plodded on. He passed the sleeping hare, and was approaching the finish line when the hare awoke with a start. It was too late to save the race. Much ashamed, he crept away while all the animals at the finish line acclaimed the winner.

Application: Slow and steady wins the race.

Aesop's Fables

Families are Forever

GEORGE WASHINGTON AND THE CHERRY TREE

When George Washington was a little boy he lived on a farm in Virginia. His father taught him to ride, and he used to take young George about the farm with him so that his son might learn how to take care of the fields and horses and cattle when he grew older.

Mr. Washington had planted an orchard of fine fruit trees. There were apple trees, peach trees, pear trees, plum trees and cherry trees. Once, a particularly fine cherry tree was sent to him from across the ocean. Mr. Washington planted it on the edge of the orchard. He told everyone on the farm to watch it carefully to see that it was not broken or hurt in anyway.

It grew well and one spring it was covered with white blossoms. Mr. Washington was pleased to think he would soon have cherries from the little tree.

Just about this time, George was given a shiny new hatchet. George took it and went about chopping sticks and hacking into the rails of fences, and cutting whatever he passed. At last he came to the edge of the orchard, and thinking only of how well his hatchet could cut, he chopped into the little cherry tree. The bark was soft, and it cut so easily that George chopped the tree right down, and then went on with his play.

That evening when Mr. Washington came from inspecting the farm, he sent his horse to the stable and walked down to the orchard to look at this cherry tree. He stood in amazement when he saw how it was cut. Who would have dared do such thing? He asked everyone, but no one could tell him anything about it.

Just then George passed by.

"George," his father called in an angry voice, "do you know who killed my cherry tree?"

This was a tough question, and George staggered under it for a moment, but quickly recovered.

"I cannot tell a lie, father," he said. "I did it with my hatchet."

Mr. Washington looked at George. The boy's face was white, but he looked straight into his father's eyes.

"Go into the house, son," said Mr. Washington sternly.

George went into the library and waited for his father. He was very unhappy and very much ashamed. He knew he had been foolish and thoughtless and that his father was right to be displeased.

Soon, Mr. Washington came into the room. "Come here, my boy," he said.

George went over to his father. Mr. Washington looked at him long and steadily.

"Tell me, son, why did you cut the tree?"

"I was playing and I did not think-" George stammered.

"And now the tree will die. We shall never have any cherries from it. But worse than that, you have failed to take care of the tree when I asked you to do so.

George's head was bent and his cheeks were red from shame.

"I am sorry, father," he said.

Mr. Washington put his hand on the boy's shoulder. "Look at me," he said. "I am sorry to have lost my cherry tree, but I am glad that you were brave enough to tell me the truth. I would rather have you truthful and brave than to have a whole orchard full of the finest cherry trees. Never forget that, my son."

George Washington never did forget. To the end of his life he was just as brave and honorable as he was that day as a little boy.

Selected

TRUTH NEVER DIES

Truth never dies. The ages come and go.
The mountains wear away, the stars retire.
Destruction lays earth's mighty cities low;
And empires, states and dynasties expire;
But caught and handed onward by the wise,

Truth never dies.
Though unreceived and scoffed at through the years;
Though made the butt of ridicule and jest;
Though held aloft for mockery and jeers,
Denied by those of transient power possessed,
Insulted by the insolence of lies,
Truth never dies

It answers not. It does not take offense,
But with a mighty silence bides its time;
As some great cliff that braves the elements
And lifts through all the storms its head sublime,
It ever stands, uplifted by the wise;
And never dies.

As rests the Sphinx amid Egyptian sands;
As looms on high the snowy peak and crest;
As firm and patient as Gibraltar stands,
So truth, unwearied, waits the era blessed
When men shall turn to it with great surprise.
Truth never dies.

Truth is eternal. Truth must be passed from friend to friend, from teacher to teacher, from parent to child.

YOUNG ABRAHAM LINCOLN

Abraham Lincoln, as a store clerk proved to be honest and trustworthy in these two incidents from his youth. One day a woman came into the store and purchased sundry articles. They footed up two dollars and six and a quarter cents, or the young clerk thought they did. We do not hear nowadays of six and a quarter cents, but this was a coin borrowed from the Spanish currency.

The bill was paid, and the woman was entirely satisfied. But the young storekeeper, not feeling quite sure as to the accuracy of his calculation, added up the items once more. To his dismay he found that the sum total should have been but two dollars.

"I've made her pay six and quarter cents too much," said Abe, disturbed.

It was a trifle, and many clerks would have dismissed it as such. But Abe was too conscientious for that.

"The money must be paid back," he decided.

This would have been easy enough had the woman lived "just round the corner," but, as the young man knew, she lived between two and three miles away. This, however, did not alter the matter. It was night, but he closed and locked the store, and walked to the residence of his customer. Arrived there, he explained the matter, paid over the six and quarter cents, and returned satisfied.

A woman entered the store and asked for half pound of tea.

The young clerk weighed it out, and handed it to her in a parcel. This was the last sale of the day.

The next morning, when commencing with his duties, Abe discovered a four-ounce weight on the scales. It flashed upon him at once that he had used this in the sale of the night previous, and so, of course, given his customer short weight. I am afraid that there are many country merchants who would not have been much worried by this discovery. Not so the young clerk in whom we are interested. He weighted out the balance of the half pound, shut up the store, and carried it to the defrauded customer.

THE CROW AND THE PITCHER

A crow, so thirsty that he could not even caw, came upon a pitcher which once had been full of water. But when he put his beak into the pitcher's mouth he found that only a little water was left in it. Strain and strive as he might he was not able to reach far enough down to get at it. He tried to break the pitcher, then to overturn it, but his strength was not equal to the task.

Just as he was about to give up in despair a thought came to him. He picked up a pebble and dropped it into the pitcher. Then he took another pebble and dropped that into the pitcher. One by one he kept dropping pebbles into the pitcher until the water mounted to the brim. Then perching himself upon the handle he drank and drank until his thirst was quenched.

Aesop's Fables

Application: Necessity is the mother of invention.

THE EMPEROR'S NEW CLOTHES

*M*any years ago there was an emperor who was so fond of new clothes that he spent all his money on them. He did not give himself any concern about his army; he cared nothing about the theatre or for driving about in the woods, except for the sake of showing himself off in new clothes. He had a costume for every hour in the day, and just as they say of a king or emperor, "He is in his council chamber," they said of him, "The emperor is in his dressing room."

Life was merry and gay in the town where the emperor lived, and numbers of strangers came to it every day. Among them there came one day two rascals, who gave themselves out as weavers and said that they knew how to weave the most exquisite stuff imaginable. Not only were the colors and patterns uncommonly beautiful, but the clothes that were made of the stuff had the peculiar property of becoming invisible to every person who was unfit for the office he held or who was exceptionally stupid.

"Those must be valuable clothes," thought the emperor. "By wearing them I should be able to discover which of the men in my empire are not fit for their posts. I should distinguish wise men from fools. Yes, I must order some of the stuff to be woven for me directly." And he paid the swindlers a handsome sum of money in advance, as they required.

As for them, they put up two looms and pretended to be weaving, though there was nothing whatever on their shuttles. They called for a quantity of the finest silks and of the purest gold thread, all of which went into their own bags, while they worked at their empty looms till late into the night.

"I should lie to know how those weavers are getting on with the stuff," thought the emperor. But he felt a little queer when he reflected that those who were stupid or unfit for their office would not be able to see the material. He believed, indeed, that he had nothing to fear for himself, but still he thought it better to send someone else first, to see how the work was coming on. All the people in the town had heard of the peculiar property of the stuff, and everyone was curious to see how stupid his neighbor might be.

"I will send my faithful old prime minister to the weavers," thought the emperor. "He will be best capable of judging this stuff, for he is a man of sense and nobody is more fit for his office than he."

So the worthy old minister went into the room where the two swindlers sat working the empty looms. "Heaven save us!" thought the old man, opening his eyes wide. "Why, I can't see anything at all!" But he took care not to say so aloud.

Both the rogues begged him to step a little nearer and asked him if he did not think the patterns very pretty and the coloring fine. They pointed to the empty loom as they did so, and the poor old minister kept staring as hard as he could – without being able to see anything on it, for of course there was nothing there to see.

"Heaven save us!" thought the old man. "Is it possible that I am a fool! I have never thought it, and nobody must know it. Is it true that I am not fit for my office? It will never do for me to say that I cannot see the stuff."

"Well, sir, do you say nothing about the cloth?" asked the one who was pretending to go on with his work.

"Oh, it is most elegant, most beautiful!" said the dazed old man, as he peered again through his spectacles. "What a fine pattern, and what fine colors! I will certainly tell the emperor how pleased I am with the stuff."

"We are glad of that," said both the weavers; and then they named the colors and pointed out the special features of the pattern. To all of this the minister paid great attention, so that he might be able to repeat it to the emperor when he went back to him.

And now the cheats called for more money, more silk, and more gold thread, to be able to proceed with weaving, but they put it all into their own pockets, and not a thread went into the stuff, though they went on as before, weaving at the empty looms.

After a little time the emperor sent another honest statesman to see how the weaving was progressing, and if the stuff would soon be ready. The same thing happened with him as with the minister. He gazed and gazed, but there was nothing but empty looms, he could see nothing else.

"Is not this an exquisite piece of stuff?" asked the weavers, pointing to one of the looms and explaining the beautiful pattern and the colors which were not there to be seen.

"I am not stupid, I know I am not!" thought the man, "so it must be that I am not fit for my good office. It is very strange, but I must not let it be noticed." So he praised the cloth he did not see and assured the weavers of his delight in the lovely colors and the exquisite pattern. "It is perfectly charming," he reported to the emperor.

Everybody in the town was talking of the splendid cloth. The emperor thought he should like to see it himself while it was still on the loom. With a company of carefully selected men, among whom were the two worthy officials who had been there before, he went to visit the crafty impostors, who were working as hard as ever at the empty looms.

"Is it not magnificent?" said both the honest statesmen. "See, Your Majesty, what splendid colors, and what a pattern! And they pointed to the looms, for they believed that others, no doubt, could see what they did not.

"What!" thought the emperor. "I see nothing at all. This is terrible! Am I a fool? Am I not fit to be emperor? Why nothing more dreadful could happen to me!"

"Oh, it is very pretty! It has my highest approval," the emperor said aloud. He nodded with satisfaction as he gazed at the empty looms, for he would not betray that he could see nothing.

His whole court gazed and gazed, each seeing no more than the others, but, like the emperor, they all exclaimed, "Oh, it is beautiful!" They even suggested to the emperor that he wear the splendid new clothes for the first time on the occasion of a great procession which was soon to take place.

"Splendid! Gorgeous! Magnificent!" went from mouth to mouth. All were equally delighted with the weavers' workmanship. The emperor gave each of the impostors an order of knighthood to be worn in their buttonholes, and the title Gentlemen Weaver of the Imperial Court.

Before the day of which the procession was to take place, the weavers sat up the whole night, burning sixteen candles, so that people might see how anxious they were to get the emperor's new clothes ready. They pretended to take the stuff from the loom, they cut it out in the air with huge scissors, and they stitched away with needles that had no thread in them. At last they said, "Now the clothes are finished."

The emperor came to them himself with his grandest courtiers, and each of the rogues lifted his arm as if he held something, saying, "See! Here are the trousers! Here is the coat! Here is the cloak," and so on. "It is as light as a spider's web. One would almost feel as if one had nothing on, but that is the beauty of it!"

"Yes," said the courtiers, but they saw nothing, for there was nothing to see.

"Will Your Majesty be graciously pleased to take off your clothes so that we may put on the new clothes here, before the great mirror?

The emperor took off his clothes, and the rogues pretended to put on first one garment and then another of the new ones they had pretended to make. They pretended to fasten something round his waist and to tie on something. This they said was the train, and the emperor turned around and around before the mirror.

"How well his Majesty looks in the new clothes! How becoming they are!" cried all the courtiers in turn. "That is a splendid costume!"

"The canopy that is to be carried over Your Majesty in the procession is waiting outside," said the master of ceremonies.

"Well, I am ready," replied the emperor. "Don't the clothes look well?" and he turned around and around again before the mirror, to appear as if he were admiring his new costume.

The chamberlains, who were to carry the train, stooped and put their hands near the floor as if they were lifting it. Then they pretended to be holding something in the air. They would not let it be noticed that they could see and feel nothing.

So the emperor went along in the procession, under the splendid canopy, and everyone in the streets said: "How beautiful the emperor's new clothes are! What a splendid train! And how well they fit!"

No one wanted to let it appear that he could see nothing, for that would prove him not fit for his post. None of the emperor's clothes had been so great a success before.

"But he has nothing on!" said a little child.

"Just listen to the innocent," said its father. And one person whispered to another what the child had said. "He has nothing on. A child says he has nothing on!"

"But he has nothing on," cried all the people. The emperor was startled by this, for he had a suspicion that they were right. But he thought, "I must face this out to the end and go on with procession." So he held himself more stiffly than ever, and the chamberlains held up the train that was not there at all.

Hans Christian Andersen

It is better to be honest than silent.

THE BOY WHO NEVER TOLD A LIE

Once there was a little boy,
With curly hair and pleasant eye –
A boy who always told the truth,
And never, never told a lie.

And when he trotted off to school,
The children all about would cry,
"There goes the curly-headed boy –
The boy that never tells a lie."

And everybody loved him so,
Because he always told the truth,
That every day, as he grew up,
'Twas said, "There goes the honest youth."

And when the people that stood near
Would turn to ask the reason why,
The answer would be always this:
"Because he never tells a lie."

Selected

YOUTHFUL GOALS AND DREAMS

*P*ossessing the ability to make wise decisions is a key to success. It is essential that you seek good and competent advice from parents, school counselor, religious leaders, or role models and mentors. If you know a champion whom you desire to emulate, seek and follow his or her advice. Try to find experienced adults, who are in the vocation you wish to pursue, who are willing to help and to guide you. Be selective and be sure they have the qualities that you desire to emulate.

Working at the vocational or professional skill level, and doing what you derive enjoyment from is a paramount objective in life. You will more easily excel in those areas of endeavor for which you are best suited. Decide what your goal in life is to be, and stay motivated. Do not feel compelled to pursue something for which you are not suited, nor do you enjoy. You should therefore derive happiness and satisfaction in your chosen vocation or profession.

How exciting it is to watch a champion excel in his chosen sport. We have all watched sports competitors, after a well executed play hold their arms skyward to God, in thanks for his help. They know a great secret through their dedication to faith in God, and sacrifice of time and effort. God gives you a dream with the talent to achieve it. It is entirely up to you to work hard to achieve your dream. Not every person receives the same timetable in life. Your friends might discover their talents much later than you do. Perhaps, your friends waste their time each day and invite you to join them. Do not allow another to manage your time or motivation. If your dream is now – use every moment you can spare to achieve your dream.

If you are in high school or college, discipline yourself to do your studies first, and pursue friendships second. Education is your road map to a great future. Developing good study habits and work habits will benefit you throughout your lifetime. It is certain that most friends you acquire in your early years seem to vanish as you approach adulthood. Do not let your friends determine the course of your life, wasting your valuable time in just "hanging out." There will be special times to enjoy them when your needed work and studies are finished. Your friends, if they are true, will respect you for your decision. In return your dream is still intact and your initiative undamaged.

Remember, your dreams may be destroyed for a lifetime when you get involved in other pursuits before adulthood. Everyone is in such a hurry to get on with life and pursue life's pleasures, they need to slow down. A person does not have to prove anything to anyone else, except perhaps parents. Learn to slow down and think about what you are getting into. I am speaking about such pursuits as drugs, sex, drinking and driving under the influence of drugs or alcohol. Teenage pregnancy has destroyed more educational plans and careers than any other problem. You have a long life to live – do not get in a hurry to live in a present rush of things.

You could repeat the following affirmation when temptation surrounds you. "Lord, help me to remember that nothing is going to tempt me today, that you and I can't handle together." Write this affirmation and keep it in your billfold, and refer to it often. An easer way is to commit the affirmation to memory and repeat it often to your subconscious mind.

Youth, you are our hope for the future. May you be anxiously engaged in seeking truth and goodness. May your labors reflect an attitude of caring for all persons. Honor our past leaders and our country too - these days many do not. May you give hope and direction by communicating with the young, the ill, the down trodden and depressed. May you hold other persons and leaders accountable for their mistakes and untruths. May you prove to be a generation in strong pursuit of excellence!

MENTORS OF YOUTH

The responsibility of being a mentor to youth carries with it gifts of knowledge, talent, and other contributions that border on a smidgen of Sainthood.

Encouraging others to be the best they can be is a fine example of unselfish compassion. Mentors especially care for those they wish to inspire to greatness. Mentors never seem to get tired or lack understanding. Mentors are never too busy to gently impart the spirit of love and a comforting personal touch.

Coaches, as mentors, inspire young men in sports. We notice that coaches are always giving their players a pat now and then, showing youth they have done well. This type of support is paramount if you wish to build self-esteem in the youth.

Mentors treasure every moment they give to others and are always most enthusiastic. Ralph Waldo Emerson said nothing great was ever achieved without enthusiasm. Those are choice words from a great writer of wisdom on how to live and accomplish greatness.

COACHES NEVER LOSE

A team can lose.
Any team can lose.
But in a sense
A very real sense
A coach never loses.

For the job of a coach
Is over and finished
Once the starting whistle
Blows.
He knows
He's won or lost
Before play starts.

219

Manna From Heaven

For a coach has two tasks.
The minor one is to
Teach skills:
To teach a boy how to run faster
Hit harder
Block better
Kick farther
Jump higher.

The second task
The major task
Is to make men
Out of boys.

It's to teach an attitude
Of mind.
It's to implant character
And not simply to impart
Skills.
It's to teach boys to
Play fair.
This goes without saying.

It's to teach them
To be humble in victory
And proud in defeat.
This goes without saying.
But more importantly
It's to teach them
To live up to their potential
No matter what this
Potential is.

It's to teach them
To do their best

And never be satisfied
With what they are
But to strive to be
As good as they could be
If they tried harder.

A coach can never make a
Great player
Out of a boy who isn't'
Potentially great.
But he can make a great
Competitor out of any
Child.
And miraculously
He can make a man
Out of a boy.

For a coach
The final score doesn't read;
So many points for my team
So many points for theirs.
Instead it reads:
So many men
Out of so many boys.

And this is a score that
Is never published.
And this is the score
That he reads to himself
And in which he finds
His real joy
When the last game is over.

Author Unknown

IF YOU WANT A THING BAD ENOUGH

If you want a thing bad enough
To go out and fight for it,
Work day and night for it,
Give up your time and your peace and your sleep for it,
If only a desire of it
Makes your arm strong enough
Never to tire of it,
Makes you hold all things tawdry and cheap for it,
If life seems empty and useless without it
And all that you scheme and you dream is about it,
If gladly you sweat for it,
Fret for it,
Plan for it,
Lose all your terror of God and of man for it,
If you'll simply go after the thing that you want,
With all your capacity,
Strength and sagacity,
Faith, hope and confidence, stern pertinacity,
If neither cold, poverty, famished and gaunt,
Nor sickness, nor pain,
Of body and brain,
Can turn you away from the thing that you want,
If dogged and grim, you besiege and beset it,
YOU'LL GET IT!

Author Unidentified

FELLOWSHIP

When a feller hasn't got a cent
And is feelin' kind of blue,
And the clouds hang thick and dark,

And won't let the sunshine thro',
It's a great thing, oh my brethren,
For a feller just to lay
His hand upon your shoulder in a friendly sort o' way.

It makes a man feel strange,
It makes the tear-drops start.
And you kind o'feel a flutter
In the region of your heart.
You can't look up and meet his eye,
You don't know what to say
When a hand is on your shoulder in a friendly sort o'way.

Oh this world's a curious compound
With its honey and its gall;
Its cares and bitter crosses,
But a good world after all.
And a good God must have made it,
Leastwise that is what I say,
When a hand is on your shoulder in a friendly sort o'way.

Author Unknown

Remember, time is crowding you, right now – pushing you through your teens to your twenties, and then your thirties and forties – and so on – sooner than you suppose. And almost before you know it, you will be one of "those who are older."

Youth isn't the permanent property of anyone. It is a corridor we pass through, without lingering very long. There is no stopping place for any of us. And all of us, young or old, should respect each other, at all ages – for our strength is not in a society of segments, but in making the most of the whole length of life.

Who is youth? When is youth? Well, it isn't a clique or a club in which we can claim perpetual place. It's a time of life we all go through, quite swiftly, quite soon.

Oh, beloved young friends: Remember life is forever – but youth doesn't last very long. Live to make memories that will bless the whole length of your life.

Richard L. Evans

ADVICE FOR SONS AND DAUGHTERS IN-LAW

*C*all your parents-in-law "Mom," or "Mother" and "Dad." Or, by some other name of affection. In most cases they'll like it and feel warmer toward you! (If you want trouble, just don't name them at all when you speak to them!)

Live alone, apart from any relatives, if you possibly can. You will want to be boss of your household, even if you must live in a shack. Only people of exceptionally warm and giving natures can live with in-laws!

Make friends with your in-laws before you marry. A girl has two strikes against her if, without warning, she walks in with her new spouse and lets him drop the bombshell: "Mother, Dad – this is my wife, Mary!" According to a study, the third strike may not be far in the offing.

Learn all you can about marriage before you marry! The study showed that wives who took marriage courses in school had a slight edge.

Choose a husband with at least as much education as you have. Things are evening up, but today he's still supposed to be the brains of the family.

Look out for interfaith marriages. It's sad but true, the study shows, that in-law trouble still breeds here.

Marry a man whose parents are happy. If they're happy together, they won't cling to him.

ADVICE FOR PARENTS IN-LAW

*D*ON'T MEDDLE. Unmasked advice stands out head and shoulders above all other trouble-makers. "My parents give us too free and too frequent advice, " is an often repeated complaint.

Yet many fortunate wives have reported over and over to this effect: "My in-laws never have interfered, but they have given us the secure feeling that they would help us if we needed it."

DON'T CLING: After your son is married, you are no longer Number One interest in his life! If you are alone, find some outside interest.

But DON'T keep hands off to the extent of ignoring your grandchildren. Proud young parents demand recognition for their children. "They ignore the baby, young mother's often wail. This, it seems, is a serious offensive.

DON'T FAIL to call your daughter-in-law by some name of affection, and encourage her to do likewise! This is top insurance.

DON'T address your letters to your son, or daughter, but to BOTH of them.

So much for the DON'TS. A now for some DO'S.

DO speak and think of your in-law son or daughter not as an "in-law" at all but as "one of the family.

DO try to give them a feeling of acceptance right from the beginning.

DO keep on trying! Among those who had most in-law trouble were people-young and -old who gave up too easily.

DO sit with the Baby (although your young folks must remember that this is often hard on you-especially as you grow older).

DO give them advice out of your experience if they ask for it, but let them decide freely whether or not to follow your suggestions.

DO give them financial help if they need it and you can spare it, but NEVER make them feel obligated to do as you suggest.

Lately I have thought a lot about 'listening,'" said Hannie Struve. "How often you hear a little child complain… 'you're not listening!' And how easily the mother replies, 'What do you want?' and mostly the child does not really 'want' anything, only to communicate."

Take time to listen – to children, young people, others! Sometimes they are reluctant to seek counsel because they receive impatient replies.

"Why do we parents so often say, 'I'm busy now,'" asked Robert M. Neal. "Why do we… not realize that a child is like a sunbeam, here for a moment and then gone somewhere else."

Talking – listening – patience, willingness to learn enough before jumping to quick conclusions: Sometimes in just letting them talk and using us for listening, they will come soberly, safely to their own conclusions. But when two people both talk at once, when they cut each other short, or when they don't talk at all, there aren't likely to be any satisfactory solutions.

Yes, it takes time to listen, but it takes more time to correct mistakes once they have been made. With too many misjudging, too many making mistakes, with too few taking time to listen, counsel cannot seem as satisfactory as it should.

"The key is communication," reported a Time essay. " 'Can't you see I'm busy?'… ought to be banned. 'Listen' ought to be [implanted] over every parent's heart."

If only we could feel we have been heard! If only we would listen when we should!

Richard L. Evans

THE HOUSE WITH NOBODY IN IT

Whenever I walk to Suffern along the Erie track
    I go by a poor old farmhouse
    with its shingles broken and black.
I suppose I've passed it a hundred times,
    but I always stop for a minute
And look at the house, the tragic house,
    the house with nobody in it.

I never have seen a haunted house,
    but I hear there are such things;
That they hold the talk of spirits,
    their mirth and sorrowings.
I know this house isn't haunted, and I wish it were, I do;
For it wouldn't be so lonely if it had a ghost or two.

This house on the road to Suffern
    needs a dozen panes of glass,
And somebody ought to weed the walk
    and take a scythe to the grass.
It needs new paint and shingles, and the vines
    should be trimmed and tied;
But what it needs the most of all is some people living inside.

It I had a lot of money and all my debts were paid,
I'd put a gang of men to work with brush and saw and spade.
I'd buy that place and fix it up the way it used to be,
And I'd find some people who wanted a home
    and give it to them free.

Now a new house standing empty,
    with staring window and door,
Looks idle, perhaps, and foolish, like a hat on
    its block in the store.

Manna From Heaven

But there's nothing mournful about it;
it cannot be sad and lone
For the lack of something within it that it has never known.

But a house that has done what a house should do,
a house that has sheltered life,
That has put its loving wooden arms
around a man and his wife,
A house that has echoed a baby's laugh
and held up his stumbling feet,
Is the saddest sight, when it's left alone,
that ever your eyes could meet.

So whenever I go to Suffern along the Erie track
I never go by the empty house without
stopping and looking back;
Yet it hurts me to look at the crumbling roof
and the shutters fallen apart,
For I can't help thinking the poor old house
is a house with a broken heart.

Joyce Kilmer

CHAPTER FIVE

Poems With Wisdom

MY TRIBUTE TO AMANDA BRADLEY

I was fourteen years old when Amanda Bradley came into my life. The first time I saw her, she was so beautifully attired, I thought she was visiting Royalty. She was a most meticulous person in her dress and color selections. She came into my parents neighborhood grocery store dressed for a special occasion, so I thought.

The next Sunday when I arrived at church, she was in the congregation. When everyone was dismissed for Sunday school, to my great surprise, she was my new Sunday school teacher. Because she already knew me, she called on me during her lesson quite a few times and later apologized for her actions. We became immediate friends.

Little would I have imagined the love and comfort she would give to me in just a few days from that special Sunday morning. My father died at a very early age, just two days later. There was so much to do within our family – I felt alone like never before. My father was our security. Dear Amanda knew that and wrote me a beautiful card. How many times I have wished that I had saved that beautiful letter.

I soon learned that she made her living by writing the poems for greeting card companies. However, it took many years for her line of cards to be uniquely marketed under, "The Inspirations of Amanda Bradley."

She was my beautiful friend until I was married. She moved from our town due to the illness of her husband. I never saw her again and our correspondence soon was lost. She always gave me advice on following my dreams and goals, her advice was immeasurable. Her poems written with the image of virtue.

Gwenith Lewis

WHEN SPECIAL PEOPLE TOUCH OUR LIVES

When special people touch our lives,
then suddenly we see
how beautiful and wonderful
our world can really be.
They show us that our special hopes
and dreams can take us far,
by helping us look inward
and believe in who we are.
They bless us with their love and joy
through everything they give - -
When special people touch our lives,
they teach us how to live.

Amanda Bradley

LORD HELP ME TO HELP OTHERS

Please help me think of all
the nicest words that I can say,
The nicest favors I can do
to brighten up a day.

Please help me be as gentle and as kind as I can be
Whenever someone turns
for warmth and thoughtfulness to me.
Please help me gladly listen, and help me truly care
Whenever someone turns to me
with special things to share.
Please help me be deserving
of lasting faith and trust,
Help me to be generous, always fair and just.
Whenever someone turns to me,
please help me to come through…
The way that You come through for me
each time I turn to you.

Amanda Bradley

THE JOY OF LIVING

Some people seem to specialize
in doing thoughtful deeds.
Before you ask, they understand
your problems and your needs.
Quietly, they do their best to help, inspire and cheer,
And everything looks brighter
right away, because they're near.
They always have a lot to do
but still find time to spare
to listen and to give advice because they really care.
They help because they want to,
They find joy in being kind,
And making others happy
is the first thing on their minds.
They make this world a better place by practicing the art
Of reaching out to others
and by giving…from the heart.

LORD, LET ME BE A DREAMER

Lord, let me be a dreamer,
and let me be a doer,
let me strive
and steadily achieve.
Let me be a learner,
and let me be a teacher,
let me give
and graciously receive.
Let me be Your follower,
let me be Your friend,
let me hear Your voice
and heed Your call.
Let me come to know
the special plans You have for me,
and let me, with Your help,
fulfill them all.

Amanda Bradley

LOVE TAKES TIME

LOVE TAKES TIME…
Time to give a hug or smile,
To stop and listen for a while,
Time to give support and praise,
To learn and grow in many ways.

LOVE TAKES TIME…
Time to celebrate good news,
To share ideas, explore new views,
To see things through another's' eyes,
To sacrifice, to compromise.

LOVE TAKES TIME...
Time to understand and share,
Time to show how much you care,
Time to make sweet memories –
Love takes time for all of these.

Amanda Bradley

FRIENDSHIP IS A PRECIOUS TREASURE

I treasure every moment
warmed by friendship,
for more and more
my heart has come to learn
How precious are the gifts
of understanding,
of thoughtfulness and mutual concern,
How precious are the ties
of love and caring
that weave our separate lives
so close together,
I treasure every moment
warmed by friendship...
for every one brings joy
to last forever.

Amanda Bradley

"A BIRTHDAY IS A GIFT FROM GOD"

A birthday is a gift from God - -
another year to grow,
a chance to learn
the wondrous things
God feels that we should know.

233

It's like a new adventure,
full of places not yet seen,
full of people we can meet
and dreams we've yet to dream.
It's like a new awakening.
a search for who we are,
and if we seek in earnest,
our discoveries take us far.
And when we put our best
into each moment that we live,
then we are truly giving God
the best thanks we can give.

Isn't it funny how some special people
Don't realize they're special at all?

They're thoughtful without thinking about it,
They're always right there when you call…

They share, not expecting a thing in return,
Yet always seem richer for giving –

Isn't it lovely how those special people
Can teach us so much about living!

Amanda Bradley

MY READING MOTHER

*J*dedicate this poem to my sweet, patient mother who read to her children. During summer vacation from school, time was set aside for us to memorize poetry, reading and singing. Although we enjoyed the time she spent with us, what she accomplished with her children in cultural pursuits, were not appreciated until we reached adulthood.

Gwenith Lewis

THE READING MOTHER

I had a Mother who read to me
Sagas of pirates who scoured the sea,
Cutlasses clenched in their yellow teeth,
"Blackbirds" stowed in the hold beneath.

I had a Mother who read me lays
Of ancient and gallant and golden days;
Stories of Marmion and Ivanhoe,
Which every boy has a right to know.

I had a Mother who read me tales
Of Gelert the hound of the hills of Wales,
True to his trust till his tragic death,
Faithfulness blent with his final breath.

I had a Mother who read me the things
That wholesome life to the boy heart brings-
Stories that stir with an upward touch,
Oh, that each mother of boys were such!

You may have tangible wealth untold;
Caskets of jewels and coffers of gold.
Richer than I you can never be-
I had a Mother who read to me.

Strickland Gillian

MEMORIES

The following poems are taken from a poetry book, Daisies from A Child's Garden of Verses by Robert Louis Stevenson, published by DeWolfe Fiske & Co. Boston, 1898. My mother was given this book in 1905. My siblings and I memorized many poems from this volume. This book now rests in my China Closet, too fragile to be read.

A GOOD BOY

I woke before the morning, I was happy all the day,
I never said an ugly word, but smiled and stuck to play.
And now, at last, the sun is going down behind the wood,
And I am very happy, for I know that I've been good.

My bed is waiting cool and fresh, with linen smooth and fair,
And I must be off to sleep, and not forget my prayer.
I know that, till tomorrow I shall see the sun arise,
No ugly dream shall fright my mind, No ugly sight my eyes.

But slumber hold me tightly till I waken in the dawn,
And hear the thrushes singing in the lilacs round the lawn.

THE LAND OF COUNTERPANE

When I was sick and lay a-bed,
I had two pillows at my head,
And all my toys beside me lay
To keep me happy all the day.

And sometimes for an hour or so,
I watched my leaden solders go
With different uniforms and drills
Among the bed-clothes, through the hills;

And sometimes sent my ships in fleets
All up and down among the sheets;
Or brought my trees and houses out,
And planted cities all about.

I was the giant, great and still,
That sits upon the pillow-hill,
And sees before him dale and plain,
The pleasant land of counterpane.

A GOOD PLAY

We built a ship upon the stairs
All made of the
back-bedroom chairs,
And filled it full of sofa pillows
To go a-sailing on the billows.
We took a saw and several nails,
And water in the nursery pails;
And Tom said, "Let us also take
An apple and a piece of cake;"
Which was enough for Tom and me
To go a-sailing on, till tea.

We sailed along for days and days,
And had the very best of plays;
But Tom fell out and hurt his knee,
So there was no one left but me.

THE LITTLE LAND

When at home alone I sit
And am very tired of it,
I have just to shut my eyes
To go sailing through the skies-
To go sailing far away
To the pleasant Land of Play;
Where the Little People are;
Where the clover-tops are trees,
And the rain-pools are the seas,
And the leaves, like little ships
Sail about on tiny trips;
And above the daisy tree
Through the grasses,

237

High o'erhead the Bumble Bee
Hums and passes.

AUTUMN FIRES

In the other gardens
and all up the vale,
From the Autumn bonfires
See the smoke trail!

Pleasant summer over
And all the summer flowers,
The red fire blazes,
The grey smoke towers.

Sing a song of seasons!
Something bright in all!
Flowers in the summer,
Fires in the fall!

TO ANY READER

As from the house your mother sees
You playing round the garden trees,
So you may see, if you will look
Through the windows of this book,
Another child, far, far away,
And in another garden, play.
But do not think you can at all,
By knocking on the window, call
That child to hear you. He intent
Is all on his play-business bent.
He does not hear; he will not look,
Nor yet be lured out of his book.

For, long ago, the truth to say,
He has grown up and gone away,
And it is but a child of air
That lingers in the garden there.

Robert Louis Stevenson

A MILE WITH ME

O who will walk a mile with me
Along life's merry way?
A comrade blithe and full of glee,
Who dares to laugh out loud and free.

And let his frolic fancy play,
Like a happy child, through the flowers gay
That fill the field and fringe the way
Where he walks a mile with me.

And who will walk a mile with me
Along life's weary way?
A friend whose heart has eyes to see
The stars shine out o'er the darkening lea,
And the quiet rest at the end o' the day, -
A friend who knows, and dares to say,
The brave, sweet words that cheer the way
Where he walks a mile with me.

With such a comrade, such a friend,
I fain would walk till journey's end,
Through summer sunshine, winter rain,
And then? – Farewell, we shall meet again!

Henry Van Dyke

FOOTPRINTS

One night a man had a dream. He dreamed he was walking along the beach with the Lord. Across the sky flashed scenes from his life. For each scene, he notice two sets of footprints in the sand; one belonging to him, and the other to the Lord.

When the last scene of his life flashed before him he looked back at the footprints in the sand. He noticed that many times along the path of his life there was only one set of footprints.

This really bothered him and he questioned the Lord about it, "Lord, you said that once I decided to follow you, you'd walk with me all the way. But I have noticed that during the most troublesome times in my life, there is only one set of footprints. I don't understand why, when I needed you most, you would leave me."

The Lord replied, "My son, my precious child. I love you and I would never leave you. During your times of trial and suffering when you see only one set of footprints, it was then that I carried you.

Author Unknown

MYSELF

I have to live with myself, and so
I want to be fit for myself to know,
I want to be able, as days go by
Always to look myself, straight in the eye:
I don't want to stand, with the setting sun,
And hate myself for the things I have done.

I don't want to keep on a closet shelf
A lot of secrets about myself,
And fool myself, as I come and go,
Into thinking that nobody else will know

240

The kind of a man I really am:
I don't want to dress up myself in sham.

I want to go out with my head erect,
I want to deserve all men's respect;
But here is the struggle for fame and pelf
I want to be able to look at myself.
I don't want to look at myself and know
That I'm bluster and bluff and empty show.

I can never hide myself from me;
I see what others may never see;
I know what others may never know,
I never can fool myself and so,
Whatever happens, I want to be
Self-respecting and conscience free.

Edgar A. Guest

A WAYFARING SONG

O who will walk a mile with me
Along life's merry way?
A comrade blithe and full of glee,
Who dares to laugh out loud and free
And let his frolic fancy play,
Like a happy child, through the flowers gay
That fill the field and fringe the way
Where he walks a mile with me.
And who will walk a mile with me
Along life's weary way?
A friend whose heart has eyes to see
The stars shine out o'er the darkening lea,
And the quiet rest at the end o' the day –
A friend who knows, and dares to say,

The brave, sweet words that cheer the way
Where he walks a mile with me.
With such a comrade, such a friend
I fain would walk till journey's end,
Through summer sunshine, winter rain,
And then? – Farewell, we shall meet again!

Henry van Dyke

LIFE'S A GAME

This life is but a game of cards,
Which everyone must learn;
Each shuffles, cuts, and deals the deck,
And then a trump does turn;
Some show up a high card,
While others make it low,
And many turn no cards at all –
In fact, they cannot show.

When hearts are up we play for love,
And pleasure rules the hour;
Each day goes pleasantly along,
In sunshine's rosy bower.
When diamonds chance to crown the pack,
That's when men stake their gold,
And thousands then are lost and won,
By gamblers, young and old.

When clubs are trump look out for war,
On ocean and on land,
For bloody deeds are often done
When clubs are held in hand.
At last turns up the darkened spade,
Held by the toiling slave,

And a spade will turn up trump at last
And dig each player's grave.

Author Unknown

DON'T QUIT

When things go wrong, as they sometimes will,
When the road you're trudging seems all up hill,
When the funds are low and the debts are high,
And you want to smile, but you have to sigh,
When care is pressing you down a bit,
Rest, if you must – but don't you quit.
Life is queer with its twists and turns,
As everyone of us sometimes learns,
And many a failure turns about
When he might have won had he stuck it out;
Don't give up, though the pace seems slow-
You might succeed with another blow.

Often the goal is nearer than
It seems to a faint and faltering man,
Often the struggler has given up
When he might have captured the victor's cup,
And he learned too late, when the night slipped down,
How close he was to the golden crown.

Success is failure turned inside out-
The silver tint of the clouds of doubt-
And you never can tell how close you are,
It may be near when it seems afar;
So stick to the fight when you're hardest hit-
It's when things seem worst that you mustn't quit.

Author Unknown

DO IT NOW!

If you've got a job to do,
Do it now!
If it's one you wish were through,
Do it now!
If you're sure the job's your own,
Do not hem and haw and groan-
Do it now!
Don't put off a bit of work,
Do it now!
It doesn't pay to shirk,
Do it now!
If you want to fill a place
And be useful to the race,
Just get up and take a brace-
Do it now!
Don't linger by the way,
Do it now!
You'll lose if you delay,
Do it now!
If the other fellows wait,
Or postpone until it's late,
You hit up a faster gait-
Do it now!

Author Unknown

I SHALL NOT PASS THIS WAY AGAIN

Through this toilsome world, alas!
Once and only once I pass;
If a kindness I may show,
If a good deed I may do
To a suffering fellow man,
Let me do it while I can.

No delay, for it is plain
I shall not pass this way again.
Author Unknown

ALWAYS FINISH

If a task is once begun,
Never leave it till it's done.
Be the labor great or small,
Do it well or not at all.
Author Unknown

THE LEGEND OF THE ORGAN-BUILDER

Day by day the Organ-Builder in
his lonely chamber wrought;
Day by day the soft air trembled
to the music of his thought,

Till at last the work was ended;
and no organ-voice so grand
Ever yet had soared responsive
to the master's magic hand.

Ay, so rarely was it built that
whenever groom and bride,
Who in God's sight were well pleasing,
in the church stood side by side.

Without touch or breath the
organ of itself began to play,
And the very airs of heaven through
the soft gloom seemed to stray.
He was young, the Organ-Builder,
and o'er all the land his fame

Manna From Heaven

Ran with fleet and eager footsteps,
   like a swiftly rushing flame.

All the maidens heard the story,
   all the maidens blushed and smiled,
By his youth and wondrous beauty
   and his great renown beguiled.

So he sought and won the fairest,
   and the wedding day was set:
Happy day – the brightest jewel
   in the glad year's coronet!

But when they the portal entered
   he forgot his lovely bride –
Forgot his love, forgot his God,
   and his heart swelled high with pride.

"Ah!" thought he; "how great a master am I!
   When the organ plays,
How the vast cathedral arches
   will re-echo with my praise!"

Up the aisle the gay procession moved.
   The altar shone afar.
With every candle gleaming through
   soft shadows like a star.

But he listened, listened, listened,
   with no thought of love or prayer,
For the swelling notes of triumph
   for his organ standing there.

All was silent. Nothing heard he save
   the priest's low monotone,
And the bride's robe trailing softly
   o'er the floor of fretted stone.

Then his lips grew white with anger.
Surely God was pleased with him
Who had built the wondrous organ
for His temple vast and dim!

Who's the fault, then? Hers – the maiden
standing meekly at his side!
Flamed his jealous rage,
maintaining she was false to him – his bride.
Vain were all her protestations,
vain her innocence and truth;
On that very night he left her to
her anguish and her ruth.

Far he wandered to a country wherein
no man knew his name;
For ten weary years he dwelt there,
nursing still his wrath and shame.

Then his haughty heart grew softer,
and he thought by night and day
Of the bride he had deserted,
till he hardly dared to pray;

Thought of her, a spotless maiden,
fair and beautiful and good;
Thought of his relentless anger,
that had cursed her womanhood;

Till his yearning grief and penitence
at last were all complete,
And he longed, with bitter longing,
just to fall down at her feet.

Ah! How throbbed his heart when,
after many a weary day and night,

Manna From Heaven

Rose his native towers before him,
with the sunset glow alight!

Through the gates into the city,
on he pressed with eager tread;
There he met a long procession
—mourners following the dead.

"Now, why weep ye so, good people?
And whom bury ye today?
Why do yonder sorrowing maidens
scatter flowers along the way?

"Has some saint gone up to heaven?"
"Yes," they answered weeping sore;
For the Organ-Builder's saintly wife
our eyes shall see no more;

"And because her days were given
to the service of God's poor,
From his church we mean to bury her.
See! Yonder is the door."

No one knew him; no one wondered
when he cried out, white with pain;
No one questioned when, with pallid lips,
he poured his tears like rain.

"'Tis someone whom she has comforted,
who mourns with us," they said,
As he made his way unchallenged,
and bore the coffin's head;

Bore it through the open portal,
bore it up the echoing aisle,
Let it down before the altar,
where the lights burned clear the while:

Poems With Wisdom

When, oh, hark! The wondrous
organ of itself began to play
Strains of rare, unearthly sweetness
never heard until that day!

All the vaulted arches rang with
the music sweet and clear;
All the air was filled with glory,
as of angels hovering near;

And ere yet the strain was ended,
he who bore the coffin's head,
With the smile of one forgiven,
gently sank beside it – dead.
They who raised the body knew him,
and they laid him by his bride;
Down the aisle and o'er the threshold
they were carried, side by side,
While the organ played a dirge
that no man ever heard before,
And then softly sank to silence
– silence kept for evermore.

Julia C.R. Dorr

God moves in a mysterious way
His wonders to perform;
He plants his footsteps in the sea
And rides upon the storm.

Deep in unfathomable mines
Of never-failing skill,
He treasures up his bright designs
And works his sovereign will.

William Cowper

SMILE

Like a bread without the spreadin',
Like a puddin' without the sauce,
Like a mattress without beddin',
Like a cart without a hoss,
Like a door without a latchstring,
Like a fence without a stile,
Like a dry an' barren creek bed-
Is the face without a smile.

Like a house without a dooryard,
Like a yard without a flower,
Like a clock without a mainspring,
That will never tell the hour;
A thing that sort o' makes yo' feel
A hunger all the while –
Oh, the saddest sight that ever was
Is a face without a smile!

The face of man was built for smiles,
An' thereby he is blest
Above the critters of the field,
The birds an' all the rest;
He's just a little lower
Than the angels in the skies,
An' the reason is that he can smile;
Therein his glory lies!

So smile an' don't' forgit to smile,
An' smile, an' smile ag'in;
'Twill help you all along the way,
An' cheer you mile by mile;
An' so, whatever is your lot,
Jes' smile, an' smile, an' smile.

Author Unknown

LOVE

I love you,
Not only for what you are,
But for what I am
When I am with you.

I love you,
Not only for what
You have made of yourself,
But for what
You are making of me.

I love you
For the part of me
That you bring out;
I love you
For putting your hand
Into my heaped-up heart
And passing over
All the foolish, weak things
That you can't help
Dimly seeing there,
And for drawing out
Into the light
All the beautiful belongings
That no one else had looked
Quite far enough to find.

I love you because you
Are helping me to make
Of the lumber of my life
Not a tavern
But a temple;
Out of the works
Of my every day
Not a reproach
But a song.

Manna From Heaven

I love you
Because you have done
More than any creed
Could have done
To make me good,
And more than any fate
Could have done
To make me happy.

You have done it
Without a touch,
Without a word,
Without a sign,
You have done it
By being yourself.
Perhaps that is what
Being a friend means,
After all.

Roy Croft

There are two ways of being happy: We may either diminish our wants or augment our means – either will do – the result is the same; and it is for each man to decide for himself, and do that which happens to be the easiest. If you are idle or sick or poor, however hard it may be to diminish your wants, it will be harder to augment your means. If you are active and prosperous or young or in good health, it may be easier for you to augment your means than to diminish your wants. But if you are wise, you will do both at the same time, young or old, rich or poor, sick or well; and If you are very wise you will do both in such a way as to augment the general happiness of society.

Benjamin Franklin

AN OLD SWEETHEART OF MINE

An old sweetheart of mine! – Is this her presence here with me,
Or but a vain creation of a lover's memory?
A fair, illusive vision that would vanish into air,
Dared I even touch the silence with the whisper of a prayer?
Nay, let me then believe in all the blended false and true –
The semblance of the old love and the substance of the new, -
The then of changeless sunny days –
the now of shower and shine –
But Love forever smiling – as that old sweetheart of mine.

This ever restful sense of home though shouts ring in the hall, -
The easy chair – the old book-shelves and prints along the wall;
The rare Habanas in their box, or gaunt churchwarden-stem
That often wags, above the jar, derisively at them.

As one who cons at evening o'er an album, all alone,
And muses on the faces of the friends that he has known
So I turn the leaves of Fancy, till, in a shadowy design,
I find the smiling features of an old sweetheart of mine.

The lamplight seems to glimmer with a flicker of surprise,
As I turn it low – to rest me of the dazzle in my eyes,
And light my pipe in silence, save a sigh that seems to yoke
Its fate with my tobacco and to vanish with the smoke.

'Tis a fragrant retrospection, - for the loving thoughts that start
Into being are like perfume from the blossom of the heart;
And to dream the old dreams over is a luxury divine –
When my truant fancies wander with that old sweetheart of mine.

Though I hear beneath my study, like a fluttering of wings,
The voices of my children and the mother as she sings –
I feel no twinge of conscience to deny me any theme
When Care has cast her anchor in the harbor of a dream –

Manna From Heaven

In fact, to speak in earnest, I believe it adds a charm
To spice the good a trifle with a little dust of harm, -
For I find and extra flavor in Memory's mellow wine
That makes me drink the deeper to that old sweetheart of mine.

O Childhood-days enchanted! O the magic of the Spring!-
With all green boughs to blossom white, and all bluebirds to sing!
When all the air, to toss and quaff, made life a jubilee
And change the children's song and laugh to shrieks of ecstasy.

With eyes half closed in clouds
that ooze from lips that taste, as well,
The peppermint and cinnamon,
I hear the old school bell,
And from "Recess" romp in again
from "Blackman's" broken line,
To smile, behind my "lesson," at
that old sweetheart of mine.

A face of lily beauty, with a form of airy grace,
Float out of my tobacco as the Genii from the vase;
And I thrill beneath the glances of a pair of azure eyes
As glowing as the summer and as tender as the skies.
I can see the pink sunbonnet and the little checkered dress
She wore when first I kissed her and she answered the caress
With the written declaration that, "as surely as the vine
Grew 'round the stump" she loved me-that old sweetheart of mine.

Again I made her presents, in a really helpless way, -
The big "Rhode Island Greening" – I was hungry, too, that day! –
But I follow her from Spelling, with her hand behind her – so –
And I slip the apple in it – and the Teacher doesn't know!

I give my treasures to her – all, - my pencil – blue and red; -
And, if little girls played marbles, mine should all be hers, instead!

But she gave me her photograph, and printed "Ever Thine"
Across the back – in blue and red – that old sweetheart of mine!

And again I feel the pressure of her slender little hand,
As we used to talk together of the future we had planned, -
When I should be a poet, and with nothing else to do
But write the tender verses that she set the music to. . .

Then we should live together in a cozy little cot
Hid in a nest of roses, with a fairy garden spot,
Where the vines were ever fruited, and the weather ever fine,
And the birds were ever singing for that old sweetheart of mine.

When I should be her lover forever and a day,
And she my faithful sweetheart till the golden hair was gray;
And we should be so happy that when either's lips were dumb
They would not smile in Heaven till the other's kiss had come.

But, ah! My dream is broken by a step upon the stair,
And the door is softly opened, and – my wife is standing there,
Yet with eagerness and rapture all my vision I resign, -
To greet the living presence of the old sweetheart of mine.

James Whitcomb Riley

BEAUTIFUL THINGS

Beautiful faces are those that wear
It matters little if dark or fair –
Whole-soul honesty printed there.

Beautiful eyes are those that show,
Like crystal panes where hearth fires glow,
Beautiful thoughts that burn below.

Beautiful lips are those whose words
Leap from the heart like songs of birds,

Yet whose utterance prudence girds.
Beautiful hands are those that do
Work that is honest and brave and true.
Moment by moment the long day through.

Beautiful feet are those that go
On kindly ministries to and fro,
Down lowliest ways, if God wills it so.

Beautiful shoulders are those that bear
Ceaseless burdens of homely care
With patient grace and daily prayer.

Beautiful lives are those that bless
Silent rivers of happiness,
Whose hidden fountains but few may guess.

Beautiful twilight at set of sun,
Beautiful goal with race well won,
Beautiful rest with work well done.

Beautiful graves where grasses creep,
Where brown leaves fall, where drifts lie deep
Over worn-out hands-oh! beautiful sleep!

Ellen P. Allerton

GOD, THE ARTIST

God, when you thought of a pine tree,
How did you think of a star?
How did you dream of a damson West
Crossed by an inky bar?
How did you think of a clear brown pool
Where flocks of shadows are?

Poems With Wisdom

God, when you thought of a cobweb,
How did you think of dew?
How did you know a spider's house
Had shingles, bright and new?
How did you know we human folk
Would love them as we do?

God, when you patterned a bird song,
Flung on a silver string,
How did you know the ecstasy
That crystal call would bring?
How did you think of a bubbling throat
And a darling speckled wing?

God, when you chiseled a raindrop,
How did you think of a stem
Bearing a lovely satin leaf
To hold the tiny gem?
How did you know a million drops
Would deck the morning's hem?

Why did you mate the moonlit night
With the honeysuckle vines?
How did you know Madeira bloom
Distilled ecstatic wines?
How did you weave the velvet dusk
Where tangled perfumes are?
God, when you thought of a pine tree,
How did you think of a star?

Angela Morgan

THE TESTIMONY

A forest, temples of blue and green
clear cut against the summer sky;
Autumn finds the trees, a potpourri
of orange and red jewels glistening
in the light;
The artist must hurry for time races by.

Comes the winter, the trees
stand silently, solemn and white;
"Time, time – there is no time,"
cried the artist;
"And I must commune with my God".

Spring – the trees brilliant in the sun,
gesture to the wind as they carry forth
a message of love for all to hear;
Bewitched, inspired, the artist
began to paint the graceful movements
one by one;
"Dear Lord," prayed the artist,
"Master of All, Here is my Testimony."

Gwenith Lewis

I HEAR AMERICA SINGING

I hear America singing,
the varied carols I hear,
Those of mechanics, each one singing
his as it should be, blithe and strong,
The carpenter singing his,
as he measures his plank or beam,
The mason singing his, as he makes ready

for work, or leaves off work,
The boatman singing what belongs to him
in his boat, the deckhand singing
on the steamboat deck,
The shoemaker singing as he sits
on his bench, the hatter singing as he stands,
The wood-cutter's song, the ploughboys'
on his way in the morning,
or at noon intermission or at sundown,
The delicious singing of the mother,
or of the young wife at work,
or of the girl sewing or washing,
Each singing what belongs to him
or her and to none else,
The day what belongs to the day – at night
the party of young fellows, robust, friendly
Singing with open mouths their
strong melodious songs.

Walt Whitman

THE CAPTAINS'S DAUGHTER

We were crowded in the cabin,
Not a soul would dare to sleep –
It was midnight on the waters,
And a storm was on the deep.

'Tis a fearful thing in winter
To be shattered by the blast,
And to hear the rattling trumpet
Thunder, "Cut away the mast!"

So we shuddered there in silence –
For the stoutest held his breath,

259

While the hungry sea was roaring
And the breakers talked with Death.

As thus we sat in darkness,
Each one busy with his prayers,
"We are lost!" the captain shouted
As he staggered down the stairs.

But his little daughter whispered,
As she took his icy hand,
"Isn't' God upon the ocean,
Just the same as on the land?"

James T. Fields

Trust in God is very strong and pure in the very young.

SENIOR CITIZEN'S PRAYER

*L*ord, thou knowest better than I myself that I am growing older and will someday be old. Keep me from the fatal habit of thinking I must say something on every subject and on every occasion. Release me from craving to straighten out everybody's affairs. Make me thoughtful but not moody, helpful but not bossy. With my vast store of wisdom, it seems a pity not to use it all, but Thou knowest, Lord, that I want a few friends at the end.

Keep my mind free from the recital of endless details; give me wings to get to the point. Seal my lips on my aches and pains. They are increasing and love of rehearsing them is becoming sweeter as the years go by. I dare not ask for grace enough to enjoy the tales of others' pains, but help me to endure them with patience.

I dare not ask for improved memory, but for a growing humility and lessening cocksureness when my memory seems to clash with the memories of others. Teach me the glorious lesson that occasionally I may be mistaken.

Keep me reasonably sweet; I do not want to be a Saint – some of them are so hard to live with – but a sour old person is one of the crowning works of the devil. Give me the ability to see good things in unexpected places and talents in unexpected people. Give me the grace to tell them so. Amen.

Author Unknown

Whatever poet, orator, or sage
May say of it, old age is still old age.
It is the waning, not the crescent moon.
The dusk of evening, not the blaze of noon;
It is not strength, but the weakness; not desire,
But its surcease; not the fierce heat of fire,
The burning and consuming element,
But that of ashes and of embers spent,
In which some living sparks we still discern,
Enough to warm, but not enough to burn.
What then? Shall we sit idly down and say
The night hath come; it is no longer day?
The night hath not yet come; we are not quite
Cut off from labor by the failing light;
Something remains for us to do or dare,
Even the oldest tree some fruit may bear; …
For age is opportunity no less
Than youth itself, though in another dress,
And as the evening twilight fades away
The sky is filled with stars, invisible by day.

Henry Wadsworth Longfellow

TOUCHING SHOULDERS

There's a comforting thought at the close of the day,
When I'm weary and lonely and sad,
That sort of grips hold of my crusty old heart
And bids it be merry and glad.
It gets in my soul and drives out the blues,
And finally thrills through and through.
It is just a sweet memory that chants the refrain:
"I'm glad I touch shoulders with you!"

Did you know you were brave, did you know you were strong?
Did you know there was one leaning hard?
Did you know that I waited and listened and prayed,
And was cheered by your simplest word?
Did you know that I longed for that smile on your face,
For the sound of your voice ringing true?
Did you know I grew stronger and better because
I had merely touched shoulders with you?

I am glad that I live, that I battle and strive
For the place that I know I must fill;
I am thankful for sorrows, I'll meet with a grin
What fortune may send, good or ill.
I may not have wealth, I may not be great,
But I know I shall always be true,
For I have in my life that courage you gave
When once I rubbed shoulders with you.

Author Unknown

LORD, MAKE A REGULAR MAN OUT OF ME

This I would like to be – braver and bolder,
Just a bit wiser because I am older,
Just a bit kinder to those I may meet,
Just a bit manlier taking defeat;
This for the New Year my wish and my plea –
Lord, make a regular man out of me.

This I would like to be – just a bit finer,
More of a smiler and less of a whiner,
Just a bit quicker to stretch out my hand
Helping another who's struggling to stand,
This is my prayer for the New Year to be,
Lord, make a regular man out of me.

This I would like to be – just a bit fairer,
Just a bit better, and just a bit squarer,
Not quite so ready to censure and blame,
Quicker to help every man in the game,
Not quite so eager men's failings to see,
Lord, make a This I would like to be – just a bit truer,
Less of the wisher and more of the doer,
Broader and bigger, more willing to give,
Living and helping my neighbor to live!
This for the New Year my prayer and my plea –
Lord, make a regular man out of me.

Edgar A. Guest

POEMS OF DAYS GONE BY

THE LITTLE BOY BLUE

The little toy dog is covered with dust,
But sturdy and stanch he stands;
And the little toy soldier is red with rust,
And his musket molds in his hands.
Time was when the little toy dog was new,
And the soldier was passing fair,
And that was the time when Little Boy Blue
Kissed them and put them there.

"Now, don't you go till I come," he said,
"And don't you make any noise!"
So toddling off to his trundle-bed
He dreamed of the pretty toys,
And as he was dreaming, an angel song
A wakened our Little Boy Blue,-
Oh, the years are many, the years are long,
But the little toy friends are true,
Ay, faithful to Little Boy Blue they stand,
Each in the same old place,
Awaiting the touch of a little hand,
The smile of a little face.
And they wonder, as waiting these long years through,
In the dust of that little chair,
What has become of our Little Boy Blue
Since he kissed them and put them there.

Eugene Fields

DUTCH LULLABY

Wynken, Blynken , and Nod one night
Sailed off in a wooden shoe,-
Sailed on a river of misty light
Into a sea of dew.
"Where are you going, and what do you wish?"
The old moon asked the three.
"We have come to fish for the herring-fish
That live in this beautiful sea;
Nets of silver and gold have we,"
Said Wynken,
Blynken,
And Nod.

The old moon laughed and sung a song,
As they rocked in the wooden shoe;
And the wind that sped them all night long
Ruffled the waves of dew;
The little stars were the herring-fish
That lived in the beautiful sea.
"Now cast your nets wherever you wish,
But never afeard are we!"
So cried the stars to the fisherman three,
Wynken,
Blynken,
And, Nod.

All night long their nets they threw
For the fish in the twinkling foam,
Then down from the sky came the wooden shoe,
Bringing the fisherman home;
"T" was all so pretty a sail, it seemed
As if it could not be;
And some folk thought t' was a dream they'd dreamed

Of sailing that beautiful sea;
But I shall name you the fisherman three:
Wynken.
Blynken,
And Nod.

Wynken and Blynken are two little eyes,
And Nod is a little head,
And the wooden shoe that sailed the skies
Is a wee one's trundle-bed;
So shut your eyes while Mother sings
Of wonderful sights that be,
And you shall see the beautiful things
As rock on the misty sea
Where the old shoe rocked the fishermen three,-
Wynken,
Blynken,
And Nod.

Eugene Fields

JEANIE WITH THE LIGHT BROWN HAIR

I dream of Jeanie with the light brown hair,
Borne, like a vapor, on the summer air;
I see her tripping where the bright streams play,
Happy as the daisies that dance on her way,
Many were the wild notes her merry voice would pour,
Many were the blithe birds that warbled them o'er:
Oh! I dream of Jeanie with the light brown hair,
Floating , like a vapor, on the soft summer air.

I long for Jeanie with the day-dawn smile,
Radiant in gladness, warm with winning guile;
I hear her melodies, like joys gone by,

Sighing round my heart over the fond hopes that die:
Sighing like the night wind and sobbing in the rain,
Wail for the lost one that comes not again:
Oh! Long for Jeanie and my heart bows low,
Nevermore to find her where the bright waters flow.

I sigh for Jeanie, but her light form strayed
Far from the fond hearts round her native glade;
Her smiles have vanished and her sweet songs flown,
Flitting like the dreams that have cheered us and gone.

Now the wild flowers may wither on the shore
While her gentle fingers will cull them no more;
Oh! I sigh for Jeanie with the light brown hair,
Floating, like a vapor, on the soft summer air.

Stephen Collins Foster

A VISIT FROM ST. NICHOLAS

'T was the night before Christmas, when all through the house
Not a creature was stirring, not even a mouse;
The stockings were hung by the chimney with care,
In hopes that St. Nicholas soon would be there;
The children were nestled all snug in their beds,
While visions of sugar plums danced in their heads;
And mamma in her "kerchief, and I in my cap,
Had just settled our brains for a long winter's nap
When out on the lawn there arose such a clatter,
I sprang out of bed to see what was the matter.
Away to the window I flew like a flash,
Tore open the shutters and threw up the sash.
The moon on the breast of the new-fallen snow
Gave the luster of midday to objects below,
When, what do my wandering eyes should appear,

But a miniature sleigh, and eight tiny reindeer,
With a little old driver, so lively and quick,
I knew in a moment it must be St. Nick.
More rapid than eagles his courses they came,
And he whistled, and shouted, and called them by name;
"Now, Dasher! Now Dancer! Now, Prancer, and Vixen!
On, Comet, on, Cupid, on, Donder and Blitzen!
To the top of the porch! to the top of the wall!
Now dash away! Dash away all!"
As dry leaves that before the wild hurricane fly,
When they meet with a obstacle, mount to the sky;
So up to the house top the courses they flew,
With the sleigh full of toys, and St. Nickolas, too.
And then, in a twinkling, I heard on the roof
The prancing and pawing of each little hoof.
As I drew in my head, and was turning around,
Down the chimney St Nicholas came with a bound.
He was dressed all in fur, from his head to his foot,
And his clothes were all tarnished with ashes and soot;
A bundle of toys he had flung on his back,
And he looked like a peddler just opening his pack.
His eyes---how they twinkled! His dimples how merry !
His cheeks were like roses, his nose like a cherry!
His droll little mouth was drawn up like a bow,
And the beard of his chin was as white as the snow;
The stump of a pipe he held tight in his teeth,
And the smoke it encircled his head like a wreath:
He had a broad face and a little round belly ,
That shook when he laughed like a bowlful of jelly.
He was chubby and plump, a right jolly old elf,
And I laughed when I saw him , in spite of myself;
A wink of his eye and a twist of his head,
Soon gave me to know I had nothing to dread;
He spoke not a word, but went straight to his work,

And filled all the stockings; then turned in a jerk,
And laying his finger aside of his nose,
And giving a nod, up the chimney he rose;
He sprang to his sleigh, to his team gave a whistle,
And away they all flew like the down of a thistle,
But, I heard him exclaim, ere he drove out of sight,
"Happy Christmas to all and to all a good night."

Clement Clarke Moore

CHAPTER SIX

On the Lighter Side

$\mathcal{A}$ proverb states that "a cheerful heart is good medicine." Many times a hearty laugh can cause us to feel
better emotionally and physically. Reading a humorous book
or watching a comedy can also really cheer us up. When life
seems overly serious, a good laugh can help our outlook in any
situation. The joy of laughing sends out vibrations that stimulate
every cell of our being with gladness.

God designed the body with natural painkillers called endor-
phins, that are released when a person laughs. So we can use
humor as a therapy for ourselves; to help lower blood pressure,
boost the immune system, and change and uplift our spirits.

Tension is always relieved in social settings and even in
awkward moments when someone makes us laugh. It is truly a
talent to develop. Making good use of laughter is a great help
when raising a family, and also is a good teaching tool. Teachers know that the most effective lessons are the fun ones, we are
all students of life, willing and ready to learn life's lessons in fun
and joyful ways.

There are great teachings in this generation. Laughter is the
universal language of joyful living. Older folks oftentimes were
raised in homes where laughter was not considered the proper

thing to do. If you came from that kind of environment, as you grew older and had friends with a sense of humor, you realized how much fun their families had together.

The first thing a fellow ought to do after he learns he's been born equal is to try to overcome it.

Author unknown

THIS WILL MAKE YOU SMILE

A little girl walked to and from school daily. Though the weather that morning was questionable and clouds were forming, she made her daily trek to the elementary school. As the afternoon progressed, the winds whipped up, along with the thunder and lightning.

The mother of the little girl felt concerned that her daughter would be frightened as she walked home from school and she herself feared the electrical storm might harm her child. Following the roar of thunder, lightning, like a flaming sword, would cut through the sky. Full of concern the mother quickly got into her car and drove along the route to her child's school. As she did so, she saw her little girl walking along, but at each flash of lightning, the child would stop, look up and smile. Another and another were to follow quickly and with each the little girl would look at the streak of light and smile.

When the mother's car drew up beside the child she lowered the window and called to her, "What are you doing? Why do you keep stopping?" The child answered, "I am trying to look pretty. God keeps taking my picture.

-The Internet

MISS FOGGERTY'S CAKE

As I sat by my window last evening,
The letterman brought unto me
A little gilt-edged invitation
Saying, "Gilhooley, come over to tea."

Sure I knew 'twas the Foggertys sent it,
So I went for old friendship's sake,
And the first thing they gave me to tackle
Was a slice of Miss Foggerty's cake.

Miss Martin wanted, to taste it,
But really there weren't' no use,
For they worked at it over an hour
And couldn't get none of it loose.

Till Foggerty went for a hatchet
And Killey came in with a saw;
The cake was enough, by the powers,
To paralyze any man's jaw.

In it were cloves, nutmeg and berries,
Raisins, citron and cinnamon, too:
There were sugar, pepper and cherries,
And the crust of it nailed on with glue.

Miss Foggerty, proud as a preacher,
Kept winking and blinking away,
Till she fell over Flannigan's brogans
And split a whole brewing of tay.

"O, Gilhooley," she cried, "you're not eating,
Just take another piece for my sake."
"No thanks, Miss Foggerty," says I,
"But I'd like the recipe for that cake."

McNullley was took with the colic,
McFadden complained of his head,
McDoodle fell down on the sofa
And swore that he wished he was dead.

Miss Martin fell down in hysterics,
And there she did wiggle and shake,
While every man swore he was poisoned
By eating Miss Foggerty's cake.

Author Unknown

CHP vs. USMC

Two California Highway Patrol Officers were conducting speeding enforcement on I-15, just north of the Marine Corps Air Station at Miramar. One of the officers was using a hand held radar device to check the speeding vehicles approaching the crest of a hill.

The officers were suddenly surprised when the radar gun began reading 300 miles per hour. The officer attempted to reset the radar gun, but it would not reset and then turned off.

Just then a deafening roar over the treetops revealed that the radar had in fact locked on to a USMC F/A-18 Hornet which was engaged in a low flying exercise near the location.

Back at the CHP Headquarters the Patrol Captain fired off a complaint to the USMC Base Commander. The reply came back in true USMC style:

Thank you for your letter. We can now complete the file on this incident.

You may be interested to know that the tactical computer in the Hornet had detected the presence of, and subsequently locked on to, your hostile radar equipment and automatically sent a jamming signal back to it, which is why it shut down.

Furthermore, an air-to-ground missile aboard the fully-armed aircraft had also automatically locked on to your equipment location. Fortunately, the Marine Pilot flying the Hornet recognized the situation for what it was, quickly responded to the missile system alert status and was able to override the automated defense system before the missile was launched to destroy the hostile radar position.

The pilot also suggests you cover your mouths when cussing at them, since the video systems on these jets are very high tech. Sergeant Johnson, the officer holding the radar gun, should get his dentist to check his left rear molar. It appears the filing is loose. Also the snap is broken on his holster.

Thank you for your concern. Semper Fi.
Classification: UNCLASSIFIED-
Caveats: NONE

The Internet

"KIDS SAY THE DARNDEST THINGS"

Art Linkletter: Questions asked a four year old on his television show.

Boy: My teacher told me that if you asked me to tell you about her, not say she's very old, because she heard a little boy on your program once who said: "What an old teacher," he had.

Art: This prompted me to ask him, "How old would you say your teacher is?"

Boy: "Oh, about ninety!"

HOPI HUMOR

While on a vacation trip, a traveler was driving through the Arizona country side and saw a huge, jolly-looking Indian mother at a stand by the side of a road selling jewelry. She was surrounded by sixteen happy laughing children ranging from the age of a toddler to a sixteen-year old.

"Are all of those children your children?" the woman asked.

"Oh, yes," replied the mother, proffering her beadwork, blankets, and baskets.

"With a big family like that, don't you have lots of fights and arguments?"

"Oh, no," declared the mother, with a chuckle, "we're just one great big Hopi family!"

THANKSGIVING HUMOR

A young man named John received a parrot as a gift. The parrot had a bad attitude and an even worse vocabulary. Every word out of the bird's mouth was rude, obnoxious and laced with profanity. John tried and tried to change the bird's attitude by consistently saying only polite words, playing soft music and anything else he could think of to "clean up" the bird's vocabulary.

Finally, John was fed up and yelled at the parrot. The parrot yelled back. John shook the parrot and the parrot got angrier and even ruder. John, in desperation, threw up his hand, grabbed the bird and put him in the freezer. For a few minutes the parrot squawked and kicked and screamed. Then suddenly there was total quiet. Not a peep was heard for over a minute. Fearing that he'd hurt the parrot, John quickly opened the door to the freezer. The parrot calmly stepped out onto John's outstretched arms and said, "I believe I may have offended you with my rude language and actions. I'm sincerely remorseful for my inappropriate transgressions and I fully intend to do everything I can to correct my rude and unforgivable behavior. John was stunned at the change in the bird's attitude. As he was about the ask the parrot what had made such a dramatic change in his behavior, the bird continued, "May I ask what the turkey did?"

The Internet

JEWISH HUMOR

*D*uring basic training our drill sergeant asked all Jewish personnel to make themselves known. Six of us tentatively raised our hands. Much to our relief, we were given the day off for Rosh Hashanah.

A few days later, in anticipation of Yom Kippur, the sergeant again asked or all Jewish personnel to identify themselves. This time, every soldier raised his hand. "Only those who were Jewish last week can be Jewish this week."

LEADERSHIP

A salesman came to call on the purchasing agent of a large corporation. The purchasing agent detected a slight foreign accent in the salesman's speech, and told him that it was the policy of the firm to buy only from American suppliers. He hastened to reassure the purchasing agent that he had been brought up in Europe only because his father had been the American ambassador to many foreign countries, and that his family could be traced back to the Mayflower.

On that basis, the two concluded a highly profitable – for the salesman – session. As the salesman was closing his briefcase, he looked at a picture of Abraham Lincoln on the wall. "Fine-looking gentleman," he said. "President of the company?"

SUBJECT

A tough old cowboy counseled his grandson that if
he wanted to live a long life,
The secret was to sprinkle a pinch of gunpowder
on his oatmeal every morning.
The grandson did this religiously to the age of 103.
When he died, he left 14 children, 30 grandchildren,
45 great-grandchildren, 25 great-great-grandchildren
And a 15-foot hole where the crematorium used to be.

FAMILY HUMOR

A family was celebrating their daughter's fifth birthday at
a local restaurant when the little girl's father noticed
her looking sadly at the moose head on the wall. Someone had
placed a party hat on its head. Her father explained why some
people hurt animals for food.

"I know all that," sobbed the child. "but why did they have to
shoot him on his birthday?

CHILDREN SPEAK THE TRUTH

*W*e rushed our four-year-old son, Ben, to the emergency
room with a terrible cough, high fever, and vomiting.
The doctor did an exam, then asked Ben what bothered him the
most? After thinking it over, Ben said hoarsely, "I would have to
say, my little sister."

LITTLE HERO

*R*emember the little Dutch boy who saved his country
by holding his finger in a hole in the dike until the
break could be repaired? They've just discovered what the boy

said when grateful citizens pressed him for a speech: "Please not to-night, folks. I've had a tough day the orifice!"

SALES HUMOR

The sales manager came in to see the boss.

"I'd like you to get rid of that salesman we hired last month," he said. "He refuses to take orders, and yesterday, when I told him I was going to report him to you, he said that both of us could jump in the lake."

"Let me see his sales record," said the boss, and when it was brought to him, he studied it carefully. "I see that he's sold over a million dollars worth of goods since he's been with us."

"I know," said the sales manager, "but he insists on doing everything his own way, and if you don't like it, he tells you to go jump in the lake. What do you think we should do about it?"

"I don't know what you plan to do," said the boss, "but I figure I can always get a new suit."

MISTAKEN IMPRESSION

Driving her two sons to a funeral, a mother tried to explain about death and their belief in the life after death.

The boys behaved well at the funeral. The mother had second thoughts at the gravesite; she discovered her explanations were not as thorough as she had thought. In a loud voice, her four year old son asked, "What's in the box?"

HAUNTED CASTLE

An intrepid photographer went to a haunted castle determined to get a picture of a ghost which was said to appear only once in a hundred years. Not wanting to frighten off the ghost, the photographer sat in the dark until midnight, when the apparition became visible. The ghost turned out to be friendly and consented to pose for one snapshot. The happy photographer popped a bulb into his camera and took the picture. After dashing into his studio, the photographer developed the negative and groaned. It was underexposed and completely blank. The spirit was willing but the flash was weak.

SCHOOL HUMOR

The teacher was conducting a class in American History, when she called on Johnny Smith.

"Johnny Smith, give me the name of one person who signed the Declaration of Independence," she said.

"I didn't do it, teacher," said Johnny.

"Just for that fresh remark, I want your mother to come and see me after school tomorrow," said the teacher.

The next afternoon, Mrs. Smith came to the classroom. Johnny had evidently told her of his problem.

She strode up to the teacher's desk and glared at her.

"Look, Mrs. Teacher!" she said, "My Johnny is a good, honest boy. Believe me, if he says he didn't do it, he didn't do it!"

A GOOD MAMA

A mother pigeon and her young son were getting ready to migrate to Florida. The baby was afraid he couldn't make it.

"Don't worry," Mama pigeon said, "I'll tie one end of a piece of string around my leg and the other end around your neck. If you tire, I'll help you along."

The baby pigeon- began to wail. "But, " he protested, "I don't want to be pigeon-towed."

On the Lighter Side

SCHOOL HUMOR

*O*n the first day of school, the teacher was calling the roll. When she got the letter S, she hesitated a minute.

"Shakespeare," she called.

"Here, teacher," said a little boy in the back row.

"What's your first name, Shakespeare?" asked the teacher.

"William, ma'am," answered the boy.

"That's a rather well-known name, isn't it?" asked the teacher.

"It should be!" said the boy. "I've lived in this neighborhood for more than ten years!"

I HAD BUT FIFTY CENTS

I took my girl to a fancy ball;
It was a social hop;
We waited till the folks got out,
And the music it did stop.
Then to a restaurant we went,
The best one on the street;
She said she wasn't hungry,
But this is what she eat:
A dozen raw, a plate of slaw,
A chicken and a roast,
Some applesass, and sparagrass,
And soft-shell crabs on toast.

A big box stew, and crackers too;
Her appetite was immense!
When she called for pie,
I thought I'd die,
For I had but fifty cents.

She said she wasn't hungry
And didn't care to eat,

Manna From Heaven

But I've got money in my clothes
To bet she can't be beat;
She took it in so cozy,
She had an awful tank;
She said she wasn't thirsty,
But this is what she drank:
A whiskey skin, a glass of gin,
Which made me shake with fear,
A ginger pop, with rum on top,
A schooner then of beer,
A glass of ale, a gin cocktail;
She should have had more sense;
When she called for more,
I fell on the floor,
For I had but fifty cents.

Of course I wasn't hungry,
And didn't care to eat,
Expecting every moment
To be kicked into the street;
She said she'd fetch her family around,
And some night we'd have fun;
When I gave the man the fifty cents,
This is what he done:
He tore my clothes,
He smashed my nose,
He hit me on the jaw,
He gave me a prize
Of a pair of black eyes
And with me swept the floor.
He took me where my pants hung loose,
And threw me over the fence;
Take my advice, don't try it twice
If you've got but fifty cents!

Author Unknown

On the Lighter Side

He who has one for the road gets a trooper for a chaser.

ONCE IN AWHILE YOU FIND A TRUE GENTLEMAN

A man and his wife walked into a dentist's office. The man said to the dentist, "Doc, I'm in one heck of a hurry! I have two buddies sitting out in my car waiting for us to go play golf. So forget about the anesthesia and just pull the tooth and be done with it. We have a 10:00 a.m. tee time at the best golf course in town and it's 9:30 already. I don't have time to wait for the anesthetic to work!"

The dentist thought to himself, "My goodness, this is surely a very brave man asking to have his tooth pulled without using anything to kill the pain." So the dentist asked him, "Which tooth is it, sir?"

The man turned to his wife and said, "Open your mouth, honey, and show him."

-The Internet

HELP WANTED

A law firm commanding
Position of standing
Requires a general clerk-
A man who's admitted
To practice, and fitted
To handle diversified work;

Must know the proceedings
Relating to pleadings,
The way of preparing a brief;
Must argue with unction
For writs of injunction
As well as for legal relief.

283

Manna From Heaven

Must form corporations
And hold consultations,
Assuming a dignified mien;
Should read each decision
And legal provision
Wherever the same may be seen.
Must analyze cases
And get at their basis,
Should never be idle or slow;
Must manifest learning
In all things concerning
The matters referred to below:

Attachments and trials,
Specific denials,
Demurrers, replies and complaints,
Disbursements, expenses
And partial defenses,
Ejectments, replevins, distraints;

Estoppels, restrictions,
Constructive evictions,
Agreements implied and express,
Accountings, partitions,
Estates and commissions,
Encumbrances, fraud and duress.
Above are essentials,
The best of credentials
Required-and handsome physique;
Make prompt application,
Will pay compensation
Of seventeen dollars a week.

Franklin Waldheim

WHEN I GET TIME

When I get time –
I know what I shall do:
I'll cut the leaves of all my books
And read them through and through.

When I get time –
I'll write some letters then
That I have owed for weeks and weeks
To many, many men.

When I get time –
I'll pay those calls I owe,
And with those bills, those countless bills,
I will not be so slow.

When I get time –
I'll regulate my life
In such a way that I may get
Acquainted with my wife.

When I get time –
Oh glorious dream of bliss!
A month, a year, then years from now –
But I can't finish this –
I've no more time.

Thomas L. Masson

SPECIAL POEM FOR SENIORS

A row of bottles on my shelf
Caused me to analyze myself.
One yellow pill I have to pop
Goes to my heart so it won't stop.

A little white one that I take
Goes to my hands so they won't shake.
The blue ones that I use a lot
Tell me I'm happy when I'm not.
The purple pill goes to my brain
And tells me that I have no pain.
The capsules tell me not to wheeze
Or cough or choke or even sneeze.
The red ones, smallest of them all
Go to my blood so I won't fall.
The orange ones, very big and bright
Prevent my leg cramps in the night.
Such an array of brilliant pills
Helping to cure all kinds of ills.
But what I'd really want to know…
Is what tells each one where to go!

Unknown author.

THE LAWYER JOKE

A guy walks into a lawyer's office and asks, "What are your rates?"

"Two hundred dollars for three questions," answers the lawyer.

"That's a pretty hefty charge, isn't it?" Retorts the man.

"Maybe," the lawyer responds, "What's your final question?"

IT'S THAT SIMPLE

Little Johnny was in his backyard filling in a hole when his neighbor asked, "What are you doing Johnny?"

"My goldfish died and I'm just trying to bury him," answered, Johnny.

The neighbor thinking that Johnny was giving him a smart answer said," That 's a pretty big hole for your goldfish."

"Not since he is inside your cat," came the answer.

IRISH HUMOR

*P*addy was driving down the street in a sweat because he had a special meeting and could not find a parking place.

Looking up to Heaven he said, "Lord take pity on me. If you find me a parking place I will go to Mass every Sunday for the rest of me life and give up me whiskey."

Miraculously, a parking place appeared.

Paddy looked upward again and said, "Never mind, I found one."

THE BLONDE JOKE

A man was mowing his front lawn when his gorgeous neighbor came out of her house and went straight to the mailbox. She opened it, slammed it shut and went back into the house.

A few minutes later she came out again, went to the mailbox and opened it and looked in then slammed the door, she seemed agitated. She came out a third time and repeated the same actions.

Curious of her actions, the man asked, "Is something wrong?"

"There certainly is…My stupid computer keeps saying, "You've got mail!"

ALL IN A DAY'S SHOPPING

*T*he scene was a shopping mall just before Christmas and Mrs. Robinson was waiting for another car to pullout of its space. Just as the car cleared the spot, a teenager in a Corvette swung around the corner and stole it. "You saw me waiting for that space," Mrs. Robinson yelled out. "I even had my signal on."

"Sorry, that's what happens when you're young and fast," the kid sneered.

With that, Mrs. Robinson backed up and then gunned her classic Mercedes into the Corvette, ramming it over and over again until the fiberglass body was nothing but a crumpled heap.

"Hey, what'd you do that for?" the teen whined.

"Sorry, replied Mrs. Robinson with a sweet smile. "That's what happens when you're rich and old. "

The Internet

SHIRLEY AND MARCY

A mom was concerned about her kindergarten son walking to school. He didn't want his mother to walk with him.

She wanted to give him the feeling that he had some independence but yet know that he was safe.

So she had an idea of how to handle it. She asked a neighbor if she would please follow him to school in the mornings, staying at a distance, so he probably wouldn't notice her.

The neighbor said that since she was up early with her toddler anyway, it would be a good way for them to get some exercise as well, so she agreed.

The next school day, the neighbor and her little girl set out following behind Timmy as he walked to school with another neighbor girl.

She did this for the whole week.

As the two walked and chatted, kicking stones and twigs, Timmy's little friend noticed the same lady was following them as she seemed to do everyday all week.

Finally she said to Timmy, "Have you noticed that lady following us to school all week? Do you know her?

Timmy nonchalantly replied, 'Yeah , I know who she is."

The little girl said, "Well, who is she"?

"Shirley Goodnest," Timmy replied, "and her daughter Marcy."

"Shirley Goodnest? Who in the heck is she and why is she following us"?

"Well," Timmy explained, "every night my Mom makes me say the 23rd Psalm with my prayers, "cuz she worries about me so much."

And in the Psalm, it says, "Shirley Goodnest and Marcy shall follow me all the days of my life," so I guess I'll just have to get used to it!"

The Internet

I HAVE TWO HORSES

I wonder sometimes how much these teachings get inside of us – wonderful teachings we hear. I heard that a man was interviewed one day, and the person said to him, "If you had two houses would you give one to a person in need who has no house?"

The man said, "Yes I think I would."

The interviewer asked, " Well if you had two cars and you discovered someone who had no car, who really needed a car, would you give him one of yours?

The man said, "Yes I think I would."

"Well, if you had two horses, and you knew someone that loved a horse and could not afford a horse , and did not have a horse, would you give him a horse?

The man said, "Well I don't think I would".

The interviewer said, " You don't think you would! Why a

horse is much less expensive than a house or an automobile. Why wouldn't you?"

The man replied, "Well, you see, I have two horses.

THE LADY SURGEON

The eminent lady surgeon was an imperious, aloof type and she finally left her husband. He was suffering from a serious internal complaint and had undergone a series of difficult operations at the hands of a team of other eminent surgeons. She left him after the fifth operation, explaining, "I'm sick of other people constantly opening up my male."

The End

CHAPTER SEVEN

America the Beautiful

THE BIRTH OF THE UNITED STATES

Five hundred years ago the American Continents were uncovered. This epochal achievement in this discovery will never come again on our planet. There are no huge, fertile, uninhabited areas left to explore.

Great men of vision lay at the helm of progress in this "New World". Such sacrificial achievements will only happen to the world again as man explores the space around us.

Christopher Columbus, man of vision, started this exploration back in 1492. A skilled Italian seaman, Columbus, was filled with energy, courage and resourcefulness. He had a dream like all men of destiny acquire. Columbus, and many of his contemporaries, believed the world was round. Scholars in that day and age believed the world was flat.

Columbus began to sell his theories, as well as himself, and pleaded for the opportunity to prove his position on the idea that the world was indeed round. His ingenuity regarding his sales presentation hit home eventually with the suggestion of riches and spoils from the Indies. His question of, "why not let me find a shorter route to East Asia by sailing westward instead of eastward around Africa," brought him success.

A Spanish Monarch gave Columbus the opportunity for such a voyage. Persistence had paid off and he was given a motley crew and three small ships. He set sail and the winds were friendly and his progress was rapid. His superstitious crew grew mutinous as the voyage ran into a period of six weeks. Land was sighted on October 12, 1492; Columbus had landed in the Bahamas.

Columbus failed to find the riches of the Indies. He died in 1506, a cruelly disappointed and discredited soul. No doubt this was his theory of himself.

Columbus's sensational achievement has obscured the fact that he was one of the most successful failures in history.

I will continue my account of the great men whose wisdom and sacrifice built our beautiful country. I shall share some history but I prefer to let you learn of their wisdom by their actual words. Therefore, I will submit their accounts at random.

Let us keep in mind that these men believed they were building a country dedicated to God above. They disagreed with each other but did not disgrace themselves by name calling as we see in government circles today. They were gentleman who were true servants of the people and for the people.

COLUMBUS

Behind him lay the gray Azores,
Behind the Gates of Hercules;
Before him not the ghost of shore;
Before him only shore-less seas.
The good mate said, "Now must we pray,
For lo! The very stars are gone,
Brave Adm'r'l speak! What shall I say?"
"Why, say, 'Sail on! Sail on! And on!' "
Then pale and worn, he paced his deck,
And peered through darkness. Ah, that night

Of all dark nights! And then a speck –
A light! A light! At last a light!
It grew, a starlit flag unfurled!
It grew to be Time's burst of dawn.
He gained a world; he gave that world
Its' grandest lesson; "On! Sail on!"

Joaquin Miller

THE FAITH OF OUR FOUNDING FATHERS

*N*one have been so brave and none so respected as the group of patriots who drafted and signed the Constitution of the United States of America.

Many people are unaware of the Founding Fathers who have drafted other works of importance that share their thoughts regarding God's hand in establishing the Constitution of our nation and the establishment of our nation under God's direction.

On May 27, 1776, President George Washington dedicated this day "...to be observed as a day of fasting, humiliation, and prayer, humbly to supplicate the mercy of Almighty God, that it would please Him to pardon all our manifold sins and transgressions, and to prosper the arms of the united colonies, and finally establish the peace and freedom of America upon a solid and lasting foundation."

In the summer of 1787, the delegates to the Constitutional Convention in Philadelphia, had been in bitter quarrels for over ten weeks. Tempers flared over issues between the northern and southern states. Delegates threatened to leave the convention leaving our fledging nation without a strong constitution.

Benjamin Franklin, 81 years old, stood to his feet and gave this contentious gathering a stirring call for prayer.

"I have lived a long time, and the longer I live, the more convincing proofs I see of this truth, that God governs the affairs

293

of men. And if a sparrow cannot fall to the ground without His notice, is it probable that an empire can rise without His aid? I also believe that without His concurring aid we shall succeed in this political building no better than the builders of Babel... Therefore, I beg leave to move that henceforth prayers imploring the assistance of heaven, and its blessings on our deliberations be held in this assembly every morning."

Thomas Jefferson, who wrote the Declaration of Independence, was among the reluctant supporters. His good friend, James Madison, was the person who was able to change the mind of Jefferson on the new Constitution.

On the other side, Alexander Hamilton, James Madison and John Jay were credited with the passage of the Constitution for they led the battle for its' passage.

When prayer was adopted the tension subsided and the men began to work together. Political issues were eradicated and peace began to reign. One of the finest civic lessons was learned, and by example, deserves to endure for all time.

THE PRICE THEY PAID

Have you wondered what happened to the men who signed the Declaration of Independence?

Five signers were captured by the British as traitors, and tortured before they died. Twelve had their homes ransacked and burned. Two lost their sons in the Revolutionary Army, another had two sons captured. Nine of the 56 fought and died from wounds or hardships of the Revolutionary War. What kind of men were they? Twenty-four were lawyers and jurists. Eleven were merchants, nine were farmers and large plantation owners, men of means, well educated. But they signed the Declaration of Independence knowing full well the penalty would be death if they were captured.

They signed and pledged their lives, their fortunes and their sacred honor.

Carter Braxton of Virginia, a wealthy planter and trader, saw his ships swept from the sea by the British navy. He sold his home and properties to pay his debts and died in rags.

Thomas McKeam was so hounded by the British that he was forced to move his family almost constantly. He served in the Congress without pay, and his family was kept in hiding. His possessions were taken from him, and poverty was his reward. Vandals or soldiers or both, looted the properties of Ellery, Clymer, Hall, Walton, Gwinnett, Heyward, Ruttledge and Middleton.

At the battle of Yorktown, Thomas Nelson, Jr. noted that the British General Cornwallis had taken over the Nelson home for his headquarters. The owner quietly urged General George Washington to open fire, which was done. The home was destroyed and Nelson died bankrupt.

Francis Lewis had his home and properties destroyed. The enemy jailed his wife and she died within months. John Hart was driven from his wife's bedside as she was dying. Their 13 children fled for their lives. His fields and his grist mill were laid waste. For more than a year he lived in forests and caves, returning home after the war to find his wife dead, his children vanished. A few weeks later he died from exhaustion and a broken heart. Norris and Livingston suffered similar fates. Such were the stories and sacrifices of the American Revolution. These were not wild-eyed rabble-rousing ruffians. They were soft spoken men of means and education. They had security, but they valued liberty more. Standing tall, straight, and unwavering, they pledged: "For the support of this declaration, with a firm reliance on the protection of the Divine Providence, we

mutually pledge to each other, our lives, our fortunes, and our Sacred honor."
Author Unknown

THINGS THAT HAVEN'T BEEN DONE BEFORE

The things that haven't been done before,
Those are the things to try;
Columbus dreamed of an unknown shore
At the rim of the far-flung sky,
And his heart was bold and his faith was strong
As he ventured in dangers new,
And he paid no heed to the jeering throng
Or the fears of the doubting crew.

The many will follow the beaten track
With guideposts on the way.
They live and have lived for ages back
With a chart for every day.
Someone has told them it's safe to go
On the road he has traveled o'er,
And all that they ever strive to know
Are the things that were known before.

A few strike out, without, map or chart,
Where never a man has been,
From the beaten paths they draw apart
To see what no man has seen.
There are deeds they hunger alone to do;
Though battered and bruised and sore,
They blaze the path for the many, who
Do nothing not done before.

The things that haven't been done before
Are the tasks worthwhile today;
Are you one of the flock that follow, or
Are you one that shall lead the way?
Are you one of the timid souls that quail
At the jeers of a doubting crew,
Or dare you, whether you win or fail,
Strike out for a goal that's new?

Edgar A. Guest

THE FAREWELL ADDRESS

*O*f all the dispositions and habits, which lead to political prosperity, Religion and Morality are indispensable supports. In vain would that man claim the tribute of Patriotism, who should labor to subvert these great pillars of human happiness, these firmest props of the duties of men and citizens. The mere politician, equally with the pious man ought to respect and to cherish them. A volume could not trace all their connections with private and public felicity. Let it simply be asked where is the security for property, for reputation, for life, if the sense of religious obligation desert the oaths, which are the instruments of investigation in Courts of Justice? And let us with caution indulge the supposition, that morality can be maintained without religion. Whatever may be conceded to the influence of refined education on minds of peculiar structure, reason and experience both forbid us to expect that National morality can prevail in exclusion of religious principle.

'Tis substantially true, that virtue or morality is a necessary spring of popular government. The rule indeed extends with more or less force to every species of free Government. Who that is a sincere friend to it, can look with indifference upon attempts to shake the foundation of the fabric? ...

Observe good faith and justice toward all Nations. Cultivate peace and harmony with all. Religion and morality enjoin this conduct; and can it be that good policy does not equally enjoin it? It will be worthy of a free, enlightened, and at no distant period, a great Nation to give to mankind the magnanimous and too novel example of a People always guided by an exalted justice and benevolence. Who can doubt that in the course of time and things the fruit of such a plan would richly repay any temporary advantages which night be lost by a steady adherence to it? Can it be that Providence has not connected the permanent felicity of a Nation with its virtue? The experiment, at least, is recommended by every sentiment, which ennobles human nature. Alas! Is it rendered impossible by its vices?

George Washington

GOD RULES IN THE AFFAIRS OF MEN

Proclamation by the President of the United States of America, March 30, 1863.

" The will of God prevails. In the great contests each party claims to act in accordance with the will of God. Both may be, and one must be, wrong. God cannot be for and against the same thing at the same time. In the present civil war it is quite possible that God's purpose is something different from the purpose of either party."

It is the duty of nations as well as of men to own their dependence upon the overruling power of God, to confess their sins and transgressions in humble sorrow, yet with assured hope that genuine repentance will lead to mercy and pardon, and to recognize the sublime truth, announced in the Holy Scriptures and proven by all history, that those nations only are blessed whose God is the Lord;

"And, insomuch as we know that by His divine law nations, like individuals, are subjected to punishments and chastisements in this world, may we not justly fear that the awful calamity of civil war which now desolates the land may be but a punishment inflicted upon us for our presumptuous sins, to the needful end of our national reformation as a whole people?

We have been recipients of the choicest bounties of Heaven; we have been preserved these many years in peace and prosperity. We have grown in numbers, wealth, and power, as no other nation has ever grown. But we have forgotten God. We have forgotten the gracious hand which preserved us in peace and multiplied and enriched and strengthened us, and we have vainly imagined, in the deceitfulness of our hearts, that all these blessings were produced by some superior wisdom and virtue of our own. Intoxicated with unbroken success, we have become too self-sufficient to feel the necessity of redeeming and preserving grace, too proud to pray to the God that made us.

It behooves us, then, to humble ourselves before the Offended Power, to confess our national sins, and to pray for clemency and forgiveness."

What I do say is, that no man is good enough to govern another man without that other's consent.

Abraham Lincoln

THE GETTYSBURG ADDRESS

*F*our score and seven years ago, our fathers brought forth on this continent a new nation, conceived in liberty, and dedicated to the proposition that all men are created equal.

Now we are engaged in a great civil war, testing whether that nation, or any nation so conceived and so dedicated, can long endure. We are met on a great battlefield of that war. We have come to dedicate a portion of that field as a final resting place for those who here gave their lives that that nation might live. It is altogether fitting and proper that we should do this.

But in a larger sense we cannot dedicate, we cannot consecrate, we cannot hallow this ground. The brave men, living and dead, who struggled here, have consecrated it far above our poor power to add or detract. The world will little note, nor long remember, what we say here, but it can never forget what they did here. It is for us the living, rather, to be dedicated here to the unfinished work, which they who fought here have thus far so nobly advanced. It is rather for us to be here dedicated to the great task remaining before us – that from these honored dead we take increased devotion to that cause for which they gave the last full measure of devotion, that we here highly resolve that these dead shall not have died in vain, that this nation under God, shall have a new birth of freedom, and that government of the people, by the people, for the people, shall not perish from the earth.

Abraham Lincoln

O CAPTAIN, MY CAPTAIN

*H*ere Walt Whitman mourns for the fallen Abraham Lincoln. To the poet, the assassination was a terrible blow to the American democratic comradeship he celebrated in so much of his verse.

America the Beautiful

O Captain! My Captain! Our fearful trip is done;
The ship has weather'd every rack, the prize we sought is won;
The port is near, the bells I hear, the people all-exulting,
While eyes follow the steady keel, the vessel grim and daring:
But O heart! Heart! Heart!
O the bleeding drops of red,
Where on the deck my captain lies,
Fallen cold and dead.

O Captain! My captain! Rise up and hear the bells;
Rise up - for you the flag is flung – for you the bugle trills;
For you bouquets and ribbon'd wreaths
– for you the shores a-crowding;
For you they call, the swaying mass, their eager faces turning:
Here Captain! Dear Father!
This arm beneath your head!
It is some dream that on the deck,
You've fallen cold and dead.

My captain does not answer, his lips are pale and still;
My father does not feel my arm, he has no pulse nor will;
The ship is anchor'd safe and sound,
its voyage closed and done;
From fearful trip, the victor ship comes in with object won:
Exult, O shores, and ring, O bells!
But I, with mournful tread,
Walk the deck my Captain lies,
Fallen cold and dead.

Walt Whitman

Manna From Heaven

THOMAS JEFFERSON

*E*very government degenerates when trusted to the rulers of people alone. The people themselves are its only safe depositories. And to render even them safe, their minds must be improved to a certain degree...By far the most important bill in our whole code, is that for the diffusion of knowledge among the people. No other sure foundation can be devised, for the preservation of freedom and happiness.

The ground of liberty is to be gained by inches; we must be contented to secure what we can get, from time to time, and eternally press forward for what is yet to get. It takes time to persuade men to do even what is for their own good.

The execution of the laws is more important than the making of them.

There are rights which it is useless to surrender to the government, and which governments have yet always been found to invade. These are the rights of the thinking, and publishing our thoughts by speaking or writing; the rights of free commerce; the right of personal freedom.

If a nation expects to be ignorant and free, in a state of civilization, it expects what never was and never will be. The functionaries of every government have propensities to command at will the liberty and property of their constituents... Whenever the people are well-informed, they can be trusted with their own government; that, whenever things get so far wrong as to attract their notice, they may be relied on to set them to rights...Where the press is free, and every man able to read, all is safe.

It is certain that though written constitutions may be violated in moments of passion or delusion, yet they furnish a text to which those who are watchful may again rally and recall the people; they fix too for the people the principles of their political creed.

I would rather be exposed to the inconveniences attending too much liberty, than those attending too small a degree of it.

I never submitted...to the creed of any party of men whatever, in religion, in philosophy, in politics or in anything else, where I was capable of thinking for myself.

LIBERTY OR DEATH

*M*r. President, it is natural to man to indulge in the illusions of hope. We are apt to shut our eyes against a painful truth – and listen to the song of that siren, till she transforms us into beasts. Is this the part of wise men, engaged in a great and arduous struggle for liberty? Are we disposed to be of the number of those who, having eyes, see not, and having ears, hear not, the things which so nearly concern their temporal salvation? For my part, whatever anguish of spirit it might cost, I am willing to know the whole truth; to know the worst, and to provide for it. ...

There is no longer any room for hope. If we wish to be free – if we mean to preserve inviolate those inestimable privileges for which we have been so long contending – if we mean not basely to abandon the noble struggle in which we have been so long engaged, and which we have pledged ourselves never to abandon until the glorious object of our contest shall be obtained – we must fight! – I repeat it, sir, we must fight! An appeal to arms, and to the God of Hosts, is all that is left us!

They tell us, sir, that we are weak – unable to cope with so formidable an adversary. But when shall we be stronger? Will it be the next week or the next year? Will it be when we are totally disarmed, and when a British guard shall be stationed in every house? Shall we gather strength by irresolution and inaction? Shall we acquire the means of effectual resistance by lying supinely on our backs, and hugging the delusive phantom of Hope, until our enemies shall have bound us hand and foot? Sir, we are not weak, if we make a proper use of those means which the God of nature hath placed in our power. Three millions of people, armed in the holy cause of liberty, and in such a country as that which we possess, are invincible by any force which our enemy can send against us. Besides, sir, we shall not fight our battles alone. There is a just God who presides over the destinies of nations; and who will raise up friends to fight our battles for us. The battle, sir, is not to the strong alone; it is to the vigilant, the active, the brave. Besides, sir, we have no election. If we were base enough to desire it, it is now too late to retire from the contest. There is no retreat, but in submission and slavery! Our chains are forged; their clanking may be heard on the plains of Boston! The war is inevitable – and let it come! I repeat it, sir, let it come!

It is in vain, sir, to extenuate the matter. Gentlemen may cry, peace, peace – but there is no peace. The war is actually begun! The next gale that sweeps from the north will bring to our ears the clash of resounding arms! Our brethren are already in the field! Why stand we here idle? What is it that gentlemen wish? What would they have? Is life so dear, or peace so sweet, as to be purchased at the price of chains and slavery? Forbid it, Almighty God! I know not what course others may take; but as for me, give me liberty, or give me death!

Patrick Henry

PAUL REVERE'S RIDE

Listen, my children, and you shall hear
Of the midnight ride of Paul Revere,
On the eighteenth of April, in Seventy-five;
Hardly a man is now alive
Who remembers that famous day and year.

He said to his friend, "If the British march
By land or sea from the town tonight,
Hang a lantern aloft in the belfry arch
Of the North Church tower as a signal light –
One, if by land, and two, if by sea;
And I on the opposite shore will be,
Ready to ride and spread the alarm
Through every Middlesex village and farm,
For the country folk to be up and to arm."

Then he said, "Good night!" and with muffled oar
Silently rowed to the Charlestown shore,
Just as the moon rose over the bay,
Where swinging wide at her moorings lay
The Somerset, British man-of-war;
A phantom ship, with each mast and spar
Across the moon like a prison bar,
And a huge black hulk, that was magnified
By its own reflection in the tide.

Meanwhile, his friend, through alley and street,
Wanders and watches with eager ears,
Till in the silence around him he hears
The muster of men at the barrack door,
The sound of arms, and the tramp of feet,
And the measured tread of the grenadiers,
Marching down to their boats on the shore.

Manna From Heaven

Then he climbed the tower of the Old North Church,
By the wooden stairs, with stealthy tread,
To the belfry chamber overhead,
And startled the pigeons from their perch
On the somber rafters, that round him made
Masses and moving shapes of shade –
By the trembling ladder, steep and tall,
To the highest window in the wall,
Where he paused to listen and look down
A moment on the roofs of the town,
And the moonlight flowing over all.
Beneath, in the churchyard, lay the dead,
In their night encampment on the hill,
Wrapped in silence so deep and still
That he could hear, like a sentinel's tread,
The watchful night wind, as it went
Creeping along from tent to tent,
And seeming to whisper, "All is well!"
A moment only he feels the spell
Of the place and the hour, and the secret dread
Of the lonely belfry and the dead;
For suddenly all his thoughts are bent
On a shadowy something far away,
Where the river widens to meet the bay –
A line of black that bends and floats
On the rising tide, like a bridge of boats.

Meanwhile, impatient to mount and ride,
Booted and spurred, with a heavy stride,
On the opposite shore walked Paul Revere.
Now he patted his horse's side,
Now gazed at the landscape far and near,
Them, impetuous, stamped the earth,
And turned and tightened his saddle girth;

But mostly he watched with eager search
The belfry tower of the old North Church,
As it rose above the graves on the hill,
Lonely and spectral and somber and still.
And lo! As he looks, on the belfry's height
A glimmer, and then a gleam of light!
He springs to the saddle, the bridle he turns,
But lingers and gazes, till full on his sight
A second lamp in the belfry burns!

A hurry of hoof in a village street,
A shape in the moonlight, a bulk in the dark,
And beneath, from the pebbles, in passing, a spark
Struck out by a steed flying fearless and fleet;
That was all! And yet, through the gloom and the light
The fate of a nation was riding that night;
And the spark struck out by the steed in his flight,
Kindled the land into flame with its heat.

He has left the village and mounted the steep,
And beneath him, tranquil and broad and deep,
Is the Mystic, meeting the ocean tides;
And under alders, that skirt its edge,
Now soft on the sand, now loud on the ledge,
Is heard the tramp of his steed as he rides.

It was twelve by the village clock
When he crossed the bridge into Medford town.
He heard the crowing of the cock,
And the barking of the farmer's dog,
And felt the damp of the river fog,
That rises after the sun goes down.

It was one by the village clock,
When he galloped into Lexington.

Manna From Heaven

He saw the gilded weathercock
Swim in the moonlight as he passed,
And the meeting house windows, blank and bare,
Gaze at him with a spectral glare,
As if they already stood aghast
At the bloody work they would look upon

It was two by the village clock,
When he came to the bridge in Concord town.
He heard the bleating of the flock,
And the twitter of birds among the trees,
And felt the breath of the morning breeze
Blowing over the meadows brown.
And one was safe and asleep in his bed
Who at the bridge would be first to fall,
Who that day would be lying dead,
Pierced by a British musket ball.

You know the rest. In the books you have read,
How the British Regulars fired and fled –
How the farmers gave them ball for ball,
From behind each fence and farmyard wall,
Chasing the redcoats down the lane,
Then crossing the fields to emerge again
Under the trees at the turn of the road,
And only pausing to fire and load.
So through the night rode Paul Revere;
And so through the night went his cry of alarm
To every Middlesex village and farm –
A cry of defiance, and not of fear,
A voice in the darkness, a knock at the door,
And a word that shall echo forevermore!
For, borne on the night wind of the Past,
Through all our history, to the last,

America the Beautiful

In the hour of darkness and peril and need,
The people will waken and listen to hear
The hurrying hoof beats of that steed,
And midnight message of Paul Revere.

Henry Wadsworth Longfellow

THE HORSE AND THE STAG

A bitter quarrel arose between the horse
and the stag in the days when both creatures
roamed wild in the forest. The horse came to the
hunter to ask him to take his side in the feud.

The hunter agreed, but added: "If I am to help
you punish the stag, you must let me place this
iron bit in your mouth and this saddle upon your back."

The horse was agreeable to the man's conditions
and he soon was bridled and saddled. The hunter
sprang into the saddle, and together they soon had
put the stag to flight. When they returned, the
horse said to the hunter: "Now if you will get off
my back and remove the bit and the saddle, I won't
require your help any longer."

"Not so fast, friend horse," replied the hunter.
"I have you under bit and spur, and from now on
you shall remain the slave of man."

Aesop Fables

Application: Liberty is too high a price to pay for revenge.

*B*ad men cannot make good citizens. It is when a people forget God that tyrants forge their chains. A vitiated state of morals, a corrupted public conscience, is incompatible with freedom. No free government, or the blessings of liberty, can be preserved to any people but by a firm adherence of justice, moderation, temperance, frugality, and virtue; and by a frequent recurrence to fundamental principles.

Patrick Henry

AMERICA FOR ME

Tis fine to see the Old World, and travel up and down
Among the famous places and cities of renown,
To admire the crumbly castles and the statues of the kings,-
But now I think I've had enough of antiquated things.

So it's home again, and home again, America for me!
My heart is turning home again, and there I long to be
In the land of youth and freedom beyond the ocean bars,
Where the air is full of sunlight and the flag is full of stars.

Oh, London is a man's town, there's power in the air;
And Paris is a woman's town, with flowers in her hair;
And it's sweet to dream in Venice, and it's great to study Rome,
But when it comes to living, there is no place like home.

I like the German fir-woods, in green battalions drilled;
I like the gardens of Versailles with the flashing fountains filled;
But, oh, to take your hand, my dear, and ramble for a day
In the friendly western woodland where Nature has her way!
I know that Europe's wonderful. Yet something seems to lack!
The past is too much with her, and the people looking back.
But the glory of the Present is to make the Future free, -
We love our land for what she is and what she is to be.

310

America the Beautiful

Oh, it's home again, and home again, America for me!
I want a ship that's western bound to plough the rolling sea
To a blessed Land of Room Enough beyond the ocean bars,
Where the air is full of sunlight and the flag is full of stars.

Henry Van Dyke

THE SWALLOWS ADVICE

A FARMER was sowing his field with hemp seeds while a swallow and some other birds sat on the fence watching him. "Beware of that man," said the swallow solemnly. Why should we be afraid of him?" asked the other birds. "That farmer is sowing hemp seed," replied the swallow. "It is most important that you pick up every seed that he drops. You will come to regret it if you don't." But of course, the silly birds paid no heed to the swallow's advice. So, with the coming of the spring rains, the hemp grew up. And one day the hemp was made into cord, and of the cord nets were made. And many of the birds that had despised the swallow's advice were caught in the nets made of the very hemp that was grown from the seeds they had failed to pick up.

Aesop

Application: Unless the seed of evil is destroyed it will grow up to destroy us.

Manna From Heaven

AN AIRMAN'S LETTER
A letter shared by the mother of a serviceman from World War II

*A*mong the personal belongings of a young R.A.F. pilot in a Bomber Squadron who was recently reported "missing, believed killed," was a letter to his mother – to be sent to her if he were killed.

"This letter was perhaps the most amazing one I have ever read; simple and direct in its wording but splendid and uplifting in its outlook," says the young officer's station commander. "It was inevitable that I should read it – in fact he must have intended this, for it was left open in order that I might be certain that no prohibited information was disclosed.

"I sent the letter to the bereaved mother, and asked her whether I might publish it anonymously, as I feel its contents may bring comfort to other mothers, and that everyone in our country may feel proud to read of the sentiments which support 'an average airman' in the execution of his present arduous duties. I have received the mother's permission, and I hope this letter may be read by the greatest possible number of our countrymen at home and abroad."

Dearest Mother, - Though I feel no premonition at all, events are moving rapidly, and I have instructed that this letter be forwarded to you should I fail to return from one of the raids which we shall shortly be called upon to undertake. You must hope on for a month, but at the end of that time you must accept the fact that I have handed my task over to the extremely capable hands if my comrades of the Royal Air Force, as so many splendid fellows have already done.

First, it will comfort you to know that my role in this war has been of the greatest importance. Our patrols far out over the North Sea have helped to keep the trade routes clear for our convoys and supply ships, and on one occasion our information was instrumental in saving the lives of the men in a crippled lighthouse relief ship. Though it will be difficult for you, you will disappoint me if you do not at least try to accept the facts dispassionately, for I shall have done my duty to the utmost of my ability. No man can do more, and no one calling himself a man could do less.

I have always admired your amazing courage in the face of continued setbacks; in the way you have given me as good an education and background as anyone in the country, and always kept up appearances without ever losing faith in the future. My death would not mean that your struggle has been in vain. Far from it. It means that your sacrifice is as great as mine. Those who serve England must expect nothing from her; we debase ourselves if we regard our country as merely a place in which to eat and sleep.

History resounds with illustrious names who have given all, yet their sacrifice has resulted in the British Empire, where there is a measure of peace, justice, and freedom for all, and where a higher standard of civilization has evolved, and is still evolving, than anywhere else. But this is not only concerning our own land. Today we are faced with the greatest organized challenge to Christianity and civilization that the world has ever seen, and I count myself lucky and honored to be the right age and fully trained to throw my full weight into the scale. For this I have to thank you. Yet there is more work for you to do. The home front will still have to stand united for years after the war is won. For all that can be said against it, I still maintain that this war is a very good thing; every individual is having the chance to give and dare all for his principle like the martyrs of old. However long the time may be, one thing can never be altered – I shall have lived and died an Englishman. Nothing else matters one jot nor can anything ever change it.

You must not grieve for me, for if you really believe in religion and all that it entails that would be hypocrisy. I have no fear of death; only a queer elation . . . I would have it no other way. The universe is so vast and so ageless that the life of one man can only be justified by the measure of his sacrifice. We are sent to this world to acquire a personality and a character to take with us that can never be taken from us. Those who just eat and sleep, prosper and procreate, are no better than animals if all their lives they are at peace.

I firmly and absolutely believe that all evil things are sent into the world to try us; they are sent deliberately by our Creator to test our mettle because He knows what is good for us. The Bible is full of cases where the easy way out has been discarded for moral principles.

I count myself fortunate in that I have seen the whole country and known men of every calling. But with the final test of war I consider my character fully developed. Thus at my early age my earthly mission is already fulfilled and I am prepared to die with just one regret, and only one that I could not devote myself to making your declining years more happy by being with you; but you will live in peace and freedom and I shall have directly contributed to that, so here again my life will not have been in vain.

Your loving Son . . .

Anonymous

The writer of this letter remains anonymous. The young flyer has written a fitting epitaph for all who shed their blood for our freedom and liberty.

THE WORLD NEEDS LEADERSHIP

We have been fortunate in having and knowing those special leaders who have accomplished so many important things for the good of our government. Men and women of goodly stature have been and many continue to be, outstanding participants at the various levels of our municipal, county,

314

state or federal government. Many of whom serve tirelessly and without accolades. We should feel a deep sense of gratitude for their service.

We will be forever indebted to those who serve and sacrifice for our country by way of military service. Thousands have made the ultimate sacrifice and hereby have become the heroes of our time. God must hold such persons in the highest regard. They may join other martyrs who have given their lives to preserve their faith, principles and their countries security. Surely their reward in Heaven will be glorious and beyond their expectations. To give your life that another may live is a great spiritual sacrifice.

There are many among us who do not understand the nature of the great Civil War that divided our country. The human sacrifice was beyond reason. A writer, named Walker Perry, gave the following description. (The Civil War) – "is like a man walking away from a mountain. The bigger it is, the farther he's got to go before he sees it. Then one day he looks back and there it is, this colossal thing lying across his past."

The Civil War was a fight over which would be adopted, the Declaration of Independence or the United States Constitution. Included was the measure of America adopting slavery in our country. It became a war where one side must win. The men who were from the North became the major victims; they questioned their true reason for fighting in such a conflict. Many were the sons of father's who fled to America for the freedom of religion and wanted only to find a peaceful life. The North men were taken from their jobs in the factories and businesses but the farmer was required to leave his farm. The Southern men had the cause of slavery as their crusade and to serve to preserve their high standard of living.

Three million men were called into this bloody conflict. When the war was resolved 700,000 men lay dead in fields soaked with their blood. More men than all the United States wars put together, with thousands of injured victims sent home to die of their injuries.

Two such brave men were both great, great grandfathers of my husband. Captain Slocum Samuel Dunn, a business man and Civic leader of Carroll County, Illinois, and Private Lyman Grove of Kosciusko County, Indiana. Both men succumbed from injury or illnesses which were incurable from this terrible conflict in our country's history. They left families with serious financial problems and broken hearted children.

The Civil War has become a great example of a dispute in which just leaders rallied to fight oppression of a few souls, in this case the African American slaves. Oppression of humans wherever they live should bring a call for help in their rescue. The United States is a wonderful country founded on the principle that all men have the right to the pursuit of freedom and happiness.

In the future, may we raise God – fearing leaders in our children – the kind of Samaritan souls that will look to do the service of man as their mission in life. May they remember God always and ask for His divine intervention in the cause of each man. Wouldn't it be a marvelous blessing if they could bring peace and freedom to all the souls of God? Perhaps we will have children who become the type of leaders who understand love and service is where greatness is won – not in the spoils of war. It is a great country that helps another fight its' battles for freedom and then picks up their tools of war and goes home to rest. It is so grand that we live in such a country that asks for nothing in return for their service and sacrifice of their men.

God Bless the United States of America – she is the shining example of what every country needs to be. We can pray that her citizens can keep God's commandments and be worthy of such a country. If not, freedom may pay the price and our government will fall as in the Roman Empire. The people in sin destroyed the greatest empire in the world.

The Lord tells us if we keep his commandments He will do as we ask. If we do not keep his commandments, we have no promise from Him.

A ONCE PROUD LAND

Dream with me a time and view
The scene preserved within my mind
Of mountain, tree and rolling land
Now filled with clutter of mankind.

Drink with me a time and taste
Pure liquid from the rock and sand
Of mountain spring whose virgin birth
Will soon be lost to growth's demand.

Sit with me a time an hear
The rustled leaves on swaying bough
And smell the pine and cedar scent
Before they drop to ax and plow.

Watch with me a time to catch
A glimpse of creatures great and small
That fill the land from shore to shore.
As one by one they fail and fall.

Walk with me a time to find
A peace to permeate my days,
Its clement hand to quench the wrath
That haunts me through this final maze.

Rest with me a time for soon
I leave with nothing left to hand
To those who tarry for their day
But memories of a prouder land.

Lawrence Lee

With malice toward none, with charity for all, with firmness in the right, as God gives us to see the right, let us strive on to finish the work we are in; to bind up the nation's wounds; to care for him who shall have borne the battle, and for his widow and for his orphan; to do all which may achieve and cherish a just and lasting peace among ourselves, and with all nations.

Abraham Lincoln

NEEDED A LIFE OF PEACE AND HAPPINESS

*I*n the New Testament, Paul instructed the Philippians: "Finally, brethren, whatsoever things are true, whatsoever things are honest, whatsoever things are just, whatsoever things are pure, whatsoever things are lovely, whatsoever things are of good report; if there be any virtue and if there be any praise, think on these things."

"Those things, which ye have both learned and received, and heard, and seen in me, do. And the God of peace shall be with you."

Philippians 4: 8-9

Embracing this wisdom, we can expect the best outcome for every circumstance. We do not need to jump to negative conclusions or "borrow trouble". We can "borrow faith" if we need to, by asking a friend to pray for us. We enjoy sharing our optimism with others. We may bring gladness into someone's life, when he or she is going through a difficult time.

If someone were to hand you a gift-wrapped box in stunning paper, and tied with fine ribbons, we would expect to find something good inside. When the rays of morning sunlight stream though the shutters of our windows, we expect to step outside to a glorious sunny day. With unyielding certainty, therefore, let us anticipate more of God's beautiful world.

Perhaps our neighborhood might not be so inviting, but we can sit on the steps of our residence, and listen to the wonderful sounds around us. Our thoughts can rise above limitations, and we can imagine many uplifting things of the past or from books and beautiful music. We can enjoy the sights and colors of the sky and clouds. As a child of God we can be trusting, willing, and deserving. We can expect goodness to come if we feel gratitude.

We will have a humble outpouring of the good in life when we have faith. We can be alive, whole, and energetic when we look for the good in our life. It is of good report when we give service and hope to others who need us.

Thank you for giving me the opportunity to share my thoughts with you.

God Bless you. May his choicest blessings be yours this day and forever!